Dr **David Torevell** is Senior Lecturer in
Theology and Religious Education at Liverpool
Hope University College.

LOSING THE SACRED

LOSING THE SACRED

Ritual, Modernity and Liturgical Reform

DAVID TOREVELL

T&T CLARK
EDINBURGH

T&T CLARK LTD
59 GEORGE STREET
EDINBURGH EH2 2LQ
SCOTLAND

www.tandtclark.co.uk

First published 2000

ISBN 0 567 08720 4 HB
ISBN 0 567 08758 1 PB

British Library Cataloguing-in-Publication Data
A catalogue record for this book is available from the British Library

Typeset by Fakenham Photosetting Limited, Fakenham, Norfolk
Printed and bound in Great Britain by Bookcraft Ltd, Avon

To my parents, without whom a love of the Christian liturgy would never have been possible, and to my nieces and nephews Elizabeth, Rachel, Jason and Gareth.

CONTENTS

ABBREVIATIONS

CCC – *Catechism of the Catholic Church* (1994) London: Geoffrey Chapman.

CG – *The Common Good* (1997) The Catholic Bishops Conference of England and Wales.

DL – *Documents on the Liturgy 1963–1979* (1982) Collegeville: The Liturgical Press.

LM – *Lumen Gentium* (1992) in Vatican Council II. *The Conciliar and Post Conciliar Documents*. Dublin: Dominican Publications.

OD – *Oxford Declaration on Liturgy* (1996) The Liturgy Forum of The Centre for Faith and Culture.

OL – *Orientale Lumen* (1995) London: Catholic Truth Society.

SC – *Sacrosanctum Concilium* (1992) in Vatican Council II. *The Conciliar and Post Conciliar Documents*. Dublin: Dominican Publications.

PREFACE

Liturgy does not receive the intellectual attention it deserves. Although a substantial amount of thought-provoking material on Christian worship has been published in America and France, work in Britain has been relatively sparse. There are, of course, notable exceptions. Important reasons exist why this is the case. For example, the emphasis on religious studies which has emerged over the past thirty years has pushed Christian theology from the central position it once enjoyed in British (and other) universities. Multifaith perspectives and understandings have advanced considerably in relation to the wealth of new courses on world faiths. Such innovations reflect the richness and diversity of a multicultural western world and are rightly welcomed and appreciated. However, within this new academic climate, it was inevitable that methodological stances towards the study of theology itself would change. Theology and Christian studies started to be written largely from neutral and objective positions, rather than proceeding from grace-inspired work emanating from praying individuals or communities.

Ironically, the study of liturgy seemed to suffer from this broadening of the religious curriculum. For some people the study of Christian worship conjures up a return to a narrow way of doing theology or religious studies and as somehow the preserve of the institutional churches, largely irrelevant, therefore, to those outside ecclesiastical camps. It has been regarded, to a certain extent, as an exclusive patch of study for committed Christians. The increase in secular ways of thinking and acting has also relegated religious and liturgical studies within secondary and higher education to a lower status, as curriculum models emphasising skills-based competences linked to the world of employment have come to dominate educational policy and practice. Because of these and many other developments, generally speaking, it is usually in seminaries that the most serious and creative thinking about liturgy tends to take place. An important strand of Christian practice has been neglected and unexamined by many as a consequence.

There are hints, however, that change towards a more positive appreciation of liturgy is taking place. For example, recent British publications on the theological implications of the postmodern debate engage specifically with liturgical studies. Graham Ward's *The Postmodern God: A Theological Reader* includes two essays on liturgy; and Catherine Pickstock's work, *After Writing: On the Liturgical Consummation of Philosophy* is devoted entirely to liturgy. Kieran Flanagan's, Eamon Duffy's and David Ford's distinguished work continue to inspire others working in liturgical fields.

My own academic interest in liturgy began as a seminarian in the mid-1970s, although as an altar boy my formative experience 'at first hand' of the beauty and majesty of the Roman Catholic Church's worship was to have a considerable impact on my later attitude towards liturgy. Living in London during the 1970s was a memorable time, especially in the wake of the Second Vatican Council; there was a good deal of excitement and hope about the renewal and revitalisation of the Church. Liturgy was taught in the seminary with vigour and assumed a central role in the curriculum. The reforms of the Council were fully endorsed, explained and encouraged. This was to be a springtime for the Church and the study and practice of the reformed liturgy was part of that renewal. Being part of this euphoria, there was little room for cynicism or criticism about the changes and most of us accepted that the kind of worship envisaged by the Council Fathers was exactly what was needed for the modern age.

After leaving the seminary as an unordained lay person, I began teaching religious education in a number of Roman Catholic comprehensive schools and sixth-form colleges. I duly attempted to encourage the liturgical recommendations of the Council in relation to policies and practices of collective worship. I worked with chaplaincy teams in the spirit of the Second Vatican Council, promoting the liturgical changes brought about during the 1960s. Obviously, working with young people meant that issues about liturgical relevance and adaptability were high on the agenda. For ten years, despite some minor criticisms, the 'new liturgy' began to take hold and I generally accepted that the changes were a move in the right direction.

However, if I am honest, I always had nagging doubts about how much of the transcendence and mystery which had characterised preconciliar liturgy seemed somehow to be disappearing from school and parish worship (and indeed that I was partly responsible for the implementation of such a retrograde move). Although the liturgy had assumed a more social and communitarian feel, I sensed it was beginning to be no different from any other community secular gatherings of which I was a part. I began to feel that liturgy was being built around the concerns of the congregation, rather than securing an experience of the glory of God and had a strong impression that the sacred was disappearing from within my own Church as well as from the culture around me. My time as an altar boy within the Roman Catholic Church was so radically different from what I was experiencing during the 1970s, 1980s and 1990s, that it was hard to see any continuous tradition in operation. As experiments in liturgy increased, the unifying form and structure to liturgical services seemed to be disrupted endlessly in favour of idiosyncratic amendments, explanations and interruptions. Doubts about the manner in which the reforms were being implemented began to trouble me.

As time moved on my unease grew. The positive responses to the 'new liturgy' which had been envisaged by us during the 1970s seemed to be replaced by uncertainty about what was happening. Murmurs of dissatisfaction began to be heard. Widely different practices occurred. The unity and uniformity of the Church's liturgy was becoming more fragmented and disparate. Church attendance was declining not increasing. Young people became bored, not engrossed by the 'relevance' being worked at so hard by priests and laity alike. Priests themselves appeared confused about the best ways forward. A small sample of interviews conducted in 1995 and 1996 with Roman Catholic priests and seminarians suggested that the options available in the light of the reforms resulted in widely different interpretations. One priest said, 'Now there is much more need for the development of a liturgical sense. It isn't that detailed what you should do any longer.' Another priest added, 'At present there are a lot more options. Now *you* have to choose. For example, at the introduction of the Mass, it is up to the priest himself whether he says good morning or not.' A third priest said, 'The mystery attached to the liturgy before was almost out of an ignorance on the part of the congregation. I don't know what the priest is doing, so it's mysterious. I would much rather people understand what we are doing.'

Therefore, when an opportunity for me to do further study emerged, I jumped at the chance of investigating what was happening to the Roman Catholic Church's liturgy in the light of the reforms of the 1960s. I knew that in order to do justice to the complexity of the issue, the study would have to be an interdisciplinary one and draw from the insights of the social sciences, (particularly ritual studies, sociology, social theory, social anthropology), as well as theology, religious studies, ecclesiastical history, philosophy and cultural studies.

This book is the result – one attempt to plot some of the important issues which have arisen in the light of the liturgical reforms of the Second Vatican Council. I offer it, not as an exercise in nostalgia, but as a contribution towards the ongoing postmodern awakening of liturgical studies.

I owe a great debt of gratitude to those who have encouraged and supported me during the writing of this book. I am particularly grateful to Dr Philip Mellor of the Department of Theology and Religious Studies at the University of Leeds who supervised extremely patiently my initial, faltering ideas on liturgy for my PhD; he was always kind, insightful and became a good friend as well as academic mentor. I would also like to thank colleagues at Liverpool Hope University College who financed and backed the project throughout, in particular Fr Bernard Bickers, Professor Simon Lee, Dr Susan O'Brien, Canon Dr John Elford and Professor Ian Markham. Thanks must also go to Michael Ford of the BBC for reading a draft of the script and offering invaluable advice, Jeanette Theaker for her wisdom and understanding and those priests who generously gave of their time to be interviewed. I am also grateful to Fr Michael Thompson, parish priest of Ss Peter and Paul, Kirkby, Liverpool and Fr Gordon Abbs, parish priest of St Stephen's, Orford, Warrington for sharing in many stimulating theological discussions, and to Stratford Caldecott for his guidance during the stages of publication. I would also like to express my gratitude to those many students I have had the pleasure of teaching in both secondary and higher education who became highly influential on my thinking – I owe them much.

INTRODUCTION

This book aims to identify and account for a number of significant shifts in patterns and understandings of Roman Catholic worship leading up to and following the liturgical reforms of the Second Vatican Council. These will be contextualised within an analysis of the debates surrounding modernity and postmodernity, in order to examine the most important influences of the modern period on the emerging models of worship in the Roman Catholic Church since the Council. In particular, discussion will focus upon the emphasis accorded to rationality and cognitivism in liturgical theory and practice over the last thirty years, in contrast to earlier premodern emphases on collective embodiment and ritual. My discussion, however, can be introduced through a consideration of the work of Emile Durkheim on the nature of religion, and in particular, his classification of distinct types of ritual expression. I shall suggest that Durkheim's work provides a theoretical lens through which to evaluate some of the crucial issues surrounding the development of modern Catholic liturgy.

The Sacred and the Profane

Durkheim's understanding of religion emphasises the absolute division between the sacred and the profane; religion is about a sense of the sacred which emanates from that which is 'set apart and forbidden'. 'Sacred beings', he writes, 'are beings set apart' (1995: 44). What distinguishes such beings is their discontinuity from profane beings; there is 'no example of two categories of things as profoundly differentiated or as radically opposed to one another' (1995: 36). The most important mechanism for maintaining this separation is the performance of rites: 'A whole

complex of rites seeks to bring about that separation, which is
essential. These rites prevent unsanctioned mixture and contact,
and prevent either domain from encroaching on the other' (1995:
303). Such rites contain a taboo element which enables them to be
'withdrawn from ordinary use' (1995: 304). The sacred cannot
emerge unless this withdrawal and distancing constantly takes
place. As Frank Parkin contends, although Durkheim believed
religion would survive because it was foundational to society, any
decline in its influence would be associated with the extent to
which the sacred became less awesome and contracted in relation
to the profane (1992: 41–58).

Other scholars of religion have emphasised the importance of
rites for securing a separation between the sacred and the profane.
Influenced by the work of Rudolf Otto as well as that of Durkheim,
Mircea Eliade calls such a separation 'the abyss that divides the two
modalities of experience' (Eliade, 1987: 14; Otto, 1958). For
Eliade, what characterises the non-religious person is his refusal to
accept any notion of transcendence, which may often result in
doubting the meaning of existence itself. Patrick Collins argues
that the 'something missing' in postconciliar liturgy is a sense of
the sacred, 'otherness seems absent' (1992: 20). This sense of the
sacred is an experience entailing worshippers being 'grasped by a
reality greater than, and indeed, beyond themselves, both individually and collectively' (1992: 22). In Durkheimian terms, this is an
experience of something added to and above the real. Without this
sense of God's otherness made present in ritual, God simply
becomes the self magnified (Hughes and Francis, 1991).

Durkheim and Ritual

Part of this book will focus on the ritual dimension of liturgy and
be concerned to demonstrate the importance of maintaining a
strong sense of rite within worship. Durkheim's belief that ritual
has the capacity to transform individuals and strengthen collective
identity and purpose when its form and distinctiveness is upheld
will be a formative influence on my argument. Ritual is the means
par excellence by which a person is transported from the profane to
the sacred world. But Durkheim also argues that ritual requires
another central element to maintain its influence and power, and
this consists primarily in the provision of assembled bodily
gatherings which take part in rituals, without which the sacred
would not emerge: 'rites are ways of acting that are born only in

the midst of assembled groups and whose purpose is to evoke, maintain, or recreate certain mental states of those groups' (Durkheim, 1995: 9). It is this collective and somatic constituent of rites which brings about the experience of the sacred and which functions as a binding force for the group, an experience Durkheim calls 'collective effervescence'. For example, commemorative rites have the capacity to revitalise the most important values and beliefs of any group and bind them together with a sense of their own identity and solidarity: 'Through the rite, the group periodically revitalises the sense it has of itself and its unity; the nature of the individuals as social beings is strengthened at the same time' (Durkheim, 1995: 379). Rites, therefore, are essentially bodily and collective ways of acting that come about in the midst of assembled groups and which evoke, maintain, or recreate the values and identity of those groups.

In summary, therefore, we can say that Durkheimian accounts of the functions of rites consist in two broad categories: first, they establish a differentiation between the sacred and the profane; second, they integrate those involved in the rite into a sense of solidarity. By participation in ritual acts, human beings feel themselves transformed and are transformed. Such transformations occur especially during initiation rites, which produce an ontological metamorphosis in the participant. This experience is transformative because it entails the neophyte passing from the profane into the sacred world. As Durkheim writes, 'This change of status is conceived not as a mere development of pre-existing seeds but as a transformation *totius substantiae*' (1995: 37). Often this entails an intense bodily experience, for example, nakedness, followed by a new ritualised reclothing into the world of the sacred.

Durkheim insists that such rites are only effective if strict codes operate. Ritual must always occur within different time and space co-ordinates. Since the gulf between the sacred and the profane is so absolute, it is always necessary for ritual acts to be divorced from any contact with profane life. Religious and profane life can never co-exist in the same space or time. He argues that 'If religious life is to develop, a special place must be prepared for it, one from which profane life is excluded', and similarly religious and profane life 'cannot exist at the same time' (Durkheim, 1995: 312–13). The dominant characteristic of the religious rite, therefore, consists in its absolute division from ordinary life, which allows a collective gathering to celebrate its identity publicly and formally, and through which an experience of the sacred emerges.

Ritual: Collective, Bodily, Dramatic

It is not difficult to see in Durkheim's work his rejection of the individualistic philosophies advocated by Enlightenment thinkers such as Thomas Hobbes and Jean-Jacques Rousseau. His disagreement with the Hobbesian emphasis placed on the individual contracting out of nature in the creation of a good society, is shown in his contention that if societal constraint is necessary, it is much more likely to spring from an experience of the collective life, rather than from a personal experience emanating from the individual psyche. And in contrast to Rousseau's emphasis on the individual will, Durkheim argued that it was the collective sense of society which ought to be studied in its own right, since the assembled group or collective gathering were the most important elements for maintaining the moral core of society. For example, representative or commemorative rites are celebrated to 'keep faith with the past and preserve the group's moral identity' (Durkheim, 1995: 375). Such rites are able to re-present the group's mythical past, allowing it (by means of such dramatic re-enactments) to live revitalised in accordance with the values it cherishes and embodies. The collective, as opposed to the individual consciousness or conscience, is made new again by such dramatic performances of rites.

This Durkheimian attention to the dramatic is important, since it allows us to identify how participants in rituals are often transported outside themselves, well away from ordinary occupations and preoccupations. Rites frequently include a ludic or 'game' quality as part of this removal from the quotidian. He writes, 'Since utilitarian purposes are in general alien to them, they make men forget the real world so as to transport them into another where their imagination is more at home; they entertain' (Durkheim, 1995: 384). As a result of this celebratory and theatrical mode, religious ritual is able to refresh a spirit worn down by the mundane and oppressive. But this entertainment mode should not blind us to a more serious ethical element in rite: 'The moral forces that religious symbols express are real forces that we must reckon with and that we may not do with as we please' (Durkheim, 1995: 386).

Religion is always concerned about this moral regeneration in society. We are made hopeful and resourceful by our participation in religious rituals. The strength and importance of embodied experience in Durkheim's analysis of religion prevents the individual from sinking into feelings of 'anomie', a term he coined to describe that state which occurs in society when there is a decline in its social regulatory mechanisms, frequently present where economic rather than religious forces predominate. What Durkheim offered, especially during a period of social fragmentation due largely to rapid industrialisation at the turn of the century, was a way of understanding social regeneration dependent upon collective ritual activity. As Ernest Gellner writes of Durkheim's theory, 'We co-operate because we think alike, and we think alike thanks to ritual' (1992a: 37).

Roman Catholicism and Ritual

The previous discussion of Durkheim is an appropriate way of introducing my critique of the liturgical reforms of the Second Vatican Council, since a large part of my analysis will entail a consideration of the devaluation of the importance of ritualised liturgy since the 1960s, in favour of a much more cognitivist, disembodied approach, centred around the engagement of the minds of the congregation. If Durkheim is right, then the advantages of securing and maintaining an experience of the sacred by means of collective, embodied rituals are clear: society and the values it rests upon will die if rituals no longer take place. I take this Durkheimian analysis as being axiomatic for a renewal of the Church itself, plotting throughout the book how this liturgical shift from the body to the mind has taken root, and the degree to which it has become increasingly problematic for the Roman Catholic Church, particularly in the light of its historical insistence on ritual collectivity, patterning and regularity.

The foremost importance of the role of the sacramental and devotional life within the Roman Catholic Church testifies alone to the significance that has always been placed on ritual practice; its teachings on salvation and its distinctive sense of spirituality, have never been divorced from their foundation in ritual practices. The claim made at the Second Vatican Council that liturgy is the summit towards which the Church's activity is directed is also a clear indication of the centrality of the sacramental life within the salvific task of the Church (*Sacrosanctum Concilium*, Paragraph 10). The New Catholic Catechism continues this emphasis: 'Sacraments are powers that come forth from the Body of Christ, which is ever-living and life-giving. They are "the masterworks of God" in the new and everlasting covenant' (Catechism, 1994: 256).

In the light of this insistence on sacramental and ritual form within the Roman Catholic tradition, I argue that it is ironic that its modern liturgical reforms should have underestimated the significance and power of ritual. I suggest that this undermining of its importance within liturgy came about partly as a result of the insistence at the Second Vatican Council that liturgy must be primarily pastoral and that priests should take on the responsibility of promoting a much more intelligible and less obscure form of worship. Previous rites were considered alienating and unhelpful in promoting a sense of the priesthood of all believers. The Council's document on liturgy indicated that it was to be a major responsibility of the ordained priesthood to put into practice, with vigour, the changes in the liturgy and help others to understand and appreciate their potential. It was also a recommendation of *Sacrosanctum Concilium* that considerable attention should be given during the training of priests to the nature and reforms of the liturgy (*SC*, Paragraph 16). Seminarians were to understand the principles underlying the reforms so that they might encourage and later implement effectively the changes which had been discussed and finally approved by the Church Fathers. Seminaries were to be wholeheartedly involved in the study of the liturgy and to be places where the worship of God would reflect the very best in liturgical scholarship and renewal. They were to be the powerhouses for discussing and implementing liturgical change.

This was a daunting task since the newness and radical nature of the reforms meant that no one knew, from experience, whether the changes would engage a congregation in more reverent worship, infuriate a devout flock who felt no need for change or even the slightest adaptation, or alienate still further already disaffected groups within the Church. Flanagan is right to suggest that the relationship of rite to the 'cultural' was far more ambiguous and complex than had been envisaged in the reforms. If liturgy was to engage successfully with the new theological emphasis on cultural praxis, then the sociological tools through which this would be done needed to be specified (Flanagan, 1991: 10). This task was made even more difficult in the light of the highly prescribed ritual role of the priest before the Second Vatican Council. The sacrificial nature of the Mass, reiterated at the Council of Trent and virtually unchallenged until the 1960s, entailed the priest and bishop, separated from the laity, in a clearly defined hierarchical structure. The performance of the Mass, essentially a sacrificial ritual, was part of a tightly structured social organisation, in which the priest, as Christ, re-enacted the one sacrifice of Christ and who acted supernaturally as a mediator between God and man (Jay, 1992: 113). This consisted in an ordained person's exclusive right to sacrifice based upon the notion of apostolic succession involving the male sacrificing priesthood. The sacrifice of the Mass was not only expiatory and propitiatory, but the basis and driving-force by which Christians came to understand their social world. After the Second Vatican Council, when the dividing line between the clergy and the laity began to be less marked, it is not surprising that a 'crisis of identity' (Jay, 1992: 119) began to occur within the priesthood. Who were they to be – sacrificial male experts with invested authority to be Christ for the world within a tightly structured hierarchy; or facilitators of the priesthood of all believers in communal celebrations? Notwithstanding this confusion, the force of criticism about the unintelligibility and alienating effect of preconciliar Roman Catholic worship was enough to convince most priests that change was necessary.

The intentions underlying the changes might be easy enough to explain and, on the surface, suggest incontestable advantages: a much more pastoral emphasis within liturgy; a renewal involving active participation, reflecting the recommendations of *Lumen Gentium* on the role of the laity; a more comprehensible and intelligible liturgy, in the vernacular; much more significant weight being given to the word as well as the sacrament; a liturgy which would be more transparent and adaptable to the needs of differing cultural groupings; a catechetical liturgy which would educate the people of God into the meaning lying behind the liturgy. However, such recommendations involved radically alternative ways of thinking and doing and any transitional period was bound to be fraught with misunderstandings and mistakes. Within the thirty years which have elapsed since the reforms, a whole range of opinions have been expressed, some openly hostile, some enthusiastically supportive and others, by far the majority, a mixture of the two, welcoming parts of the renewal, while regretting the rest.

This diversity of reaction to the reforms can be seen most vividly in the attitudes of Roman Catholic priests themselves: those who have lived through the reforms and known the 'before and after' story; and those who have been trained, both in England and abroad, into the theology and practices of liturgical renewal since the mid-1960s. Many priests understood the principles and meaning of the liturgical reforms in significantly different ways and from widely contrasting perspectives. It is not surprising, therefore, that the style of worship and ritual patterns which have emerged over the last thirty years have moved in noticeably different directions. A Catholic Mass in one parish church is often very different from another in a neighbouring parish.

Insights from Social Anthropology

Leading social anthropologists have pointed to the dangers involved in associating a more pastoral liturgy with any devaluation of ritual expression. Indeed, they argue the reverse. For example, in his critique of modern Roman Catholic liturgical developments, Victor Turner recognises that the ritual traditions of Roman Catholicism have always been able to represent the collective understandings of many generations and were able to prevent the individual from slipping into secular ways of thinking and doing. He argues that ritual arenas of sacred space-time enable participants to 'confront eternity which is equidistant from all ages' (1976: 524). Ritual 'communicates the deepest values', and 'can anticipate change as well as inscribe order' in participants (1976: 506). In his comparison of the preconciliar rites of the Catholic Church with the rites of the Ndembu tribes in Zambia, he attempts to demonstrate this function by showing how both 'referred frequently to traditional narratives and beliefs, of which the rituals were partly a dramatic enactment' (1976: 506). He writes that 'Theorists of the new discipline of "communications" might regard ritual as an extreme case of "redundancy" saying the same thing in numerous ways. But this is precisely where ritual ceases to be merely "cognitive". Ritual allows the participant to be "supersaturated" with "existence" by which the whole person is engaged' (1976: 510).

Turner argues that most Catholics before the reforms were so highly accustomed to ritual procedures that they hardly noticed them. For centuries the Mass had been divided into the Mass of the Catechumens and the Mass of the Faithful. The first – originally possibly a separate service – concentrated on instruction to non-baptised adults, but the second was essentially a dramatisation of the sacrifice of Calvary. The first was addressed to the mind of the participant, the second, through symbolic action, to the body. Turner argues that the reforms were too strongly influenced by structural-functionalism, the view which accepts that ritual structure reflects social structure and should therefore change in response to social structural changes. Such a theory sees the social function of ritual as having to 'reanimate periodically the "sentiments" on which a given social formation depends for its successful running' (Turner, 1972: 392). One of the major strengths of the Catholic Church before the Second Vatican Council had been its liturgical ability to develop community and collective identity through ritual regularity. Its possession of a single body of ritual meant that it had a unique ability to form social and collective bonds.

Mary Douglas has complained that the Catholic hierarchy has demonstrated a clear undermining of the expressive function of ritual leading up to and beyond the Council. She argues that there have been three distinct movements away from ritual: the Church's contempt of external ritual forms; a more private internalising approach to religion; and an emphasis on humanist philanthropy (Douglas, 1970: 25). Using the example of the Catholic Church's changed teaching towards the Friday abstinence of eating meat, she concludes that there has been a war waged against ritual by the Church itself.

Liturgy as Ritual

Although the practice of ritual within the Roman Catholic tradition has always been prevalent, theoretical discussion of its potential has remained limited and therefore may partly account for its neglect at the time of the reforms. Historical studies in liturgy have generally emphasised its theological nature and underpinnings, or what has been referred to as 'a theology of worship' has dominated debate on the subject. Studies and theories which have appreciated its significance essentially as a ritual act are much less common and it is only relatively recently with the work of Ronald Grimes and Mark Searle that ritual studies has emerged as a formidable discipline within liturgical studies (Grimes, 1982, 1990; Jones, *et al.*, 1992). Searle writes that this neglect might have occurred because 'the very idea of ritual was suspect' (1992: 52).

However, the growing realisation and acceptance that ritual expressions of religious traditions are often prior to doctrinal and theological formulation have resulted in an increased status being given to ritual studies within theological debate. Liturgy cannot be understood fully without a thoroughgoing analysis of the role that ritual plays (Kavanagh, 1984, 1990). Traditionally, of course, the

Church has always addressed the dilemma of the relationship between *lex orandi* and *lex credendi* and in this regard is not unfamiliar with discussions of this kind. But, what was glaringly omitted in such debates was a detailed analysis of how the specific ritual dimension of liturgy operated within the worshipping life of the Church, and how that dimension related to overall patterns and formulations of worship. More anthropological interpretations of how ritual can open up rather than close down meaning are only recently being realised. As Flanagan points out, rituals 'are deemed to have enhancing rather than reductionist tasks in handling meanings. This has led to an acceptance of what these rituals strive to represent' (1991: 239). Once the inclusion of ritual is accepted, important questions emerge. For example, what particular features does ritual contain that might resist or allow alteration? Do any rules and codes govern its practice? What is the relationship between ritual practice and theological formulation and understanding? There is no evidence that such questions were ever addressed leading up to and during the reforms.

Contemporary scholarship is beginning to identify the close relationship between ritual and theological study (Kavanagh, 1984; Loughlin, 1996). A good example of this interrelationship can be seen in Gerard Loughlin's work on narrative theology. He argues that liturgy has always carried the responsibility of telling God's story to succeeding generations in word and action. Ritual participants are called upon to re-enact this Christian narrative and make present through ritual retelling and participation, an ancient myth which will exist until the end of time: 'The participants' absorption into the story is made possible through their absorption of the story in and through its ritual enactment. They are not simply witnesses of the story, but characters within it' (1996: 223). For Loughlin, Christianity itself is founded upon the performance of story. Such performances are central to the life of the Church. Never able to defend themselves against other stories by reason, Christian liturgy enacts its own distinctive tale again and again in the hope that others will be drawn in: 'Christianity is postmodern because it is not founded on anything other than the performance of its story. It cannot be established by reason, but only presented as a radical alternative, as something else altogether' (Loughlin, 1996: 21; see Slee, 1996).

Early forms of worship support such arguments. The first celebrations of the Eucharist were conditioned by an already existing Jewish ritual which became adapted to an act of remembrance of the death and resurrection of Jesus. Paul Bradshaw argues that the already established ritual patterning enabled converts to Christianity to tell their own 'new' story within an existing ritual framework, '... the command, "Do this in remembrance of me" (1 Cor. 11.24, 25), was not intended to initiate some novel ritual pattern that the early Christians would not otherwise have done, but was instead a direction that when they performed the customary Jewish meal ritual, they were to do so in future with a new meaning – as a remembrance of Jesus' (Bradshaw, 1996: 40).

It is my contention in this book that the unique power and potential of ritualised liturgy to transform individual and collective identities and to reaffirm the values and beliefs on which a religious community is based, was forgotten about or underplayed in debates leading up to and beyond the reforms of the Second Vatican Council. What dominated discussion was an overriding concern for the pastoral nature of liturgy, a theme the Council as a whole was keen to stress. This led to a commonly held view that earlier ritualised liturgical forms were anachronistic and incomprehensible and therefore, must be replaced by more dynamic celebrations, which would engage the congregation more actively and help them to understand the meaning of the liturgies in which they were involved.

Such an approach, partly influenced by the prevalent cultural and social assumptions of modernity, and partly by the existing marginalisation of ritual within liturgical debate, led, not surprisingly, to the conclusion that an appeal to the minds of the worshipping community was most likely to achieve the renewal in worship the Church sought and considered long overdue. Consequently, the mind began to replace the body as the focus of attention within Roman Catholic liturgy. The liturgical pastor was no longer the ritual expert, but the person who saw to it that worshippers understood exactly what they were doing and why they were doing it.

To substantiate this claim, I argue my case in three ways. First, by a detailed discussion of the nature and transformative potentialities of ritual expression itself. Second, by contrasting premodern understandings of Christian liturgy and experience with modern understandings, focusing particularly on the shifting emphasis accorded to the mind as opposed to the body. And third, by demonstrating the impact of modern cultural and social assumptions upon much of the theological and liturgical thinking leading up to and beyond the liturgical reforms.

Losing the Sacred

Theoretical Perspectives on Modernity

In what follows, then, I draw upon a whole range of disciplines and theoretical perspectives to trace the changes involved in the move from an overtly ritualised and embodied understanding and performance of liturgy before the reforms, to an increasingly rationalised and cognitive approach to worship thereafter. In order to do this satisfactorily, I give considerable attention to some of the characteristic expressions of worship in the premodern and especially medieval period. I contend that these reflected the Middle Ages' overriding involvement with an embodied experience of the sacred. Medieval spirituality and religious identity were rooted in the centrality of the body as a site and route for an experience of the sacred, which in turn became reflected in the highly ritualised practices and liturgies of the Church. I show how it was impossible to understand much of medieval worship as separate from, or opposed to, somatic experience.

I go on to discuss how this emphasis on the ritualised body became eroded in the modern period. I do this in a number of ways. From a philosophical perspective, I plot how the impact of René Descartes' writings on new understandings of the self had significant bearing upon the emergence of the prioritisation of the mind over the body and I emphasise the pivotal position that the mind has assumed in the modern period. Although Aquinas had identified the body as having no part in the intellective principle in a person, he clearly rejected any Platonic dualist belief in favour of the Aristotelian notion of *hylomorphism,* which advocated the intrinsic unity of the body and soul. Such understandings, however, were to be abandoned during modernity, as the mind, totally separate from the body, came to dominate all other locations, including God, for the attainment of knowledge, truth, power and self-identity. As Grace Jantzen writes in her analysis of the modern period, the way forward was always centred around looking into the 'mirror of the human mind, to polish its powers of reflection so that the world may be known, since it is knowledge, for Bacon as for Locke and Descartes. . . which gives power' (1996: 10). The contention by Philip Mellor and Chris Shilling that during the modern period 'Knowledge became an increasingly mental phenomenon in which the mind, experienced as divorced from the prejudices of the body's passions and senses, provided valid knowledge' (1997: 24), is discussed in relation to the main shifts in epistemological methodology and thinking about worship which were to emerge during the modern period.

I argue that the reasoning given about the methods to be used in securing a more pastoral liturgy was influenced by many of the rationalist assumptions embedded within the Enlightenment project and became strongly rooted in an approach centred around the mind and cognitive assimilation, with the body and the senses playing little part or having no significance. The ritualised body of premodern liturgy was no longer given any of the recognition or status it had previously held. I show that what became much more pivotal was the meaning and intelligibility of worship, which in turn was to endorse the view that more didactic and catechetical approaches to Christian liturgy should operate. If there were to be any references to the 'religious body', they were to be largely in terms of control and taming (Seidler, 1994a, 1994b).

The Protestant Reformation and Ritual

Such emphases were seen especially in Protestant conceptualisations of the self, which gave due warnings about the sensual temptations of the body. I discuss how such theological reappraisals about the place of the body within Christian identity were to have considerable influence on later thinking about the sense of the sacred and the practice of worship during modernity. The Reformation altered the way in which ritual came to be viewed, with many of the Reformers challenging any status which had previously been given to ritual expression. The Protestant emphasis on a sense of the sacred as the sublime (brought about by reading the word of God), rather than as a consequence of collective experience instigated through ritual engagement, became a hallmark of much Protestant thinking. The Protestant Reformers, keen to lay emphasis on the free gift of grace divorced from any ritual expression, meant that many of the ritual and liturgical objects which had previously held significance for the Christian community were removed or destroyed. As Euan Cameron argues, such 'iconoclasm' was '... not a campaign against "graven images" as such, but a campaign against the veneration of all that detracted from the free and sufficient grace of Christ – so relics or mass vestments, not "images" as such, might none the less be denounced and destroyed as "idols"' (1992: 249). The sacraments too, were no longer seen as being essentially ritual events or actions performed apart from faith, (as they were for late medieval thinkers), but rather became associated with alternative ways of proclaiming the word of God. Like most other things, the sacraments were to undergo cognitive scrutiny and become things explained and made sense of, with each one being accompanied by an explicit and unambiguous preaching of its purpose in the vernacular. The emphasis given by the Protestant Reformers to the formation of an authoritative statement of beliefs similarly produced a growing sense that Protestant identity entailed a far more intellectualist and mentalist understanding of Christianity than had previously existed in Catholic circles.

This rise of a more rationalised and explanatory approach to Christianity, separated from any status given to the body, became widespread and influential. Weber's analysis of Protestantism and in particular his association of Calvin's doctrine of predestination with the development of what he called 'an unprecedented inner loneliness of the single individual' (1992: 104), similarly rested upon the erosion of ritual devices and support. The individual, alone and isolated, could no longer rely upon the priest, the sacraments, or the Church for any help in solving the existential problems which naturally arose as part of everyday existence. For Weber, this lack of mediation between God and man was the decisive difference between Catholicism and Protestantism. It reached its climax in the Puritans' complete renunciation of any hint of ritual, even at death. As Weber comments, 'The genuine Puritan even rejected all signs of religious ceremony at the grave and buried his nearest and dearest without song or ritual in order that no superstition, no trust in the effects of magical and sacramental forces on salvation, should creep in' (1992: 105). The Calvinist and Puritan emphasis on the sinfulness of the flesh and its related antagonism to any forms of sensual engagement exacerbated this approach and resulted in a heightened sense of individualism and loneliness.

This process of individualism identified by Weber as being directly consequent upon the Protestant attitude towards religion, was also shared by Durkheim. He argued that the suicide rates were much higher in Protestant than in Catholic countries because of the central role ritual played within Catholicism, which released a sense of unchanging tradition, closely allied to an unquestioning of doctrine (1951). In contrast, the more cognitivist Protestant approaches to truth tended to instigate change by its encouragement to engage in greater self-reflection, which according to Durkheim, frequently resulted in adherents withdrawing from community involvement. He believed that this Protestant spirit of 'free enquiry' led to an undermining of religious and societal integration, which in turn had a substantial effect on the promotion of feelings of anxiety and ultimately upon acts of suicide. He argued that the Protestant denigration of ritual (for example, the abolishing of confession) was born of an attitude towards religion which had separated the individual from the community of believers. As Ken Morrison writes, 'This process of withdrawal from external ideas is evident in the Protestants' abandonment of religious confession. In that confession serves the function of drawing the individual into the centre of religious life by creating a link between private thought and public faith, it places a claim on the individual to practise greater morality and, therefore greater faith' (Morrison, 1995: 170). A much more privatised and individualistic understanding of religion developed as the anti-ritualistic influence of Protestantism grew and became widespread.

Sociological Perspectives

In what follows I also draw upon other sociological perspectives and discuss some of the work of leading social theorists who have identified many of the problems associated with the overriding modern concern for exclusively cognitivist and mentalist approaches to knowledge and meaning-construction. For example, I refer to the work of Zygmunt Bauman (1991, 1992a, 1992b, 1993) to outline some of the harmful and disturbing cultural effects which emerged in the modern period as the process of instrumental reasoning took hold. I then turn to Michel Foucault (1965, 1981, 1991) to demonstrate how newly formed social understandings within the modern period became largely organised around non-bodily discourses, often in relation to emerging operations of power. I indicate this development with particular reference to Foucault's writings on punishment to show how modern models of rationalisation became crucial in gaining knowledge. As such discourses of power took root, a process of abstraction occurred, separate from the bodily experience of the individual. In the case of crime and punishment, Foucault shows how the category of criminalisation became invented by an efficient society intent on keeping control. The body, as a result, simply became docile in the process. Foucault's analysis of discipline centres on the demise of ritual expression.

With reference to the work of Peter Berger (1974, 1990) and Anthony Giddens (1990, 1992), I highlight the growing sense of isolation and individualism, allied to feelings of anomie and anxiety, which were to develop as the 'sacred canopy' of the premodern world collapsed under the weight of increasingly secular and rationalist accounts of the world. This process of self-reflexivity and growth in personal strategies to construct narratives of the self, was to follow naturally upon the heels of the collapse of the religious frameworks of the world, often secured by ritual devices. This identification of an increased isolation and individualism associated with the demise of ritualised approaches to religion has been discussed by Giddens. He suggests that during the 'post-traditional' order, the self became a 'reflexive project' (1992: 33). Traditionally 'psychic reorganisation' had been inextricably bound up with rites of passage and the future tended to be clearly staked out in unchanging cultures. With the emergence of a deritualised modern culture, the self had to be explored, analysed and constructed. No rites were available to assist or even recognised as being able to assist in such personal transitions and transformations.

According to Charles Taylor (1992), the sense of the rational which emerged during the eighteenth century became associated with a view of human identity as defined and discovered within individuals themselves. Unlike the premodern world, nothing was passed on from one generation to another or taken for granted. Everything in the modern period, had to be discovered afresh within the individual psyche. And as Giddens argues, it is not only the absence of rites which characterise the modern period, but the prevalence of what he calls the 'reflexively mobilised trajectory of self-actualisation' (1991: 79). The telling point here is that the 'modern' individual began to construct a narrative of the self which was purely 'internally referential', with no external reference points coming into play; the key reference points are set 'from the inside' (1991: 80). In this description of the construction of the self, we see a definitive characteristic of modern culture: the self comes to rely, not on an external pregiven order of things, but on an inner process of self-authentification. This process of individualization, by which the self is constantly being 'thrown back' upon itself, results in a fragile process of self-refuge, as it is forced to seek comfort in its own subjectivity, even at the most difficult times in life. As Robert Bellah argues, such individualism leads to a position that what really matters is listening to inner voices which come from the inner self, not external voices of authority (1985).

Inevitably, with this shift from the external to the internal, traditions underpinned by strong ritual practices come to be viewed with suspicion and even hostility. Berger's work identifies this process as resulting in 'homeless minds' which become lost and confused as the 'sacred canopy' of the premodern world collapsed (1974, 1990). Religion had always interpreted the world in terms of an all-encompassing sacred order which prevented individuals from plunging into anomie. In the modern period when individuals go against society as legitimated by religion, they tend to '... make a compact with the primeval forces of darkness' (Berger, 1990: 39). Ritual serves to prevent such slips into meaninglessness and employs mnemonic devices to prevent such states occurring. It reminds people that the world has a meaning and purpose: 'Religious ritual has been a crucial instrument of this process of "reminding". Again and again it "makes present" to those who participate in it the fundamental reality-definitions and their appropriate legitimations' (Berger, 1990: 40). Ritual restores continuity between the present moment and the past. Berger argues that because Catholicism maintained such an insistence on the variety of ways in which the sacred could be mediated (the sacraments, the saints, the miraculous), it prevented the community from losing its sense of identity and purpose. In contrast, Protestantism seemed to divest the world of such support (except for the Bible) and paved the way for a process of secularisation after the world had become '... amenable to the systematic, rational penetration, both in thought and activity, which we associate with modern science and technology' (Berger, 1990: 112).

Modern Theology

In order to demonstrate the influence of dominant theological trends upon modern liturgical thinking, I also trace the rise of the major trajectories in Roman Catholic religious thinking during the twentieth century. I take Ferguson's claim that a central characteristic of twentieth-century theology became centred around anthropomorphic concerns and that what dominated much theology was an investigation into the nature of humanity itself, as the locus of revelation (Ferguson, 1992). This shift to a more immanent existential exploration, drawn from personal experiences within both the secular and religious worlds, rested on a much more self-referential, internalised and experiential understanding of religion. The modernist movement and Karl Rahner's theological anthropology serve as good examples of this kind of trend within the Roman Catholic tradition. I trace such theological

developments and suggest that their approaches are consonant
with the dominant anthropomorphic emphases advocated by the
Fathers throughout the Second Vatican Council and which were
inevitably to become highly influential in postulating the more
pastoral and subjectivist approaches to worship.

Criticisms of the Reforms

Towards the end of the book I suggest that it should come as no
surprise that the reforms of the liturgy were to promote such bitter
attacks from within both the 'traditional' and 'liberal' wings of the
Roman Catholic Church. The move towards a more cognitivist,
deritualised and less embodied approach to Christian liturgy
resulted in both feminist and masculinist accusations of bias, issues
which require more careful study in the future. Attacks from those
more associated with a 'conservative' ecclesiastical approach rested
upon the claim that reformers had betrayed the liturgical tradition
of the Church, which for centuries had rested upon a highly
ritualised form of worship. Attacks from more 'progressive' wings
argued that the overriding attention given to the mind as separate
from the body set up harmful dualist models within Christian
worship. Both parties appear united in their view that the reforms
have resulted, and continue to result, in further fragmentation and
a loss of a sense of the sacred.

Formal and public appraisals of the liturgical reforms have
already happened. The *Oxford Declaration on Liturgy*, issued in June
1996 by the Liturgy Forum of the Centre for Faith and Culture,
while referring to some of the positive effects of the changes, was
not reserved in highlighting grave areas of concern. The
Declaration was clearly keen to emphasise the fruits of
Sacrosanctum Concilium: the introduction of the vernacular, the
more widespread and open use of sacred scripture, the increased
participation in the liturgy, the enrichment of the process of
Christian initiation; all these are highlighted as substantial
improvements. But the statement also contained a more critical
and exhortative tone, concluding that 'the preconciliar liturgical
movement as well as the manifest intentions of *Sacrosanctum
Concilium* have in large part been frustrated by powerful contrary
forces, which could be described as bureaucratic, philistine and
secularist' (*OD*, paragraph 1). What was now urgently required
was a revival of the liturgical movement itself, to restore the
'sense of the sacred' (*OD*, paragraph 3), sadly lacking in much

contemporary liturgical practice. This could only be achieved by a renewal of liturgical eschatology, cosmology and aesthetics. The Forum also hoped that future liturgical reform would not be imposed on the faithful but would proceed, 'with caution and sensitivity, to the *sensus fidelium*, and from a thorough under-standing of the organic nature of the liturgical traditions of the Church' (*OD*, paragraph 6). In this regard, it reflected the mixed blessings which many acknowledged about the changes in contemporary Roman Catholic liturgy over the last thirty years.

A similar development and emphasis, this time instigated primarily by American authors, began in 1995 with the inaugu-ration of The Society for Catholic Liturgy. This multidisciplinary association of Catholic scholars, teachers, pastors and ecclesiastical professionals, is committed to promoting the scholarly study and renewal of the Church's liturgy. Like the Oxford Declaration, the Society reflected the same tension between the obvious fruits of *Sacrosanctum Concilium* and its more unsettling developments. For example, the Society states in its 'General Philosophy' section in its information leaflet that it will take 'a critical attitude regarding any liturgical "restorationism" which rejects or is fundamentally suspi-cious of the reforms set in place by the Second Vatican Council', while at the same time it advocates, 'an awareness of the problems of the dilution of liturgical practice and spirituality by cultural forces inimical to Catholic Christian tradition; thus a critical assessment of the challenges involved in the cultural adaptation of liturgy'. Like the Declaration, too, the Society is keen to emphasise the intrinsically conservative and organic nature of liturgy, recom-mending that a renewal of the liturgical movement is called for if the liturgy of the Church is to be improved in the future. The Society also advocates the importance of the aesthetic in liturgical renewal, especially in the areas of music, art and architecture, so that ceremonial dignity and artistic beauty may be fostered.

Eamon Duffy, one of the leading members of both initiatives, has cogently expressed his concern about some of the recent developments in Roman Catholic worship and speaks for a growing number of people who are concerned about the future of Roman Catholic worship. In July 1996 (on this occasion with reference to the introduction of the vernacular into the liturgy), he wrote 'the actual moment at which the transition to the vernacular occurred could hardly have been less propitious. The post-conciliar transformation of the liturgy coincided with a period of profound cultural dislocation in the west. Genuine theological

renewal became inextricably tangled with a shallow and philistine
repudiation of the past which was to have consequences as disastrous in theology as they were in the fine arts, architecture and city
planning' (Duffy, 1996: 882). He argues that although many of
the changes in theological thinking rightly replaced some of the
stale aridities of neo-scholasticism, the embracing of the 'signs of
the times' was to be nothing more than the absorption of 'some
of the least happy developments within the secular culture of the
1960s and the early 1970s' (1996: 882).

   Such claims – and the two recent developments I have already
mentioned – clearly point to a need for a thorough evaluation of
the historical, theological, philosophical and cultural assumptions
underpinning the changes to the Roman Catholic liturgy. This
book is one contribution to this evaluation, arguing that it is
impossible to understand the reforms and their consequences
without first of all taking into account the dominant cultural forces
which influenced their final draft and their inattention to the
place and significance of ritual in liturgical expression. It therefore
analyses the importance of ritual in fulfilling religious and human
potential and in so doing argues for its centrality in liturgical
expression and theological debate. To a certain degree, therefore,
it is concerned with those 'powerful, contrary forces' which have
dominated liturgical thinking and practice by tracing the rise of
formative anti-ritual, 'disembodied' approaches to truth and
knowledge during modernity.

   In Chapter 1 I discuss the nature and function of ritual, pointing
to its human and religious potentialities. I do this in order to show
how ritual as a constituent dimension of liturgy has specifically
defining characteristics which must be adhered to if its form is to
be maintained. In Chapter 2 I seek to show how in the premodern
age ritual practices and embodiment were central to the Church in
securing Christian identity and unity. I also indicate the beginnings of a shift in the importance given to ritual and embodiment
consequent upon the Reformation and philosophy of Descartes.
Chapter 3 discusses the rise of instrumental reason and new
approaches to the body during modernity, indicating the
continued expansion and dominance of cognitivism over ritual
and embodied experience. Chapter 4 analyses the emergence of
the liturgical movement in the light of such 'modern' developments and seeks to show how secular and theological thinking
influenced a much more rational and subjectivist approach to
worship, undermining its ritual nature and character. Chapter 5

demonstrates how the recommendations of the conciliar document *Sacrosanctum Concilium* reflected this 'modern' emphasis on classification, meaning and cognitivism, attenuating its transformative potential, formerly secured by ritual embodiment. In Chapter 6 I discuss and critique the central issues of participation, symbolism and embodiment in the light of the reforms. I conclude by arguing that the revitalisation of Catholic liturgy and the Church itself depends on a recovery of its former positive engagement with the embodied potentialities of ritual.

1

RITUAL'S FORM

In my Introduction I suggested that an important constituent of Christian liturgy was its ritual dimension and discussed Durkheim's notion that the moral vitality and self-identity of human communities were significantly strengthened by individuals' participation in ritual acts. In this chapter I focus on the chief features of ritual itself, considering in detail its defining and distinctive form. I hope to show how the central character-istics, codes and rules which govern its operation, are inextricably linked to its creative potentiality and power. By paying attention to the nature and potential of ritual itself, I prepare the ground for my subsequent discussion of the dangers involved in devaluing or replacing its importance by more cognitivist, explanatory and disembodied approaches to Christian worship.

Ritual as Performative Bodily Action

The importance of ritual in religion cannot be over-estimated. The modern Western habit of trying to appreciate the nature of religion by simply looking at and referring to religious beliefs (as they became formulated in creeds) has not been helpful in giving a balanced picture (Smith, 1889). As Gavin Flood contends when discussing the notion of religion and the sacred, 'The category "religion" has developed out of a Christian, largely Protestant, understanding, which defines it in terms of belief' (Flood, 1997: 8). What is required is a more comprehensive approach which testifies to the myriad of practices religious traditions are engaged in and the impact they have on people's religious lives (Segal, 1998). Ritual is an important strand to be considered in relation to this debate about religious *practices*; its importance lies in what it can achieve for the community and the individual. However, the human and religious potentialities of ritual are only secured by careful attention being given to its defining features and characteristics; to safeguard what it can do, it is necessary to safeguard what it is; to this issue I now turn.

All religious and social anthropological writings on ritual emphasise its unique *bodily* qualities (Turner, 1967; Tambiah, 1979; Kavanagh, 1990; Nichols, 1996; Searle, 1992; Lewis, 1980). Rituals always place importance on the physical actions of bodies as they enact important symbolic performances by means of highly formalised and prescribed action, movement and gesture (Kavanagh, 1984, 1990; Collins, 1992; De Coppet, 1992); speaking, understanding and verbal explanations assume secondary roles (Roose-Evans, 1994). This emphasis accorded to symbolic action entails an 'extra-ordinary' way of doing things. Actions, movement and gestures are performed in a stylised and deliberate manner within a carefully chosen and separated space added to a new ritualised timescale, as participants are transported beyond the mundane and ordinary, outside themselves (Searle, 1992). Ritual can never unleash its latent power to capture the imagination and transform the consciousness of participants without such an emphasis on this somatic and 'extra-ordinary'. Ritual brings to life in the mind only those things which have first been located in the body and the senses, *'nihil in intellectu nisi prius fuerit in sensu'* (Searle, 1992: 57). Evelyn Underhill agrees, suggesting that worship always involves the dynamism and engagement of the sensual body (1937: 37–38). Its natural habitat, therefore, is found within debates about embodiment, the fleshy self and the senses, not discourses about rationality, cognitivism or epistemological classification.

Gilbert Lewis' discussion of ritual partly focuses on the establishment of a 'peculiar arena' which seems to alert human attention by demands of 'look and see' much more than simply 'see and hear' (1980: 20). It is due to the formalised nature of ritual expression that the attention of the audience can be beckoned and captured; ritual has an 'alerting quality'. As a result, this kind of action becomes associated with theatrical performance and drama, regularly situated within a primarily performative mode of doing. Indeed, John Huizinga states that all rites are essentially *dromenons,* 'something acted, an act, an action' (1949: 14). In carrying with them this performative dimension, the bold theatricality of ritualised action is able to transform the participants who share in its dynamics (Collins, 1992: 32–33). Ritual 'temporally structures a time-space

environment through a series of physical movements thereby
producing an arena' in which formality, fixity and repetition
become key characteristics of such performances (Bell, 1992:
109). And it is only due to the deliberate staging of such
stylised action that ritual has the potential to transform moral
attitudes and perceptions: 'the purpose of ritual is to ritualize
persons who deploy schemes of ritualization in order
to dominate (shift or nuance) other, nonritualized situations to
render them coherent with the values of the ritualizing
schemes' (Bell, 1992: 108).

The Performativity of Ritual

This tightly structured performative dimension of ritual is an
essential part of its distinctiveness. According to Stanley Tambiah,
ritual is primarily performative due to three things: first, even
when it says something, it is also doing something (Austin, 1975),
second, in its intensity of experience by the audience; and third,
in the manner in which it is attached to, and inferred by, the
actors during the performance (Tambiah, 1979). What makes
ritual a distinctively performative occasion is this marriage of form
and content, whereby communication is able to flow naturally
from a carefully structured and organic sequence. The message is
to be found in the medium itself, its form indispensable in
communicating the meaning and significance of the act. But the
particular cultural contexts within which rituals emerge and their
distinctive formal features are not analytically mutually exclusive,
but rather become 'integrally implicated in the form that
ritual takes', the marriage of form and content being essential 'to
ritual action's performative character and efficiency' (Tambiah,
1979: 119–20). Formality, conventionality, stereotypy and rigidity
characterise this form, ensuring that ritual embodies a distinctively 'traditional' character. If ritual is concerned with
'cosmological constructs' (by which Tambiah means they embody
specific beliefs about the world), then 'it is a necessary corollary
that the rites associated with them be couched in more or less
fixed form', and 'be transmitted relatively unchanged through
time' (Tambiah, 1979: 122–23). Rappaport also argues that
formality and performativity are the *sine qua non* of ritual form.
The relationship between the performer and the audience is also
central to the performance and in delineating the form and
impact of a ritual (1979).

Ritual Codes and Rules

Embedded within this notion of fixity and formality is the importance attached to following rules which govern the action, movement and gesture. These codes seek to specify and determine the process of embodied expression, delineating the spatial direction, movement and gesture within the ritual arenas. Stephen Lukes contends that 'Most writers agree in seeing ritual as rule-governed in the sense of being both patterned and usually involving normative pressure on its participants' (1975: 290). The rules which govern the bodily action of ritual need to be taught, even if, at times, they appear arbitrary or somewhat artificial. Indeed, one overriding condition of ritual is that people expect there to be rules and expect them to be followed. Such prescribed rules generate distinctions between what is and what is not acceptable in ritual performances. Clear parameters prescribe the type of action that will take place, which if gone beyond or broken, may cause the spectacle to be punctured and lose its symbolic and theatrical potency. For Lewis, such prescription goes some way towards defining what ritual actually is: 'To say the action is prescribed, that there is some ruling about the circumstances for its performance, moves closer to an answer' (1980: 11). Informality may take the place of a more formal structure, but this will only be acceptable if it reflects a deliberate and conscious attempt to flout or parody more traditionally prescribed patterns.

The kinetic relations between those 'on stage' and those in the audience in ritual performances are highly significant and purposeful. The spatial positioning and sense of movement between actors and audience are determining aspects which produce and extend the full force of ritual occasions. The corporeal actions, gestures and movements assume a symbolic signification. Ritual is itself an action that can only 'be understood as bodily movement towards or positioning with respect to other bodily movements and positions' (Parkin, 1992: 12). It is precisely because of this emphasis on bodily movement and spacing that ritual 'full of spatial movement and gestural performance would make the evolutionary transition to drama and theatre based at first on mime rather than dialogue' (Parkin, 1992: 17). The symbolic, kinetic body is its primary source of communication and 'in-formation'.

This establishment of a keen sense of opposition between ritualised action and space and their 'ordinary' counterparts distinguishes ritual. The sense of distancing between the 'extra-ordinary' or different and the everyday or quotidian is achieved by the physical and spatial strategies employed. Within ritual spaces, sacred objects and movement entail a deliberate polarity or contrast with each other, which determine and strengthen the values, attitudes and social relations the ritual symbolises. The raised altar or the elevated host, the act of genuflecting or bowing, all perform this function by their spatial alignments and inter-action. The body or object is able to interact with its environment only through such deliberate positioning and carefully planned co-ordination. This produces a ritualised and highly sym-bolic patterning, which structures the action and renders it symbolic and persuasive. Or as Bell puts it, 'ordinary physical movements generate homologies and hierarchies among diverse levels and areas of experience, setting up relations among symbols, values and social categories' (1992: 104).

It seems logical in the light of this recognition that ritual entails prescribed action, movement and spatial patterning that 'experts' will be called for, those who know and are able to safeguard the prescribed codes and patternings which are required. Plainly, those 'in charge' of any ritual performance must ensure that the actions, spatial positions and directions of the enactment are followed carefully. Who does what, when and how is paramount. Inevitably this coincides with the manner in which ritual sets up and reflects how human existence is morally and socially intended, since the ritualised values symbolically advocated by the performance are those to be aspired to. Rituals fail in this regard when they are unable to secure consensus or when they become driven by unauthorised illegality or individual interference. In such circumstances, safety devices may come into play. For example, when slippage from prescribed ritual codes occurs the momentum of the action may itself insist on correction or as Parkin puts it, 'may scold and insist on proper reordering' or, 'if a growing number of ritual participants take the new direction, such officials may instead tacitly accept the spatial shift and even claim it is the real way – allowing new agency by default' (1992: 20). But it must be remembered that such moments are inevitably fraught with danger and fragility.

The encoded form which ritual maintains to ensure its unique powers of transformation is related correspondingly to its own exercise of formality, fixity and prescription. There is always a basic code to ritual which must be followed. Such prescription does not imply a slavish regularity or monotony since often the real challenge and goal of any ritual is to make a performance dynamic and original within the code which controls it. In fact, its originality is crucially interconnected to its own ease with formality and unfaltering fixity and repetition.

Roy Rappaport suggests that essentially two categories of information are transmitted in rituals, what he terms the 'indexical' and the 'canonical' (1979). The first is characterised by the current psychological state of the participants, the second with the enduring aspects of nature, society and cosmos. Referring specifically to liturgical practice, he contends that, 'canonical messages' are carried by that which is invariable in the liturgy and in contrast, indexical transmissions rely upon whatever opportunities invariant liturgy offers for variation' (1979: 179–82). Securing the right integration between the two is fundamental and ensures the success or failure of a ritual. This is a particularly important issue to consider during periods of liturgical reform (Nichols, 1996).

Tambiah's research into the nature of ritual is illuminating in regard to this notion of code in ritual. Unity and harmony are established due to the performance of symbolic action within a highly condensed and prescribed code. Three characteristics define ritual: it possesses an ordering or procedure that structures it tightly; it embodies a communal or collective dimension which is purposive; and it appears different from 'ordinary' everyday events (Tambiah, 1979). The unifying function of ritual is emphasised by contrasting it (in partial response to Huizinga), with play:

> Games... appear to have a disjunctive effect: they end in the establishment of a difference between individual players or teams where originally there was no indication of inequality.... Ritual, on the other hand, is the exact inverse; it conjoins for it brings about a union... or in any case an organic relation between two initially separate groups, one ideally merging with the person of the officiant and the other with the collectivity of the faithful (Tambiah, 1979: 118).

The performative rules and sequence of events within rituals establish this unity and stand in stark contrast to the unpredictable and unequal outcomes of games and sports. Tambiah's eventual attempt at defining ritual is worth stating in full since it summarises the main characteristics I have discussed so far:

> Ritual is a culturally constructed system of symbolic communication. It is constituted of patterned and ordered sequences of words and acts,

often expressed in multiple media, whose content and arrangement are characterised in varying degree by formality (conventionality), stereotypy (rigidity), condensation (fusion), and redundancy (repetition) (1979: 119).

This maintenance of form ensures that the ritual is able to communicate what it needs to. Any aberrations in this process unsettle and puncture the values, beliefs and messages to be conveyed, rendering the ritual less effective and powerful.

Ritual and Mystery

Although ritual behaviour may involve highly prescriptive ways of doing things, the meaning or 'message' of a performance is not classified unproblematically. A rite is never exhausted, its meaning never fully resolved. Participants share in repetitious forms of rite in order to engage in a constantly renewable experience of the divine, one never fully explained nor finally understood (Scruton, 1997); ambiguity and mystery remain dominant impressions. It is through the performance of rite that 'an opening, one that facilitates the coming of a presence from outside the limits of rite is secured' (Flanagan, 1990: 237). Rites invite potential participants to be involved in this endless series of disclosures of the divine and create experiences which are never identical. The divine becomes present and given shape through the experience of the rite far more than in theological discourse. That is why any changes or disruptions in the liturgy must be taken with enormous care, because they impinge on the central, deeply embedded notion participants have of God or the divine presence by which they have been formed and in which they have come to believe (Scruton, 1997: 460). Familiarity, routine and repetition are essential when developing this formation: 'You enter the frame of mind in which you cannot get enough of it; not because you look forward to it – on the contrary, you might like Amfortas, dread it to the point of preferring death – but because you belong to it, and it to you' (Scruton, 1997: 460).

It is through the maintenance of the form that mystery is able to emerge and envelop the participant: 'contrived and peculiar, asking for attention, the mind may attend to the thing as a sign or symbol which may yield up information about a mystery that seems to come within grasp when invested with perceptible form' (Lewis, 1980: 30–31). The experience of the holy is always beyond human manufacture, but liturgical expressions require a predictable social form if their unpredictable effects are to be realised (Flanagan, 1991:

70). Like icons, they open up 'a sense of presence of the Divine through social actions that are believed and intended to be endowed with holy purpose' (Flanagan, 1991: 70). The social form and human agency inevitably involved in ritual expression are the means by which the re-presentation of the holy becomes possible, but they must always remain serviceable to the participants' engagement with the sacred. This is never easy to maintain: 'The difficulty is that the form of rite can take on a life of its own, where its beauty and order can become inherently attractive in a way that renders the performance an end in itself' (Flanagan, 1991: 163). The use and importance of silence emerging during the gaps and pauses during liturgy testify to this requirement of the stability of form in experiencing a sense of the sacred; but they also point to its limits: 'The limits of liturgical form need to be marked to allow a content to be noticed, a phenomenon that might pass unsignified and unheard' (Flanagan, 1991: 250). Lest an idol be created in place of God, the use of silence establishes a crucial apophatism in which mystery is veiled and a sense of the sacred experienced (*OL* 1995: 32).

Ritual also embodies the unique ability to combine both a sense of mystery with the propensity to enable the participant to come some way in being absorbed by that mystery. Rather than affirming clear and dogmatic values, ritual is more likely to present an argument or a set of tensions, offering infinite possibilities for interpretation (Parkin, 1992: 18–19). Not concerned about securing specific objectives or goals, it is differentiated from mere craft, skill or technique by its refusal to make sense of an action in terms of precise classificatory diagnosis, or what Lewis calls, 'means-end relationship' (1980: 13). 'Words that recur in discussion of the distinction between ritual and craft or skill are "irrational" or "non-rational" where rationality implies Weber's sense of the "methodological attainment of a definitely given and practical end by the use of an increasingly precise calculation of adequate means"' (Lewis, 1980: 13). Such observations allow us to differentiate ritual expression from other more classificatory and unambiguous approaches to knowledge and meaning-construction which I move on to discuss in later chapters.

Ritual and Non-Rationality

Thinking operates in a different manner during rituals. Symbolic objects and action 'ungate' our usual way of seeing, releasing a markedly different operation of understanding, often at a distance from our 'normal' means of perception (Lewis, 1980: 31). This involves thought making a kind of 'leap' in order that usual causal connections become somehow short-circuited (Huizinga, 1965: 195). Symbolic actions and objects of attention stimulate the senses away from conceptually mundane thought and from an overemphasis on rational formulation and the process of *mathesis*. One might describe this unique experience of participation within a rite as being part of a mystery greater than oneself, allied to a sense of the presence of powers or spirits which lifts participants into an experience of the sacred and transcendent. As Tom Driver writes, 'Ritual is not about itself but about relation to not-self. Secular or religious, ritual is always concerned with powers that are understood to have their being outside the ritualisers, even though it is ritual that gives the powers their being, instantiating them within its circle of magic' (1991: 99).

This non-rational dimension of ritual is worth emphasising. Although ritual action often takes place within a narrative framework (Loughlin, 1996; Segal, 1998), invariably 'the narrative frame dissolves, the action is just, "done", not thought about' (Schechner, 1993: 240). In neurological terms, properly conducted rituals are said to be able to achieve a synchronization of excitement within both the right and left hemispheres of the forebrain' (Schechner, 1993: 240). For Richard Schechner there is always a dynamic tension between the cognitive and affective in performance, but full cognitive understanding is never necessary for an audience to be enraptured by a performance.

Eugenio Barba's work on the 'dilated body' in performance emphasises this non-rational aspect of ritual and shows how many actors have an 'elemental energy' which automatically attracts the observer to their performance. Sometimes a spectator by simply 'Seeing a performance whose meaning he cannot fully understand and whose manner of execution, he cannot competently appreciate, he suddenly finds himself in the dark. But he must nevertheless admit that this void has a power which holds his attention, that it "seduces" in a way which precedes intellectual understanding' (1991: 54). Barba's analysis of ritual within theatre anthropology also points to the different world the dramatic performer inhabits. It is never 'ordinary' bodily action. The way the body is used in performance is substantially different from that in everyday life. Performers need to master techniques whereby the body can 'attract the spectator with an elementary energy which "seduces" without mediation. This occurs before the spectator has either deciphered individual actions or understood their meanings' (1991: 54). But the purpose of the actors' technique is 'in-formation' and communication. They literally put the body in-form and allow it to become a means of communication, achieved after many years of work.

Ritual – Public and Objective

Rituals are public, collective and objective experiences. Although private ritual acts do take place, the usual setting for a performance is a public arena in which an assembled group takes part. As a result, it is rare for subjective expressions and private feelings to become integral or rest easily within the public domain of ritual acts. This sense of objectivity is again secured by its endeavours to distance the action from the usual and familiar. Richardson argues that Catholic liturgy has historically used the priestly vestments of the cope, alb and surplice to separate ecclesiastical and liturgical offices from the non-sacral and 'ordinary' (1995: 223). His comparison of Roman Catholic and Baptist worship identifies how, since performance, (by its very nature), stresses the exterior rather than the interior, Catholic unlike Baptist worship, is much more akin to a performance mode, 'It is the location of the sacred external to the worshipper that places Catholicism parallel to performance' (1995: 233). This public and performance mode can be seen in the ritual dress and setting of Catholic worship, often a primary means used to construct a new sacred self in relation to the selves embodied in statues which dominate Catholic places of worship. Intensity combines with distancing to convey this distinguishing feature of Catholic worship:

> Thus the *iglesia* becomes peopled with selves embodied in statues that portray scenes of agony, despair, and occasionally bliss; these are performances frozen at the moment of their most intense reality. Corresponding to the acts in ceramics are the flesh and blood performances of the priest and the communicants (Richardson, 1995: 233).

Richardson's argument is not dissimilar to Tambiah's about the stereotypical and conventionalised nature of ritual: 'Stereotyped conventions... act at a second or further remove; they code not intentions but "simulations" of intentions. People can act meaningfully in stereotyped ways because they have "learned to learn" in Bateson's sense of deutero-learning, and because the enactment of ritual is the guarantee of social communication' (Tambiah, 1979: 124).

No Pretence

As I have already argued, at its core, ritual is primarily about symbolic action, movement and gesture. This is what dominates the performance dimension of its expression and establishes its difference from 'ordinary' action; as such, it involves conventionalised or stylised action, which results in a form of intense communication. Without such stylised somatic action and the creative and intelligent organisation of space, there could be no sense of the dramatic or theatrical and therefore no sense of rite. As bodies move in order to enact their performances, attention invariably falls on how the body 'works' within such arenas. A 'good performance' entails the most skilful use of the body and how it is able to utilise the space provided for it.

Communication in ritual, therefore, is likely to come substantially through the bodies of the actors. Actors and participants come to be involved in a process of communication primarily through their bodies. Such 'bodily' performances are correspondingly received through the bodies of the audience, before any 'knowledge' or understanding is cognitively assimilated. As I have suggested, ritual is never a precisional or analytical form of cognitive communication, but works by appealing primarily to the sensual and fleshy bodies, emotions and feelings of the participants. One might term, therefore, with Winifred Whelan, this form of communication 'bodily knowing'. 'Bodily knowing is a kind of knowing that is felt by the body before, after, or alongside the understanding of the mind' (1993: 274).

Such ritual communication, however, is never achieved by mere pretending. On stage, I may perform the action of sweeping the stage or I may simply pretend to do it, or even mime the action. Similarly, in everyday life, I might perform or pretend to do certain actions for effect or to gain the attention of those around me. Erving Goffman's work on this aspect of an individual's performance in everyday interaction is instructive (1990). To perform implies that there is an 'audience', some others who will observe what I am doing. It is about self-consciously knowing that one is performing something, that such actions will have a particular effect on any observers. Goffman uses the word 'front' to describe the individual's performance, 'which regularly functions in a general and fixed fashion to define the situation for those who observe the performance' (1990: 32). If an individual's activity is to be significant to others, then such activity must be galvanised so that it expresses what he or she intends. In other words, it has to be performed dramatically: 'While in the presence of others, the individual typically infuses his activity with signs which dramatically highlight and portray confirmatory facts that might otherwise remain unapparent or obscure' (1990: 40).[1] And yet if the actor becomes self-conscious in an awkward or embarrassed way, the performance becomes less effective and may fail to have any impact on the audience at all. It was only during the early modern period when civic peace, (established by 'good manners') became substituted for ritualised peace that a sundering of the outward sign from the inner meaning occurred within ritual expression (Elias, 1982; Bourdieu, 1997). As Pickstock notes, 'The civic peace achieved through good manners might be a mere *apparent* peace which cloaked insincerity, and, indeed, the disguise of one's real intentions could itself be seen as a *politique* means of sustaining civic order in the long run' (1998: 148). Once ritual became viewed on the model of polite manners, cut off from the drama of life, 'mere ritual' began to be seen as a method of concealing rather than revealing the truth (Asad, 1993). This non-sacral mode of living according to civilised manners disrupted the premodern sacral realm which had so successfully secured the integration of 'real' life with ritual performance.

'Pretending' is never appropriate in religious ritual (Huizinga, 1949: 8). For instance, in the Roman Catholic rite of the Mass, the priest is both the official priest of the Church and Christ. This is not in any sense 'make believe' but 'actual believe'. The priest is never pretending to be Christ at the altar, but is Christ, just as the consecrated host during the Mass is not symbolic bread, but always the 'actual' body of Christ.[2] Nothing is faked. As Richardson suggests:

[1] Schechner comments on how markedly different is the performance of the 'professional performer' to the kind of everyday performance that Goffmann speaks about, since such 'acting' is largely unreflective and done without any self-conscious awareness of its significance and possible impact on others: 'The situation of the "professional performer" a person who reflexively masters the techniques of performance... is very different from the Goffmann performer who is likely to be unaware of her/his performance' (1990: 28).
[2] A sense of transformation is emphasised by Yi-Fu Tuan in his analysis of ritual, in relation to space and context: 'Officiants at a ritual transform rather than perform. A priest by his gestures and incantations acts on

To perform, the actor has to construct a self other than the everyday
self the performer ordinarily claims as her or his own. The actor must
become that other, theatrical self to the extent that it is credited as
having life. The magic of the moment, so to speak, is when the
performance achieves a reality of its own. For the performing self to be
credited as real it must be an objective, external self so that others,
actors and audience, may respond to it (1995: 233).

To conceive of religious ritual as mere theatrical show or display
is to misunderstand its nature; a ritual can never be primarily an
entertainment. Rituals do not simply engage in illusion, nor do the
actors in the sacred space simply 'pretend' to do the actions. They
are performed with as much seriousness and holiness that the
'actors' can evoke. As Driver notes, 'When a priest lifts a chalice, or
a New Guinea man greases a sacred stone, each actually does what
she or he is doing. Such a performer does not only pretend, as
might an actor on a proscenium stage' (1991: 98). Ritual is work
of the utmost seriousness done playfully, never simply a mimic of
real life, but within a specific context, a performance which
becomes transformative and 'real'. Driver concludes: 'In Christian
theological perspective, work done playfully is a sign of grace. That
is, it cannot be accounted for rationally, for it is transformative
work accomplished through play' (1991: 99). This transformation
occurs through a performance which calls into being the awesome
power of the Wholly Other. This is not to undermine but recognise
that liturgical performance is one of the most authentic means of
poiesis or 'making up'. Ritualised symbolic action brings about what
it signifies. The shaking of a hand in friendship cannot be
separated from friendship itself: the action is the friendship. There
might well be possibilities available for dissembling in
performance, but these often result in 'bad performances'.

Comic and Serious – The 'Play' Element in Ritual

This 'authentic' characteristic of ritual should not imply that ritual
is always serious. A strong 'play' element resides within ritual since
it is action that is 'played out' within certain limits of time and

reality as an architect-builder may be said to act on it. Is Pope John Paul II
acting? Note how ambiguous that word is – and disturbing to those who
want their sacerdotal figures to act but not to put on an act. Ritual places
people in contact with reality – with divine potency. Hence the moments
of danger from which only the consecrated and those who know precisely
what to do are protected' (1990: 242).

space. Huizinga argues for an inseparable connection between play and ritual since,

> the consecrated spot cannot be formally distinguished from the playground, the arena, the card-table, the magic circle, the temple, the stage... tennis court... etc. are all in form and function play-grounds ie. forbidden spots, isolated, hedged round, hallowed, within which special rules obtain. All are temporary worlds within, but distinct from, the ordinary world, dedicated to the performance of an act apart (1949: 10).

Huizinga maintains that play itself is ritualised action, a mode of performance set in a special arena of space and time which incorporates a new formality and dimension of bodily action. It is a world of authentic illusion where the 'beauty of the human body in motion reaches its zenith' (1949: 7). It entails a stepping out of the real world and entering another, one which can be as equally or even more serious and absorbing for the participants. Its repetitive nature contains the ability to transform it into a custom or a tradition, since events can be performed again and again without losing any of their significance. It involves contrasts, tensions, variation, poise and resolution within a magical circle and has a 'disposition all of its own' (Huizinga, 1949: 8). Those who are involved in rite must play this particular game fairly and the spoilsport is dealt with in a more severe way than the false player, since such action shatters the illusion of the performance itself.

What characterises religious performance is the added dimension of making present a sacred event of the past which has the potential to transform both the present and the future. All those involved must be prepared to be changed by those things which underpin every sacred performance. For Huizinga, sacred play is not merely representation but rather 'identification, the mystic repetition or re-presentation of the event' (1949: 15). Consequently, a religious rite is not simply an imitative re-enactment of a potentially life-changing event, but the magical reliving of that event, materialised anew each time it is performed. It causes the worshippers to be part of the event again, to participate in the sacred happening itself. Characters within this play mode become part of 'the sublimest forms of action' (Huizinga, 1949: 18). This form of pretence does not signify a lack of seriousness since 'Frivolity and ecstasy are the twin poles between which play moves (Huizinga, 1949: 21).

The Efficacious Nature of Ritual

The more serious dimension of ritual is connected to its efficacious character. Schechner writes that 'Whether one calls a
specific performance "ritual" or "theatre" depends mostly on
context and function. If the performer's purpose is to effect transformations – to be efficacious – then the qualities listed under
the heading "efficacy" will most probably also be present, and the
performance is predominantly a ritual' (1977: 120). His list under
efficacy includes: results, link to an absent other, symbolic time,
performer possessed in trance, audience participates, audience
believes, criticism discouraged, collective creativity established;
and under entertainment: fun, only for those here, emphasis now,
performer knows what she is doing, audience watches, audience
appreciates, criticism flourishes, individual creativity. Such an
analysis draws attention to the centrality of the efficacious within
ritual and adds the notion that ritual invariably gathers its meaning
by its potential to transform those involved.

   Driver's work echoes Schechner's in its location of religious
ritual within a predominantly efficacious mode: 'The dominant
functions, the ones that constitute ritual as ritual, have to do with
efficacy, with bringing about some change in an existing state of
affairs' (1991: 95). Schechner's idea of an absent other becomes
for Driver the central characteristic in religious ritual: 'A ritual is
an efficacious performance that invokes the presence and actions
of powers which, without the ritual, would not be present or active
at the time and place or would be so in a different way' (1991: 97).
Symbols are the means by which these hidden agencies are
depicted (1991: 27).

Ritual and the Body of Christ

Within Christianity, the ritualised performances of the liturgy are
the supreme means by which the Church, the new body of Christ,
is constituted and formed by the saving action of the Holy Spirit,
the divine presence invoked through the ritual. Participants
during a Eucharist are not simply gathered around the sacrificial,
saving victim on the altar, but share in his redemptive work by their
physical and mystical participation *in his body*. They *become his body*,
a body which has been transposed into other forms since the
ascension, the most important being the form of bread and wine,
a form they are invited to eat and drink. The corporeal

transformations which take place concerning the body of Jesus, become responsible, in the words of Ward, for an 'ontological scandal' (1999: 168), since time and space are redefined to accommodate the varied transpositions of Jesus' physical body. This physical, broken and sexed body of Jesus becomes liturgically contextualised as a different and yet same body, as a new assembly, as a thin wafer snapped and distributed, as the mystical union of all peoples 'called together from every nation' (*CCC*, 1994: 183). The Church, his body, comes to share in that same but transposed body of the Eucharist, in order to strengthen and sustain it in its own work of redemption.

Liturgical and ritualised spaces are particularly sacred because they are often the most concentrated arenas for the presence of such transpositions of the body of Jesus. The Church enacts and is united with Christ in the saving mission of the Church, in his joys and sufferings, (*CCC*, 1994: 182); by making present throughout the liturgical year those things which the body of Christ endured itself when constituted as a physical male form – its birth, its joy, its temptation, its suffering, its death, its resurrection – it becomes the new yet same broken body of Christ, distributed for the salvation of the world. This relationship between Jesus and his Church is always processional – one abides in the other, as members of the Trinity abide in one another (Ward, 1999: 177).

The manner in which liturgies unfold and take place, therefore, not only reflect this bodiliness and physicality, but always use the body in the fullest and most reverent manner since their task is to remind participants of the redemptive self-giving action brought about through, and in, Christ's body. The assembly enact through their 'prayer-bodies' (their gestures, postures, bodily submissions), their own potential for sacrificial self-giving, the ultimate example of which they participate in and see before their eyes on the altar. Christian worship, at its best, is always concerned with this bodily self-giving to the Father. As Prokes notes, 'When liturgical life is at-one with the eucharistic Self-gift of Christ, it is authentic' (1996: 145).

Ritual in the Middle Ages

Nowhere is this interplay between corporeality, theatrical performance, entertainment, efficacy and liturgical ritual seen more startlingly than in the liturgy and performance of the *Corpus Christi* play during the Middle Ages. Kolve has traced the use of the

word 'play' in his depiction of this medieval drama, a text written
by local clergy enlisting ordinary townspeople which had a span of
about fifteen hours acting and was performed for over two
hundred years. Whereas the word 'perform' might be used in this
century, the verb in the Middle Ages was always 'play'. But this did
not imply that such dramas were not performed with ritual
seriousness and correctness. The order of the *Corpus Christi* play
was set down in a playbook which had to be strictly followed and
fines were given to individuals and guilds for playing badly or
inaccurately.

The drama sought not to imitate but to 'pattern human
experience, to give to the history of men an order that would
reveal its meaning' (Kolve, 1960: 20). The intention was not to
reflect ordinary life but to make sense of life within the framework
of *heilsgeschichte*. It translated everyday living into a game mode.
That is why the word 'play' became contrasted with the word
'eyrnest' which means the world of everyday reality. There was
never any attempt to invite a suspension of disbelief: 'Their
function was to enclose the action, whether natural or mythic, in
a frame of commentary which put the playing unmistakably at
a distance from reality' (Kolve, 1960: 27). As a result of watching
the play, ordinary lives had been given a framework of meaning
and significance. The characters who agreed to play the parts were
ordinary men who never attempted to get inside the character but
simply to mimic certain actions and gestures of the person they
were representing. As Kolve says,

> These townsmen would have been astonished by Stanislavsky. They
> were ordinary townsmen engaged in a certain type of game, distin-
> guished from their fellows only by a more generous mimetic gift...
> those who played God would not have sought... to be God nor to get
> inside His personality; such a notion would have seemed to them
> blasphemous and absurd. They presented not the character of God but
> certain of His actions (1960: 24).

Their acting was both formalised and in a style divorced from the
world of 'real' life.

The unlearned and illiterate came to know the great truths of
Christianity through the engagement of their bodies and senses in
response to such dramatised performances. The action took place
outdoors and took on a mythic quality. The play was not a philosophical or theological treatise (although it was used for didactic
purposes), but primarily a 'bodily' pageant of salvation history,

indicating what God had done in history and would continue to do. The appeal was not primarily to the intellect but to the feelings and the senses of the audience since it was a type of affective education performed with grand gesture and symbolic force. Emotions of pity, grief, sorrow and joy were called forth as the play became a means of renewal in devotion – it was more important to feel the sorrow of the crucifixion than to understand its theological meaning. To 'know' about Christianity was to experience its pains and joys in the body and heart. As Kolve states, 'The lesson is less to the mind than to the heart, but it too is part of the medieval "knowing of God"' (1960: 6; Krondorfer, 1993).[3]

In the light of the importance of such pageants as *Corpus Christi* it is not difficult to realise how it was primarily through the body and senses that a person came to know the Godhead. Kolve's attempt to describe the essence of the play comes very close to Driver's definition of what religious ritual is in part, 'It played action in "game" not in "eyrnest" within a world set apart, established by convention and obeying rules of its own' (Kolve, 1960: 32). Religion was conveyed primarily through the ritualised actions of the body and the overlaps and links between dramatic ludic performance and church liturgy clearly testify to this at the end of the Middle Ages. Para-liturgical dramatic re-enactments were

---

[3] Krondorfer also argues that if we look at the development of Christian drama through the eyes of performance studies then it is apparent that the sacred texts of Christianity are not based on disembodied speculative thought, but reflect a catalogue of stories, plots, and imagery in which the body takes a central place. What occurred was a discourse of disguise through the theology of play. He argues that play theology becomes disembodied by its use of allegorical and metaphorical approaches. This could be, he maintains, a result of attempting to protect itself against vulnerability by rendering that theology safe and harmless and by disguising the sexual and violent body. The development of the Feast of Fools was one parody of, and counter to, this development in the Middle Ages. Here the dissolute body was displayed in carnival grotesquesness. These were performed by schoolmen and lower clerics on the feast of St Stephen, on New Year's Day, on the feast of Holy Innocents, on the Epiphany and the feast of St John. Eventually they became banned from the churches at the end of the Middle Ages. The Feast of Fools became an occasion for parodying and ridiculing the solemn and at times censorious world of the Church. They gave expression to the bodily nature of human nature with gluttony, drunkenness, orgies, disrobing and indecent gestures characterising these episodes (Krondorfer, 1993: 365–80).

widespread and reached their most theatrical in the Candlemas and Holy Week services. Duffy argues how, 'the gild of the Blessed Virgin Mary at Beverley, founded in the 1350s, moved from liturgical re-enactment to dramatic impersonation' (1992: 20). The appropriate guild would assemble each morning on the annual feast of Candlemas, one member dressed as the Queen of Heaven carrying a doll representing Christ. Alongside would be Joseph and Simeon, the whole spectacle accompanied by celebratory music and procession to the church. This would be followed by members of the guild each carrying a candle of substantial weight. It is likely that after the Virgin had offered her Son at the high altar, a Mass would follow. Other guilds would similarly dramatise the biblical salvific events, enhancing the imaginative and performative dimension of the prescribed liturgy. This is not to say that the liturgical pattern did not, in a parallel fashion, inform the dramatic works of the late Middle Ages. For example, the East Anglian *Ludus Coventriae* play of the purification includes a speech when Simeon receives the child Jesus which is identical to the opening Psalm of the Mass of the feastday. What is evident here, at this period in the Middle Ages, is that drama informed liturgy and vice versa. It was also primarily the lay participation in the Church's liturgy which enhanced its theatrical potential, infusing it with a ludic and ceremonial quality with dance and drama becoming creative and pedagogic ways of representing the saving events recorded in the Bible.

The Work of Victor Turner

As I have already suggested, rituals are partly characterised by their potential to restore and transform the attitudes and values of the participants. The twentieth-century social anthropologist Victor Turner has done much influential work on this dimension of ritual and his fieldwork has important consequences for understanding religious rites of passage and liturgy in general. His research into the Ndembu tribe in north-western Zambia in Africa, has triggered off important implications for liturgists. In his first chapter of *The Ritual Process*, Turner reveals his concern,

> Rituals reveal values at their deepest level... men express in ritual what moves them most, and since the form of expression is conventionalised and obligatory, it is the values of the group that are revealed. I see in the study of rituals the key to an understanding of the essential constitution of human societies (1969: 6)

Strongly influenced by Van Gennep's accounts of rites of passage, Turner's analysis of the concept of liminality divided stages of human development into three distinct phases: separation, the margin and aggregation. His primary focus is on the second stage, the margin or threshold period, *limen* in Latin. The characteristics of this stage are ambiguous and elusive since, 'these persons elude or slip through the network of classifications that normally locate states and positions in cultural space' (Turner, 1969: 6). This second stage is a transitional one, a period of potentiality for the participant, before reaggregation into the final stage of the cycle occurs. Behaviour here is normally passive and humble since participants are being fashioned anew for a more structured stage in life. Strong bonds of comradeship and a sense of egalitarianism characterise this time, while secular distinctions of rank and status disappear. Gerard Arbuckle gives a modern equivalent when he refers to passengers on an airline who experience severe turbulence. Often all talk of rank or distinction disappears. Once the aircraft lands safely, social status and groupings reappear (1990: 74).

Turner discovered this systematised progression in the highly formalised and symbolic ritual context of the Ndembu tribe. He claims that 'almost every article used, gesture employed, every song or prayer, every unit of space and time, by convention stands for something else' (1969: 95). The tribe organised much of its social meaning around the expressive functions of ritual; it was a *chijik-ijilu*, a hunting term which meant a landmark, blaze or beacon. It therefore carried two symbolic representations: a hunter's blaze (and an element of connection between known and unknown); and a blaze or beacon conveying the notion of structured as opposed to the unstructured or chaotic. For Turner the crucial stage is the liminal one, that betwixt-and-between time when liminal entities are neither one thing nor the other. It exists like the territory between mapped certainty and the unknown, it is uninvestigated ground, shade or mystery. Referred to as a wilderness or to being in the womb, it is neither born nor unborn. And as Flanagan suggests, 'liminality always carries an antinomal quality, an element of standing before, but between elements such as the sacred and the profane' (1990: 241). Clothing and appearance become significant in this liminal phase. Entities may be disguised as monsters, or wear only a strip of clothing or even go naked. They do not possess property, have no status and have no insignia that reflects rank, role or position. They are able to live a

communitas existence without any sense of division or separation.
This undifferentiated character is partly shown by the discontin-
uance of sexual relations. Another central feature of the second
stage is the transition to a higher status once the participants have
experienced the lowliness of the second, 'Liminality implies that
the high could not be high unless the low existed, and he who is
high must first experience what it is like to be low' (Turner, 1969:
97). The final trait involves a radical ontological change as participants move out of the second stage. The experience refashions the
very being and nature of the candidates. Turner's research has had
considerable impact on understanding what religious ritual can
achieve within a person's life and within the social group. His
critique of the reformed Roman Catholic liturgy centres around his
research into this notion of liminality and the power and potential
of ritual to secure ontological change. The ability of the Roman
Catholic tridentine rite to secure this liminal phase through its
attention to ritual structure is contrasted with modern worship
which has no such propensity or inclination (Turner, 1972).[4]

Emile Durkheim and the Function of Ritual

Durkheim's analysis of the totem similarly attempts to develop this
unifying and bonding function of religion (Durkheim, 1995). The
totem is the name for an object from which beliefs and rites flow,
an 'emblem' which represents the group. Three kinds of activity
may be associated with the concept: a system of beliefs and rites
which bind the social group together; a system of interdictions
which prescribes obligations towards the totem; and a system of
rites for worshipping the sacred object. The totem is also able to
make the group itself sacred and project its own sense of the sacred
onto the natural world, thereby providing a complete system of
religious understanding of the universe in relation to itself and its
own classifications of what is sacred as opposed to what is profane.

---

[4] Schechner echoes Turner's argument about transformation from a
theatrical perspective: 'what happens is that a person enters training or a
workshop as a "fixed" or "finished" or "already made" being. The training
consists of "breaking down" the neophyte, rendering her/him
psychophysically malleable' (1995: 41). He uses the word 'bits' (meaning
the smallest repeatable strip of action), to describe this deconstruction.
Once this has occurred, the 'bits' can be rearranged, 'almost as the frames
of a film being edited are rearranged – to make new action' (1995: 41).

Durkheim demonstrated the positive effects rites would have on individuals and society through his identification of four types: sacrificial, imitation, representative and piacular. Rituals re-enact important values and beliefs, reconstitute the social identity of the group and strengthen the participants in a social purpose. Sacrificial rites specify the obligations individuals have towards certain objects of the group which help the clan or are fundamental to life. Imitation rites are organised to imitate the movements and habits of animals whose reproductive powers are wanted. Representative rites bring into the present the collective values of the participants' ancestors, thereby renewing the understanding the group has of itself, bringing about social integration:

> Here, then is a whole collection of ceremonies whose sole purpose is to arouse certain ideas and feelings, to join the present to the past and the individual to the collectivity. In fact, not only are these ceremonies incapable of serving other ends, but the faithful themselves seek nothing more from them. ... I have already shown that they are closely akin to dramatic performances (Durkheim, 1995: 382–83).

What mattered most, argued Durkheim, was that individuals were assembled and that feelings were expressed through actions performed in common.

Piacular rituals assert the religious significance of misfortune, loss and death. Their function is to renew the group to its former unity and collectivity after a period of lamenting. At key periods, rites put into action the central myths of the group, an invaluable exercise in collective memory by which a common social purpose is reinforced and sustained. The collective consciousness engendered by the social group allows the participants to undergo a metamorphosis. It was society which raised individuals above themselves and made its influence felt when the individuals of which it is composed are assembled together and act in common. Common faith is revitalised in the social group, dispelling private doubts and anxieties. The recognition of the sacred by the social cohesion of the assembly becomes the means by which personal anxieties can be overcome.

William Pickering suggests that for Durkheim everything turns on this being together and acting together. Those who are involved in rituals are left with feelings of euphoria and strength: 'They take away with them feelings of well-being, the causes of which they cannot clearly see, but which is well-founded' (1984: 337). At an 'effervescent' assembly levels of feeling can be intense, engendering new ideas or a level of excitement which can be so strong that members at the close of the ritual feel morally strengthened. This recreative function is indispensable to religion, without which it becomes listless. Durkheim understood ritual primarily as having this overwhelming power to dramatise collective representations and endow them with a mystical ethos (1995). In the course of the communal experience acceptance of those representations is established as well as deep-seated affective responses to them. This belief in the transformative energy latent within ritual underlines its social power. The social efficacy of the message is maintained by the participation involved.

Although participants in ritual events may at times react against such institualised ritual norms (as I shall demonstrate at the close of this chapter) their very involvement secures a significant degree of endorsement to the things acted, spoken about and represented. Rituals reinforce the social relationships they represent. But there can be disadvantages, as Denise Newton rightly points out:

> This includes not only the symbolic aspects designed by the religious specialists, eg. kiss of peace, priest facing congregation representing corporateness and egalitarianism in recent Church of England and Roman Catholic liturgical reforms, but the empirical reality expressed in terms of the social positions of those who play key roles, eg. the exclusion of women, social background of clergy/lay leaders, etc. and how roles are allocated prior to worship, and link into the ranking structure of wider society, reinforcing or challenging it (1986: 496).

Ritual defines as authoritative certain ways of seeing society, since it serves to 'specify what in society is of special significance, it draws people's attention to certain forms of relationships and activity – and at the same time, therefore, it deflects their attention from other forms, since every way of seeing is also a way of not seeing' (Lukes, 1974: 175).

For Lévi-Stauss ritual performs a strong communitarian function, being able to re-etablish social connectedness and harmony. It reasserts the connectedness of things and the conti-nuities of life (1966, 1981), and fuses together a moral and aesthetic understanding of culture with a sense of the really real, the cognitive and existential. It has a unique capacity to integrate both conceptions of order and dispositions for moral action (Geertz, 1973). The notion that rituals can substantially bring about resolutions of conflict is supported by Max Gluckman (1963); rites act as a kind of safety value for social tension. René

Girard also emphasises that ritual sacrifice can control and finally repress human violence, enabling ordered social life to continue (1977). Such important theories about the positive functions of ritual point to its restorative and reconciliatory power.

Difficulties and Challenges

Although I have argued throughout this chapter that ritual possesses a unique power to strengthen collective values and identity, in this final section I wish to draw attention to some of the difficulties which might arise if the values and beliefs underpinning the ritual are no longer shared or considered meaningful by the ritual participants themselves. In other words, to raise the question, what happens when ritual fails to resonate with the experiences, values and beliefs of the participants? Patricia Curran's persuasive study of two religious orders, the Dominicans and the Sisters of Notre Dame, has emphasised the importance of this issue by tracing the demise of food ritual within these two Roman Catholic communities. She argues that, 'their dining place, the refectory, is a ritual arena where the sisters portray their understanding of discipleship; using gesture, posture, movement, silence, and speech to give thanks to God for all that sustains them – food and faith, life and grace' (1989: ix)

She describes the preconciliar era as one of complete acceptance of the prescribed codes for food ritual. The refectory was regarded as a stage where performances were acted out, reflecting a deep-seated theological worldview and an attitude to the body and the senses which was unambivalent. A turning point arrived about 1960 Curran argues: inner resistance to such rituals and public performances started to occur, with hostility to such ritual re-enactment becoming widely prevalent. In the past, the refectory stage came ritually alive at meal times, with each of the Sisters acting their parts, 'The Dominican refectory was a fixed space: the tables were set in the room in a horseshoe pattern that was obligatory for every house, and the seating pattern followed precise rules' (1989: 111). This was an essential part of their disciplined life to direct the self more substantially towards God by means of ritual action and gesture.

Curran has highlighted in this study the importance of ritual enactment for securing personal and community identity, but suggests that when the actors rejected the understanding of reality played out in the performance problems occurred. In this case, the difficulty became manifest in the demise in the number of candidates entering the Order and the increase in those leaving the community. 'No-one knows when precisely the rituals died, when the actors rejected the construction of reality rendered in the performance, when the forms became empty, because no-one inquired at the time' (1989: 144). New postulants began to question the value in some of the community's rituals. If Ortner's model of ritual (1977) was to claim that it dramatises the fundamental assumptions of a culture, then those assumptions (eg. the ascendance of grace over nature, mind over body, common good over individual interest), were no longer easily accepted.

The previous dining rituals had portrayed an ambivalent attitude towards food, (as being both gift from God and source of temptation) coupled with a distinct theological worldview. The spatial staging of the dining area itself reflected the cosmology of a divinely inspired universe. Order and design in the chapel and refectory were essential. Everyone knew their place. In the Dominican 1923 Constitutions mention is made of how the 'visible Church upon earth regulates minutely the order of the hierarchy, from the humble acolyte to the Vicar of Christ. The same is true in human society, even within the narrow limits of the family circle. Any disregard or neglect of this custom would everywhere result in chaotic confusion' (Curran, 1989: 113).

The ritualised rules of the refectory were also meant to control the indulgences of the senses. The formality of bodily politeness was a means of centring the self on God. Spontaneous actions and gestures were forbidden. Sense stimulation was to be avoided. For instance, the eyes were to focus downward, and actions were to avoid any abruptness of movement. The performance here was one of control and serenity, the senses being restricted and regulated. Hearing was to be awakened only by the readings from the Bible, saints or martyrs. Hands, stated the Dominican Order, were to be placed under the scapular when not in use and eating was to be done without showing any preference for food. 'The rituals of convent dining were cultural performances that attempted to reestablish the fundamental facts and values of religious congregations' (Curran, 1989: 141).

Curran's research shows that after the Second Vatican Council a significant erosion in the ownership of refectory customs was underway. What the study reveals is not only the shifting understanding of religious life within the contemporary Roman Catholic Church, but the need for rituals to enact and embody a view of the world which is cognisant with the actors involved in the performance. Ritual has the power to sustain and develop 'the self' and community identity if it can sustain at least some agreed meaning by its adherents. Actors have to recognise and appreciate the importance of the performance for their own existence. Candidates in the 1960s had entered a new, 'sensory world, a foreign land where space is structured differently' (1989: 144). 'Personal orientations that derived from the novices' culture conflicted with religious orientations of the congregation over the value of the self' (1989: 144). The research does not question the need for rituals in community living, but rather what rituals represent about the self and, in particular, their relation to the senses and the body. It underlines the view that rituals have the power to disorientate and undermine, as well as to build up a community, if their significance rests upon assumptions no longer accepted by the actors. Its creative power, therefore, is partly based on an acceptance of those actions and what they rest upon and signify.

Having discussed the dominant features and characteristics of ritual, I am now in a position to show in my next chapter how ritual and liturgical practices in the premodern world were central to the life of the Church and to the individual's and community's Christian self-understanding.

2

THE BODY, RITUAL AND LITURGY IN THE PREMODERN WORLD

In the previous chapter I examined the distinctive features of ritual, pointing to those characteristics which would need to be maintained if its potentiality and power were to be released and secured. In this chapter I focus initially on the place and significance of embodiment and ritual expression in the premodern Christian world to show the pervasiveness and ease with which liturgies were carried out in relation to 'the ritualised body' and somatic experience. In particular, I refer to how the medieval Church sought to incorporate the 'religious body' into the very core of its ritual expressions, emphasising the importance of corporeal and collective experiences of the sacred. Liturgical practice and meaning was to be found through, not in spite of, the body. I then move on to outline the marginalisation of ritual expression which occurred during the time of the Protestant Reformation. Finally, I conclude with a discussion of the influence of René Descartes' philosophy on the dismantling of any notion which sought to attach importance to embodied experience.

The Body and Ritual in Early Christianity

The premodern Church placed the human body at the centre of its speculations about Christian life, identity and faith. It is impossible to understand how early and medieval Christianity functioned without considering the status the Church gave to notions of embodiment (Brown, 1991; Thomas, 1991; Mellor and Shilling, 1997). Not surprisingly, this emphasis became reflected in the liturgical and ritual practices governing the life of the early and medieval Church (Swanson, 1997; Prokes, 1996). The overriding majority of ritual undertakings (fastings, exorcisms, ascetical disciplines) combined with the 'physicality' of sacramental practice and devotions, to affect the body in perceptible ways. Christians in the premodern world could both feel and see the extent of their spiritual endeavours and aspirations (Stuart, 1996). The physical marks etched on their bodies reflected their spiritual earnestness and became indispensable means and signs of purification and preparation for their ongoing encounters with God.

Accounts of baptism in the fourth century record this insistence on bodily practices for conversion and the striving for more purified Christian living. The ceremony itself was specifically organised to bring about a dramatic conversion in the candidate by inducing a distinctive physical effect, with emotional and psychological consequences. Instruction about the meaning of the sacrament, known as *mystagogy*, was only given after the ceremony had taken place and was never part of the ritual event itself. Easter was the time for such baptismal rites, a period symbolically attuned to emphasising the death and resurrection of Christ, and an obvious time for stresssing corporeal identification. St Cyril of Jerusalem referred to the newly baptised as 'undergoing a corporeal transformation: stripped naked... you were imitating Christ naked upon the cross... You were conducted by the hand to the holy pool of sacred baptism, just as Christ was conveyed from the cross to the sepulchre' (quoted in Bradshaw, 1996: 25).

St Ambrose's understanding of baptism during the fifth century was correspondingly couched in terms of a bodily transformation, emphasising a transition from a state of self-indulgence (where the soul was commonly being forced to 'slip') to a new state of innocence, prefigured in the pure body of Christ. His preaching in Milan emphasised how baptism would transform potential converts, if only they would allow their skins to be touched by the holy water from the sacred pool outside the city's basilica. Baptisms of this kind involved a somatic and ontological transformation since to 'put on Christ' meant to exchange the weakness of the human flesh for the pure flesh of Christ. Christ's flesh was 'a pool of shade, which has cooled the high fevers of our desires, which has slaked the fires of our lusts' (quoted in Brown, 1991: 350). As Peter Brown notes of such occasions, 'Ambrose presented conversion and baptism in terms of an intimate participation in the perfect flesh of Christ' (1991: 350). A central strand within the sacramental life of fifth-century Milan had clearly become associated with an emphasis on spiritual transformation brought about by a corporeal experience of baptism.

The anointing of various parts of the body was an important part of baptism during the fourth and fifth centuries. Described in highly sensual terms by St Cyril, the ears were touched so that candidates may hear the divine mysteries, the nose that it may smell like 'the aroma of Christ' and the chest to arm the candidates against the devil (Bradshaw, 1996: 30). St John Chrysostom from Antioch imagines such anointing as an armour for the limbs of the candidates, which would become strong, like soldiers, able to fend off the wiles of the devil (Bradshaw, 1996: 27). It was also common practice for the naked baptismal candidates to be clothed in white garments following their immersion in water, to signify their transfigured and purified state, St Ambrose even insisting on a purificatory washing of the feet after the anointing. The head was anointed as a related but separate action. Peter Ackroyd's account of the baptism of Thomas More in 1478 records a similar emphasis on bodiliness: The priest, 'placed some salt in the baby's mouth, according to custom; then the priest exorcised the devil from its body with a number of prayers, and pronounced baptism as the sole means to obtain grace… The priest spat in his left hand and touched the ears and nose of the child with his saliva. Let the nose be opened to the odour of sweetness' (Ackroyd, 1998: 1).

Margaret Miles describes such early Christian initiations as essentially ontological transformations of the self, emphasising how Christian understanding always followed and never preceded bodily experience: 'The aim of religious practices was thus not to "act out" previously held ideas or beliefs, but to realise – to make real – in a person's body, the strong experience that, together with the religious community's interpretation of that experience, produced a counter-cultural self' (1992: 24). The nakedness involved became an important part of the initiation, a visible and bodily means of developing a newly formed 'subjective' self. Such nakedness, particularly for women, became a symbolic representation of opposition to the prevailing secular approaches to the flesh (Stuart, 1996). The aspiring counter-cultural body, due to its identification with the soul and Christ's spirit, was rescued from the ravages of the world and was able to be reborn. The clothing (white linen robe and slippers) and ritual food (milk and honey) symbolised an ontological transformation and strengthening of the self. Consequently, the sacrament of baptism, not unlike the rite of extreme unction at the moment of death, centred around a corporeal experience, considered essential for the formation of a new Christian self.

St Augustine, too, not unlike earlier African Christian writers, also gave considerable attention to the physical and bodily nature of baptism. The feats to be done during the time of sacramental preparation were often seen in terms of physical challenges and metaphors, reflecting stringent bodily activities – the body was the stadium, the wrestling ground, the race-course, the boxing ring (Miles, 1992: 40). St Ambrose also described the ceremony of pre-baptismal anointing in strongly somatic terms: candidates must be 'rubbed with oil like an athlete, Christ's athlete, as though in preparation for an earthly wrestling match' (quoted in Bradshaw, 1996: 26). In fact, one of the most important signs by which Christians would be assured that they were progressing in the spiritual life was their ability to master physical feats, for example, sexual abstinence, fasting and vigils. The new body given in baptism, could only be offered once the old body had been physically affected and altered. Such bodily self-abnegation became a reliable measure of the dedication with which the catechumen desired baptism. It is not surprising in the light of this that St Augustine could happily describe the newly baptised as the actual body of Christ: 'You are what you have received' (quoted in Miles, 1992: 41).

The sensual body featured strongly in the spiritual experiences of the early Christians. St Augustine believed that knowledge of the created world automatically entailed knowledge of God. The bodily senses bring knowledge to the inner self, where it sifts and monitors the information given. The senses are then able to act as messengers to the inner self: 'With my bodily powers I had already tried to find Him in earth and sky, as far as the sight of my eyes could reach, like an envoy sent upon a search. But my inner self is the better of the two, for it was to the inner part of me that my bodily senses brought their messages' (St Augustine, 1985: 212). Christian endeavour for St Augustine is never to allow the senses to become slaves to the created order (and thereby indulge in distractions) but to recognise that by reason, individuals (unlike animals, not guided by this faculty) can 'sift the evidence' relayed to them by the senses (1995: 212). Both the senses and the inner self have important roles to play in the acquisition of knowledge and in ensuring an experience of the love of God.[1]

At times St Augustine does record a more cautious and ambivalent attitude to the senses. In *The Confessions* he claims that they can be distractions for the soul, since they are often not content to work in harmony with reason. They may become jealous and wish to take precedence. Interestingly, the experience of music in worship can lead to such indulgence since it is primarily a sensual activity: 'So I waver between the danger that lies in gratifying the senses and the benefits which, as I know from experience, can accrue from singing' (1985: 239). He also admits that his weakest moments often come through the sense of sight, but such temptations never convince him that the senses are unimportant, since it is God who has given to human beings an added power in the soul to discern and reach God through such means and 'By it I not only give life to my body but also give it the power of perceiving things by its senses' (1985: 213).

The Body and Ritual in Medieval Christianity

An important medieval figure who similarly acknowledged the importance of the sensual body in the process of Christian formation and identity was the twelfth-century Franciscan, St Bonaventure. Knowledge of God was always mediated through bodily experience: 'The best way to know God is through the experience of sweetness; this more perfect, excellent and delightful than through rational inquiry' (quoted in Dreyer, 1983: 54). A member of a Franciscan Order which stressed the importance of affectivity in devotional practices, St Bonaventure's frequent use of affective language is testimony to his

---

[1] However, St Augustine does acknowledge at the same time, the superiority of the inner self, 'But my inner self is the better of the two, for it was to the inner part of me that my bodily senses brought their messages' (1985: 212). The inner soul judges the material the senses bring, being their final arbiter and controlling agency. For St Augustine, the love of God is experienced within the inner self, sensed as light but of a different kind to bodily sensation, 'a voice, a perfume, a food, an embrace; but they are of a kind that I love in my inner self, when my soul is bathed in light that is not bound by space; when it listens to sound that never dies away; when it breathes fragrance that is not borne away on the wind; when it tastes food that is never consumed by the eating; when it clings to an embrace from which it is not severed by fulfilment of desire' (1985: 212).

understanding that knowledge of the divine and ritualised devotion to God, must always centre around a 'bodily' encounter. In his Prologue to the *Tree of Life* he demonstrates this emphasis, as he takes as his scriptural foundation St Paul's letter to the Galatians 2:9, 'with Christ I am nailed to the cross', a quotation he uses in his *The Soul's Journey to God*. Here he suggests that the authentic worshipper is the one who is able to 'truly feel in himself' what St Paul must have felt (quoted in Cousins, 1978: 119). He or she must carry in his/her flesh the cross of Christ and in order to imprint on the memory the power of the crucifixion, the believer must 'enkindle his/her affection' (1978: 119).

Later in this work he prays that he might be like his Saviour, 'fixed with my beloved to the yoke of the cross' (1978: 49). This stress on the bodily brutality of the crucifixion, a devotional depiction for the individual Christian to imitate and have compassion towards, is described boldly by St Bonaventure: 'Jesus was dripping with blood... first from the bloody seat, then from the lashes and thorns, then from the nails and finally from the lance' (1978: 156). The description is given so that Christians throughout time, may 'experience toward you... that feeling of compassion which your innocent mother... experienced at the very hour of your passion' (1978: 158). It is also in the *Tree of Life* that he was able to reveal most explicitly the purpose of his devotional method based on the expiatory 'physicality' of Christ – to soften the hardness of people's hearts: 'O human heart you are harder than hardness of rocks, if at the recollection of such great expiation you are not struck with terror, nor moved with compassion, nor shattered with compunction, nor softened with devoted love' (1978: 154).

Such bodily, empathetic identification with the suffering of Christ was one of the most effective means of ensuring entry into higher contemplative meditation, a clear passageway to a higher state made possible through the doors of affectivity. The soul's journey into God came about by sensing the full impact of the things of creation. The essence, power and presence of God can only be satisfactorily felt and perceived through sensation. If for St Augustine the inner soul of a person converted and processed the phenomena of the created order captured by the senses, then for St Bonaventure that created world became itself a vestige, a distant, but authentic and telling representation of God. Indeed, for St Bonaventure, there is a vestige of the Trinity in every single creature: the created world is like a book in which the Trinity is able to shine forth and be read (Cousins, 1978: 69–78). The whole of the created world enters the human soul through the doors of the senses becoming vestiges in which we can see God and it is primarily through this created order's impression on the senses that we come to acknowledge its ultimate source. This strongly Aristotelian notion (that everything that moves is moved by something else) led St Bonaventure quite naturally to the conclusion that things perceived by the senses are ultimately enjoyed as knowledge of the spiritual world. Experiencing the bodily and corporeal things of the created order entails enjoying the world of spiritual truth. The 'smaller world' of the physical universe, known by the five senses through apprehension, pleasure and judgement, is an icon of the things of God, since 'from the creation of the world, the invisible attributes of God are clearly seen, being understood through the things that are made' (quoted in Cousins, 1978: 70).

It is not surprising to find in the light of this emphasis by St Bonaventure on the redemptive bodiliness and physicality of Christ, that he was the first Christian to formulate and encourage devotion to the Sacred Heart, a meditation which first began as a reflection on the wound in Christ's side. Devotional practices emerged which entailed aligning one's own body with the body of Christ, endeavouring to feel the pain that Christ would have felt. One feature of this devotional method was an attention placed on the incidents involved in the passion as themes for meditation, to be developed later into the Stations of the Cross, a devotion still evident in Roman Catholic churches today. As Duffy writes,

> The liturgical centrality of the Crucifix in the surroundings of late medieval English men and women was matched by a similar emphasis on the passion as the centre of their private devotion. In England, as elsewhere, the Bernadine tradition of the affective meditation on the passion enriched and extended by the Franciscans, had become without rival, the central devotional activity of all seriously-minded Christians (1992: 234–35).

Devout Christians were encouraged to empathise with the details of their Saviour's passion with a later branch of medieval devotion being characterised by association with the actual wounds of Jesus. This emphasis accorded to Jesus' humanity and suffering gave medieval men and women confidence to acknowledge relation to their suffering Saviour. In Christ's human suffering, they saw a loving brother from whom they could claim the rights of kin and salvation (Duffy, 1992; Swanson, 1995; Pickstock,

1998). Gordon Wakefield suggests that such devotional practices occurred when 'human feelings burst the bonds of a rigid social order and yearned for a God, who in spite of the impassability theologians averred, shared our human nature' (1983: 347). Christ was not to be seen as an iconic image, but as a human person who bled, cried and suffered and with whom Christians were exhorted to identify.

A notable difference occurs, however, between St Augustine and St Bonaventure in their theological approach to the senses. The latter believed strongly that the senses have the power and ability to act directly upon the soul: the action of a material object upon the soul itself creates a sensation whereby the individual is able to know God's presence directly through contact with the external world. In contrast, for St Augustine, it is the soul itself which forms the content of sensation from its own resources and substance. St Bonaventure always maintained that the soul was the form of the body, only being modified and changed by it through the experience of the sensible world – in other words, the senses were able to communicate directly the presence of God – the finite revealed the infinite, including the wisdom and beauty of God. St Bonaventure became famous for this developed theology of the senses whereby 'the soul hears, sees, touches, and tastes the sweetness of God' (Dreyer, 1983: 54). Nevertheless, despite this difference, what is apparent in the writings of both saints, is a belief that a divine order is clearly manifest in the created order of the universe and that this is discoverable and discernible by the senses.

Ritual and Liturgy in the Middle Ages

Because the Church's liturgy and ritual practices were at the centre of medieval religion they inevitably reflected this grounding in the bodily human suffering of Jesus. Although the medieval intellect constantly wrestled with the philosophical dilemma brought about by the belief in the separation of the soul from the body at death, there was never any dispute about the assumption that the soul was unable to exist for long outside the body. If the predominant modern view now is that all we are is the body, then the medieval world acknowledged this too, but with a crucial difference – the soul is a constituent part of the body. For example, St Bonaventure regarded the soul as an actual material thing and

St Thomas Aquinas believed that the separation of the soul from the body temporarily at death was one of the most unnatural states of being that could exist (Davies, 1982: 120–21).

Such metaphysical understandings dominated speculations about personhood during the Middle Ages and had consequences for ritual practices. Within this conceptual framework there existed a hierarchical attitude to the body parts with the soul, heart and head assuming superior positions. Ritual traditions echoed this understanding of the body. Competitive pursuits invariably occurred when deceased body parts or relics of saints became available. Since these relics played a central role in medieval devotional life, when it became known that a saint's body was to be given as a gift (or possibly taken by theft) much interest was aroused. Offence would be caused if the less sacred parts of the anatomy were donated to a particular person or religious house. For example, Roger of Wendover states that Richard I's grant of his guts to the Abbey of Chaluz caused much alarm! Often, too, the heart was donated to the religious order which was favoured by the family for devotional reasons. But whole bodies were never claimed, since a small part of the body of a saint was acknowledged as representing the whole; and as early as the fifth century it was widely accepted that any dividing up of a saintly body was seen as a sign of triumph over death and as a source of healing (Binski, 1996: 63–69).

The Eucharist in the Middle Ages

It was the Mass, however, which held the superior ritual position within religious devotion during the Middle Ages (Bossy, 1985; Duffy, 1992; Swanson, 1994; Pickstock, 1998). The celebration was primarily an action, referred to as 'doing the eucharist' (*eucharistiam facere*) and 'performing the mysteries' (*mysteria telein*). The sacring (the occasion when the host was raised by the priest above his head for all the kneeling congregation to see) was the most sacred moment during the Mass when individual and corporate harmony was restored. This elevation was accompanied by the drawing of a dark curtain from behind in order to set the event in dramatic relief. Since this action of elevation ceremoniously re-enacted the passion and resurrection of Christ (and partly because many Masses took place at the same time), a warning bell was rung to enable the congregation to rush forward to the high altar and witness the sacring for themselves. Seeing the body of

Christ and receiving it once a year at Easter were devotionally crucial times when the holiness of God was experienced, grace bestowed and faith strengthened. As John Bossy writes, 'For the devout as for the average soul, the elevation of the Host at the end of the Middle Ages was a moment of transcendental experience' (1985: 68). Any refusal to respond to the sacring in a humble and devotional manner was frequently regarded as a sign of the presence of Lollards, a heretical group of people who held beliefs opposed to the official Church.

The distancing of the sacring by the roodscreen (and during the Lenten season the added appearance of an imposing veiled crucifix) heightened the importance of the host. The screen became a kind of window through which the worshipper could see the body of Christ lifted high in the form of a host; as a result, the sacring became a moment of intense drama and redemptive meaning. But the laity were not isolated or alienated from such liturgies, since at important times the Gospel texts, paxbread and holy water would be brought down into the congregation. Lay texts, produced to help the laity respond to the actions of the Mass, indicated a corresponding patterning between the actions of the priest and the actions of Christ in the Gospels. For example, the procession at the start of the Mass would echo the journey of Christ to Calvary, the maniple on the priest's arm recall the rope which dragged Christ to his death and the wearing of a purple chasuble a reminder of the vestment in which Christ was mocked. The Mass itself was a sequence of meditations on the bodily passion of Christ. It was also the supreme act of sacrifice, the sacrament of Christ's blood, a ritual re-enactment of an expiatory event. This redemptive spilling of blood was commonly depicted on medieval seven-sacrament windows. Paid for by lay donations, the stained glass often displayed Christ's wounds, from which his precious blood flowed in rays of red glass.

Texts stressed this notion of bodiliness and physicality. The most frequently printed prayer in early sixteenth-century primers was the *Salve salutaris hostia*, which emphasised the bodily suffering of Jesus as a focus for ensuring the bodily renewal of individual Christians and the Church itself. The words clearly reflect the emphasis that the ritual body had assumed in the medieval liturgy of the Mass: Before receiving communion the worshipper prays that he/she 'may be worthy to be incorporated into Your Body, which is the Church. ... May I be one of Your members, and may You be my head, that I may remain in You, and You in me, so that in the resurrection my lowly body may be conformed to Your glorious body.' It is not surprising that manuals of instruction came to be written for the clergy in order to help them perform the sacred mysteries well. The *Secreta Sacerdotum* of Henry of Hesse during the mid-thirteenth century recommended prudence in the extension of the arms and that care be taken at the elevation of the host. The head should not be bent backward at the sacring to look at the host, since this would increase the possibility of being overcome by dizziness. Priests were frequently admonished for any sloppiness or inappropriate movements or gestures made during the Mass. John Leonard and Nathan Mitchell suggest that it was particularly between the ninth and twelfth centuries that a more biblical and allegorical interpretation of the Mass began, as the liturgy assumed a more dramatic representation of the life of Christ: 'One manifestation of this shift was the addition of several new gestures, such as those done in imitation of Jesus' actions at the Last Supper: Some priests began to pick up the host at the words *acceptit panem* (he took bread) and to bless it with a sign of the cross' (1994: 68).

Eucharistic belief and devotion was also much concerned with the development of social harmony and integration during the Middle Ages, with rituals often fulfilling an integrative and community-making function. Miri Rubin argues that,

> the language of religion provided a language of social relations, and of a cosmic order; it described and explained the interweaving of natural and supernatural with human action, in a paradigm which from about 1100 was one of sacramentality, with the eucharist at its heart (1991: 98).

Many liturgical processions at the beginning of Mass reflected the social positionings of the people of the towns and villages. The sacrificial and bloody body of Christ became an indispensable focus for much medieval devotion and the means through which the social world was retored to harmony. As Pickstock notes, 'it was at the Mass that the social realm received itself as the union of the social limbs of the Body of Christ, a theme of reconciliation which was symbolised by the great procession at Mass of the craft guilds and fraternities leading up to the canopied Host' (1998: 147). All members of the procession knew and kept their place. Bossy reiterates the view that the words and actions of the Mass were of enormous significance and power, 'What that power procured was the salvation of man; or to recapture the larger overtones of the word *salus,* the deliverance of the Christian from the whole concatenation of dooms, dangers, anxieties and tribulations which loomed over him in his corporeal as in his spiritual existence' (1983: 33).

Sacramental involvement intertwined with social integration and harmony. Confession was a matter of community responsibility to one's neighbour, rather than an act of individual self-examination. In 1408 the Prologue of the Ordinances of the York *Corpus Christi* guild tells how the body of Christ is the *medium congruentissimum*, the instrument of harmony within the community. Receiving communion at Easter meant claiming one's place in the community and exclusion from the rite was a sign of social ostracism. It is small wonder that Nicholas Tyting, who had quarrelled with the rector and therefore been banned from receiving communion, should be found weeping in the churchyard and then after Mass, became a target of consolation for fellow parishioners. Exclusion from the rituals of the Church was tantamount to social death (Duffy, 1992: 94–95). In the light of all this, it is fair to say that the Mass was broadly understood during the Middle Ages in three distinct but overlapping ways: as a time when the eucharistic presence was brought about at the consecration by the actions of the priest; as a ritual sacrifice re-enacting the offering of Christ himself allowing the living and the dead to be assisted; and as a dramatic performance of the whole economy of salvation. Geoffrey Dix's work on liturgy is famous for its emphasis on the second and indicates that there were seven actions of Jesus at the Last Supper which were condensed into four – taking, blessing, breaking and giving – and which gave shape to the Mass and remained unchanged until the Reformation (1980).

Palm Sunday and Holy Week services were the most elaborate of the liturgical year and outshone other rites. Palms were distributed, processions of the blessed sacrament took place, with some parishioners even dressed as Old Testament prophets, adorned with 'flowing wigs and false beards' (Duffy, 1992: 24). The host would be carried in procession and flowers and unconsecrated Mass-wafers would be strewn ritually before the blessed sacrament. Scripture was sung. In many parishes the custom of hammering on the west door of the church with the foot of the cross came to symbolise Christ breaking through the gates of hell. The veiled crucifix positioned high above the roodscreen during Lent would be lifted and while parishioners knelt, the clergy would kiss the ground, followed by the singing of St Matthew's Gospel. In Europe, particularly Germany, the host would be replaced by a life-size representational wooden cross of Christ.

But it was the liturgy of the *Triduum* which became the most spectacular performance in the whole liturgical calendar. The creeping to the cross took place every Good Friday and involved a highly stylised gradual movement, barefooted, eventually culminating in the solemn kissing of the feet of Christ. Even more compelling than this, was the burial of Christ in the sepulchre on Holy Saturday. A consecrated host would be placed in the tomb with a crucifix, followed on Easter morning by the placing of the host in the hanging pyx on the high altar. This sepulchre remained in the church throughout Holy Week and candles and incense would burn while all-night vigils took place. Burnham states that the Church of England is only just beginning to restore the dramatic significance of the Holy Week ceremonies so central to 'enactic' and 'iconic' learning:

> The traditional ceremonies... were not to be found in the first Prayer Book of the Reformed Church in 1549, nor indeed in any of the subsequent prayer books. The acting out of Holy Week was not officially restored in the Church of England until... less than ten years ago (1994: 1150).

Ritual and Death

The medieval attitude to the deceased particularly echoed the significance the body and ritual held for Christians during the Middle Ages. Based firmly on the Christian belief in the resurrection of the body, the bodies of saints were invariably placed within churches, near the altar. Previously the deceased would have rested outside the city walls. Saintly bodies became associated with shrines and assumed a central place within devotional practice and liturgy. Regarded as having healing qualities, pilgrims believed that they could be cured of sin and sickness if only they were able to touch their bodies. St John Chrysostom writes, 'where the bones of martyrs are buried, devils flee as from fire and unbearable torture' (quoted in Binski, 1996: 18). It eventually became enshrined in Canon Law that a relic of the titular saint should be inserted in the high altar of every church. Saints were invariably treated as if they were still alive, which technically they were.

By the twelfth century, as the affective tradition of devotion grew, personal identification with the suffering body of Christ became a major source for Christian penitence and healing. The tortuous deaths of martyrs (closely identified with the death of

Jesus) were emphasised and admired. Although the cross had always been a sign of triumph, it soon became combined with a depiction of salvific horror. The Italian Golgotha paintings of the thirteenth century portrayed groups of onlookers surrounding the passion scene to enable later generations of men and women to identify imaginatively with the tortuous sufferings of Jesus. Paul Binski writes of such developments:

> the Gothic Crucifixion showed a dead Christ with nails through each hand, and one through both feet, hanging uncomfortably from the tree... To either side stood growing numbers of witnesses in ever more distressed condition... These witnesses were important, because their affective gestures and expressions of despair marked out a mode of response relevant to the audiences of such images (1996: 45).

The ecclesiastical management of death itself during the Middle Ages also affords important insights into the ritual and bodily practices of the medieval Church. There is no doubt that the single most influential factor the Church had to deal with until the Reformation was the centrality and management of death. Late medieval life was saturated with the procedures governing the passage of an individual's life from this world to the next, with particular attention being given to purgatory. Such attention did not entail a morbidity about death, however, and Huizinga's classic study of medieval France and Spain has been rightly criticised for being too heavily reliant upon the despair associated with mortality (Duffy, 1992; Huizinga, 1965). The wills of fifteenth- and sixteenth-century folk give witness to a vigorous relish for life. It was the exuberance of everyday living that had to be cherished, even if this entailed making skilful preparation for the next life. The Church had consoling messages and fitting ritual practices in the face of death: this life was uncertain and brief, the next was blissful and eternal. It therefore made sense to plan carefully for the next life with all the optimistic rigour and zeal that one could find. The key biblical text for understanding all this was Matthew 25, the parable of the sheep and the goats. Above every roodscreen stood an image based on this New Testament message, destined to remind all church-goers of their destiny – be prepared, for judgement and death come to all. Christians were never totally prepared to meet their Saviour, but through the Church's mediation, rituals and sacramental life, the soul was being prepared for the hour of death.

Ritual practices were the stuff of such good deaths in the Middle Ages, with penance, anointing and *viaticum* being the essentials. A person near to death would have confession heard, followed by extreme unction and then communion. *Viaticum* (literally one for the road), probably reflecting the pagan practice of putting coins into the mouths of the dying person, prepared the body for its final journey. The laity frequently sought the intercessions of the saints at this hour of death and in *articulo motis* men and women paid overriding importance to the authority and ministrations of the clergy as ritual experts. Although the macabre horror of death is seen in medieval times, the comfort and support of the priest at the bedside of the seriously sick or dying person was evident with much emphasis placed on the power and goodness of God to save the individual by means of the ritual power of the Church.

Liturgical gestures often symbolised this compassionate concern. The gesture which accompanied the use of the *Ordo Visitanti* was the priest's raising of a small crucifix in front of the eyes of the afflicted, so that they might identify their own suffering with that of their Saviour's. Medieval death rituals can generally be divided into three parts: those of purification and separation which entailed the washing of the body, physically and spiritually; the anointing of the body; and the separation which consisted in the actual burial of the deceased. Once the dead had been received, funeral Masses and offices were performed which completed the cycle. Such patterns can be seen appropriately within a 'liminal' ritual model. The *Ars Moriendi,* a treatise which sought to remove needless anxiety about death and prepared the afflicted for any struggles with the devil, was well known. A popular iconography at the time was St Michael weighing souls on the scales of justice, while behind him appeared the Virgin Mary laying her rosary on the sinner's side. A particularly good example of this is the relief on the west portal of Bourges cathedral completed in the mid-thirteenth century. Angels also featured prominently in deathbed iconography, often in battle against the wiles of the devil, with St Michael and the angels representing powerful protectors at the hour of death.

Burial rituals similarly reflected important notions about the body in relation to sacred space. Consecrated ground, allocating prescribed areas for burial, reflected social position and hierarchy. Lepers, Jews, suicides and the unbaptised were never allowed on holy ground, while infants going to limbo found their position on the periphery. The cemetery, therefore, reflected the social demarcations in medieval society, with only a few protesting voices ever being heard. For example, it is recorded that the egalitarian liturgist, Durandus, Bishop of Mende, wanted all the dead to be buried with heads to the west and feet to the east so that they might echo the communal sense of the resurrection and the last judgement (Binski, 1996: 55–58).

After the burial, too, the Church's worship played its full part in recalling the dead person's memory. Remembrance of the dead played an important role in the Church's liturgical life with All Souls Day being a key event in the calendar. What was crucial here was the perpetual memory of the dead in the life of the living community, since the deceased depended on the supplicatory prayers of the faithful to help them in purgatory. As early as the third century it was recognised that the living could help those in purgatory. For example, in the *Passion of Perpetua* an account exists of how she saw her dead brother trying to help those in thirst in hell by giving them cool water and how she assisted him by her prayers.

The Body and Spiritual Development During the Middle Ages

An important development in the twelfth and thirteenth centuries was the drawing together of two separate traditions in religious practice based on the cult of relics in the western Church and the centrality of icons in the eastern Church. The spread of images of Christ and the Virgin often associated with liturgical and devotional practices, resulted in the 'relic-image'. Instead of onerous pilgrimages to relic sites, the relic-image afforded an opportunity for imaginative association with the sufferings of Christ on the doorstep. Sometimes such images detailed the disconnected parts of the body of Christ along with the weapons of torture – the nails, spear, crown of thorns – and were often depicted in a disjointed, almost surrealist manner. The *Arma Christi* of the fifteenth century and the *Five Wounds of Christ* by the Carthusian abbot, Willem van Bibaut which shows the heart, feet and hands of Jesus severed and placed around a cross, are good examples of this trend. Such seemingly macabre obsession with the suffering body of Christ reflected the spiritual desire of medieval Christians to identify with their Saviour, as well as testifying to the central place the body of Christ played in medieval spirituality. Binski seems to underestimate this spiritual thirst when he writes, 'there is something neurotic in the fetishizing scrutiny of Christ's body in late-medieval images, the history of passion painting in this period is partly one of sophisticated, obsessive-compulsive

voyeurism' (Binski, 1996: 126). But clearly there is no doubt that
Christianity was the first universal religion to isolate the body as an
object of veneration and devotion, liturgically and ritually centred
around the suffering and tortured body of Jesus.

The use of the body in medieval spiritual practices (although
differing in the demands it placed on the spiritual life between
male and female) also illustrates the significance the body held for
religious meaning, personal identity and spiritual progress. As I
have already discussed, it was only possible to demonstrate the
varying degrees of loyalty to the Christian faith, by participating in
practices designed to affect and limit the potential danger the
body might have upon the spirit. This was particularly the case for
women, whose bodies were regarded as the most formidable sites
for tempting men and for sexual indulgence leading to sin. Miles
suggests, 'Medieval women, as well as many women that came
before and after them, designed their religious practices around
introjected images of their own bodies as figures of sin, sex and
death' (Miles, 1992: 13). Caroline Bynum Walker's work on
medieval women's religious practices gives impressive evidence of
this trend (1987; 1991).

One consequence of this socially constructed identification of
female bodiliness with sin was that women martyrs and ascetics
strove to become like men through their religious and spiritual
practices. The body became the central pivot around which
notions of spiritual advancement took place and by which,
according to gendered constructs, the true self was defined and
identified. This was particularly the case when it came to ascetical
practices for women involving nakedness. Female nakedness was
used by ascetics as a rejection of sexuality. Women's bodies were to
be controlled and their physical appearances neglected so that
they would not create temptations for Christian men. The body, as
a result, became both the location and the symbol of a religious
self (Miles, 1992). If a woman did succeed and was able to conquer
her innate tendencies for sexual pleasure and sin, then she was
regarded as being 'manly'. It was inconceivable that a woman
would conquer such female weaknesses for sexual indulgence,
unless she had become like a man. Women as women, could never
achieve spiritual progress, for as Jantzen argues,

> This was unthinkable, partly because it would have required an
> unlinking of all the concepts regularly associated with femaleness:
> passivity, bodiliness and sexuality, and above all, inferiority. None of

these concepts could possibly be allied with spirituality; so it was easier to say that a woman of spirit had transcended her womanly character-istics and had become 'manly' (1995: 53).

Many female medieval mystics identified their spiritual experi-ences as embodied, without any of the dualism associated with modern understandings of the self. Because of the emphasis accorded to the incarnation and the sacraments during the Middle Ages, there was an established ease with embodiment which resulted in describing spiritual experiences as overtly bodily (Stuart, 1996). Many mystics experienced being held and kissed by Christ and having their bodies physically affected by his embrace. Benedicta Ward's study of Christian spirituality from Hildegard of Bingen to Teresa of Avila points to the way in which spiritual experiences were spoken about in distinctively non-dualistic terms (1990). As I indicated earlier, one clear demonstration of people's responsiveness to God was the way in which their bodies were affected, 'Where people were peculiarly open to God it was expected that the effect would show in their bodies through taste, smell, touch and hearing' (Stuart, 1996: 80). It was quite natural, therefore, for women mystics in the Middle Ages to identify spiritual experiences with bodily changes associating the impact on their bodies as a reliable measure of the genuineness of their experience. For men, too, spiritual growth was identified with the conquering of the flesh (but they had none of the innate disad-vantages women had). 'By learning to become more manly, they aspired to the manliness of Christ in order to conquer the flesh and live according to the spirit' (Jantzen, 1995: 53–54).

Social Theories About the Body

Two recent sociological studies by Pasi Falk and Richard Sennett have highlighted some of the differences which occurred due to different approaches being taken towards the body in the premodern and modern periods (Falk, 1994; Sennett, 1994). Falk's work suggests that in the premodern world, where social bonds were stronger and where there was a more secure cultural order, the body was free to be more 'open' to its surroundings and environment: 'the stronger the cultural order and the community bonds in which the subject is constituted, the more "open" is the body, both to outside intervention and to a reciprocal relationship with its cultural/social context' (1994: 12). In 'primitive' society, this entailed the constitution of a 'group-self' which defined the boundaries between the inside and outside primarily in collective terms. In the weaker communal bonding of the 'modern world', the individual articulates the inside/outside distinction primarily at the boundaries of the individual self and mainly on the body surface. This shift has implications for sensory organisation. In the restructuring from the collective to the individual, the modern mouth becomes the site for individual judgement and taste. Falk gives an example with reference to the ritual practice of consuming food. A strong cultural order in which alimentary codes are clearly established defines what can and cannot be eaten, the sense of taste being defined at the boundaries of the culture, the community and the social. In the modern era, taste cannot be disputed because it is based on the nature of individual being (body) and not in culture.

In premodern societies, the ritual sharing of food entailed an act in which the partaker was incorporated or could be said to be 'eaten into' the community. The eating together transformed the eaters into companions. In the modern period as the individual self developed, the body became more closed, as the quick modern privatised lunch-break replaced the shared ritual meal. As the body becomes more closed, the more language becomes detached from bodily states. This leads Falk to conclude that when verbal messages are sent and received, the more the body is reduced 'into an oral-verbal means of expression' (1994: 32). In other words, there is a separation between a person's language and body in the modern period due to the autonomy of the self and the corresponding closing of the body.

Sennett's recent work also maps out a shift from a premodern civic and bodily self-identity to a modern isolated self-bewildering body, by reference to the history of the city told through people's bodily experience. Like Falk he contends that bodies were previously much more open and able to respond sensorily to the urban landscape in which they lived. Now they have become 'passive'. What startles Sennett in particular about modern architecture is its lack of sensory stimulation, all the more surprising in a culture noted for exploiting so effectively the senses in consumerist ways: 'As urban space becomes a mere function of motion, it thus becomes less stimulating in itself; the driver wants to go through the space, not to be aroused by it' (1994: 18). How unlike ancient Greece where Pericles was able to celebrate an Athens in which harmony reigned between flesh and stone.

Buildings then reflected an understanding of the body which included inhabitants' social and physical needs. It was impossible for Periklean Greeks to understand their identity as separated from the fate of the city. By contrast, in the loose hanging together of the modern city, a strong sense of the Other is replaced by a weak sense of others (Sennett, 1994; Harvey, 1990).

Deritualisation and the Protestant Reformation

As the influence of the Protestant Reformers grew, any assigning of potency to the ritualised body and ritual *per se* became associated with magic, 'charming' and superstition. Cameron argues that 'the reformers abolished the "reliable" value of a ritual performed in the face of a sacrificing Church to aid human salvation... and gave fair warning that the meaning of being a "good Christian" was to change' (1991: 400). The avowal of a form of Christianity without the comforts of ritual practices and the saints characterised much of the Reformers' task. The characteristic identity of being a 'good Christian' was inseparably linked to this devaluing of ritual (Thomas, 1991). The individual was no longer to be given any external support to strengthen Christian belief, an ecclesiastical change particularly unsettling at times of crisis and uncertainty. One homilist writing in 1563 speaks of this need to strip away any external or objective support and protection, and gives a representative description of the kind of approach that underpinned many of the reforms in relation to ritual objects and practices:

> Alas, gossip, what shall we do now at church, since all the saints are taken away, since all the godly sights we were wont to have are gone, since we cannot hear the like piping, singing, chanting and playing upon the organs that we could before. But, dearly beloved, we ought greatly to rejoice, and give thanks, that our churches are delivered of all those things which displeased God so sore and filthily defiled His Holy House (quoted in Chadwick, 1964: 185).

For Luther and like-minded Reformers, the imparting of grace had nothing to do with sacred objects or actions performed. Salvation came through the unearned gift of grace: 'In the reformation, the sacraments depended for effect not upon rituals or intentions, but upon [given] faith', notes Cameron (1991: 157).

The extent of the attack on traditional rites and customs can be seen in a proclamation issued by Henry VIII in 1538 criticising some of the excesses of the onslaught. Specific ceremonies are mentioned for having come under severe attack – holy bread, holy water, processions, creeping to the cross on Good Friday and Easter day, the setting up of lights on *Corpus Christi,* the Candlemas ceremonies, besides ceremonies such as the churching of women. Much of the material in Thomas Cranmer's dossier also concerns the devaluation of ritual practices. His commissary, Nevinson, spent much of his time visiting dioceses, the sole purpose of which was to condemn ritual customs. He forbade the distribution of holy water and Candlemas candles, attempted to prevent candles being placed in the hands of the dying, limited outdoor processions, criticised auricular confession, and tried to prevent absolution being given to those who could only recite their *Pater* and *Ave* in Latin (MacCulloch, 1996).

The cultural and social repercussions were significant. Berger's analysis of the post-Reformation society highlights how the entire collective and institutionally held assumptions about the universe were severely dislodged as a result of such minimalist approaches to ritual. Using Durkheim's term 'anomie' to describe the emerging feelings of terror which were to emerge in the light of the rift between the previously held conception of the world sanctioned by the Catholic Church, he argues that new Protestant understandings occasioned an intense loneliness and feeling of isolation. The previously established 'nomos' broke down and was unable to offer any shield against the threats of everyday existence. Consequently, a sense of the meaninglessness of life was never far from such changed attitudes towards the universe (Berger, 1980). Pre-Reformation cosmological understandings of the universe rested squarely upon notions of security and comfort, since underlying their position was the widely held assumption that the 'earthly' community and the individual affairs of men and women were always intimately connected to the 'heavenly' affairs of God and his providence. Such assumptions contained within them strong and effective barriers against 'anomie'.

Berger contends that religious ritual is the most obvious collective device for maintaining such a continuity between the things of earth and the things of heaven. Catholicism was able to make this unique and unassailable bridge between God's world and the human world. The 'crucial Catholic doctrine of the *analogia entis* between God and man, between heaven and earth, constitutes a replication of the mimesis of archaic, pre-Biblical religion' (1980: 121). In this sense, the Catholic universe was always a most comforting and stable one for its inhabitants. It was able to set an individual's life within, 'an all-embracing fabric of meanings that, by its very nature, transcends that life' (1980: 54). Rituals reinforced the ultimate meaning and teleology of the world, ensuring that the view of the cosmos as taught and defined by the Church lived on from one generation to the next. Life could never become futile since the 'sheltering canopy of the nomos extends to cover those experiences that may reduce the individual to howling animality' (1980: 55).

Protestantism entailed seeing the universe in a radically new framework which was to have consequences for the location of the sacred. Protestant theology began to stress the 'idolatry of place' rather than its sacredness. Liturgical and holy things became transmuted into mere material objects which were only to be valued for their function in stimulating faith, not in themselves (Chiffley, 1998: 22). Sacred buildings and furnishings were to become merely symbolic of interior dispositions of faith. No space was considered to be sacred or different in a religious sense from any other space in such a theology (Chiffley, 1998: 22). There occurred as a result an 'immense shrinkage in the scope of the sacred in reality' (Berger, 1980: 111). No longer was the reciprocal relationship between the living and the dead possible, since praying for the departed and the intercessions of the saints were to be discontinued after the reforms. The sacramental life of the Church was to be truncated in favour of a theology which stressed the radical transcendence of God and the utter fallenness of humanity. Berger states that Protestantism 'cut the umbilical cord' between heaven and earth (1980: 112). As a result, individuals inhabited a much more lonely and bare universe. Scripture was the only channel for communication with God, with the modern world quickly becoming more open to rational investigation.

Berger plots this 'modern' shift in terms of a crushing bureaucratisation and oppression and argues there was no going back once the process had begun, 'Any attempts at traditionalistic *reconquista* thus threatens to dismantle the rational foundations of modern society' (1980: 132). One evident consequence of this was the growth of a new form of privatised religion, where choice of a religious form came to dominate allegiance. Since religion could no longer fulfil its traditional task of 'constructing a common world within which all of social life receives ultimate meaning binding on everyone', what ensued were fragmented worlds of disparate meaning, constructed out of people's preferences and endeavours whose plausibility structure became no larger than the nuclear family (1980: 133–34). The common meaning whereby individual actions were always directed towards an integrated social order, disappeared – the objective 'nomos' becoming internalised during a period of rapidly changing socialisation. The Church had always been the guardian of that 'nomos' but with the emergence of an increasingly lonely existence, the extent to which a person could construct his/her own meaning became an issue of considerable importance. At its most dangerous level an individual may seek death in preference to life.

Other consequences followed as the devaluing of a ritually constructed framework to the universe became widespread. Previously to step outside the universe as defined by the Church was to step into a pool of uncertainty and social estrangement. During modernity however a religious supermarket emerged whereby religious institutions began to market their products, becoming bureaucratic and competing with others in the marketplace. And further to this trend was the adoption of secular modes of operating as 'there is a global tendency for religious contents to be modified in a secularising direction' (Berger, 1980: 138). A significant factor became the standardisation and marginal differentiation of religion, once the dynamics of a religiously free market were set up. Berger uses the example of a Catholic priest being less likely to talk about Fatima than to engage in a dialogue with a psychologist on mental health since such 'conscious' strategies increased the chances of the religious product being bought. With increased secularisation and the reduction in the cosmic meaning afforded by religious underpinnings, a process of rationalisation occurred which was to have important consequences.

It was Weber, however, who was to highlight most trenchantly the individualistic and lonely characteristics of the 'protestant man'. The ascetic individualism which had grown out of the seedbed of the Reformation, particularly encouraged by the puritanism of Calvin, opposed strongly any form of ritual or emotion in Christianity. Solitary figures emerged, in obeisance to the severe presence of God who in turn were to become an indication and reflection of the guiding spirit that eventually characterised 'capitalist man' (Weber, 1971). Weber saw in Calvinism the most fitting form of religion for the emergence of seventeenth-century capitalism, based as it was on rationalist individualism. Both capitalism and socialism were to change under the influence of a process of rationalisation and both became polarised from the more traditionally religious forms of life. The moral severity of Calvinism appealed in a particular way, and as Robert Bocock comments, 'It provided the taboo on pleasure and gratification, Weber argued, compelled the capitalists to save, accumulate and invest and drove them to a sober and frugal rather than a spendthrift style of life' (1981: 81). Weber demonstrated clearly in his work, *The Protestant Ethic and the Spirit of Capitalism*, that when asceticism was carried out of the monastic cells into everyday life and began to dominate the world's economy, it did its part in building the modern economic order (1971).

Gellner epitomises some of the features of Weber's analysis of Protestant individualism and its influence on capitalism by suggesting that members of this tradition worry more about 'the future of their souls as well as of their investments' (1992a; 45). They cannot bring about their own salvation since 'the dismantling of spiritual hierarchy deprives them of the mediators who could have solaced and reassured them and would have received the appropriate prestations' (1992a: 45). The clearest sign of their calling therefore is not in their involvement in ritual, but in the right performance of their worldly calling, throwing themselves into work to allay their own worst fears. Such entrepreneurs could be relied upon never to turn their honestly earned wealth into a surge for power, for as Gellner puts it, 'From the viewpoint of those first engaging in it, there was nothing in the least rational about capitalist society: on past form, the fruits of industrial labour were destined to be taken away from them by those endowed with political power' (1992: 47). Calvinism, too, founded on a much stricter moral code, would never lead to manipulative power.

Gellner proposes that a new and distinct form of *ritualism* started to develop in the modern period as each and every moment in life assumed a kind of ritualised importance. There were no longer any seasonable times set aside for ritual celebration since 'The special occasion is replaced by the view that all occasions are equally sacred... Nothing in the world is more sacred than anything else' (1992: 48). Everyday tasks became performed with all the sacredness of a holy act, but such forms of personalised endeavour always carry with them an inherent criticism of tradition and authority. What was to emerge was a free spirit of enterprise, where the shackles of former religious practices, allegiance and countenance, were discarded in favour of a self-propelled, asocial pursuit of meaning. Meaning and self-identity were no longer to be discovered and strengthened by involvement in the social and ecclesiastical rituals of the Church but through the rational workings of the mind and the honest pursuit of labour.

In such a 'disenchanted' universe, the task of finding meaning became problematic and unsettling, since earlier structures had been rudely discarded (Flanagan, 1996). As Bryan Turner writes, 'Rationalisation makes the world orderly and reliable, but it cannot make the world meaningful' (1996: 6). Indeed, Weber's views about the process of rationalisation in the modern world resulted in important evolutions of some of the residue features within contemporary living. Ritzer's work on the 'McDonaldization' of present-day society, demonstrates some of the more dehumanising effects of a highly rationalised and bureaucratic management system. Such systems, based on efficiency, quantifiability, calculation, predictability and control, invariably result in an unhealthy control of human agency. His critique is not based on a romantic longing for the past, but on a hope for the future wherein a less rationalised, or even, derationalised world 'people would be able to live up to their human potential' (1993: 13).

Descartes and Modernity

If the medieval notion of self-knowledge and self-identity was centred around ritual and the body, then the emergence of the 'modern spirit', became most closely associated with the philosophy of René Descartes and was to re-orientate and revise things for good. But well before the impact of Cartesian philosophy it is possible to trace the roots of modern individualism in the medieval period. The Franciscan, John Duns Scotus (1266–1308), became part of an intellectual and religious movement that challenged the classical, neoplatonic notion of an abstract form of *genus* or *species* within which individuals participated and replaced it with a view that the *individual was a form in itself*. Giving intelligibility to the individual by making *haecceitas* (Latin for 'thisness') of the same logical type as the universal, he claimed that knowledge proceeded by being thoroughly acquainted with *individual* form. It was futile searching for something beyond the form, since it resided as a constituent part of the individual. This was a significant development, for as Dupré notes about this change: 'If the essence of all ideas resides in an individual, the weight of knowledge shifts from the abstract universal to the singular' (1993: 38).

With the work of the English Franciscan, William of Ockham (1258–1347), and the nominalists (who argued that universals have no existence independently of being thought and are simply names representing nothing that really exists), the importance attached to the *species* became broken. Previous Christian thinking had always postulated the idea that the divine could be recognised in the form. With the nominalist claim that the form was no more that a construction of the human mind, any attempt to secure a bridge between the finite and infinite collapsed. A far more scientific and secular mode of thinking developed as an understanding of form became dislodged from any divine signification; knowledge became aligned to the workings of the mind's independence. The early medieval notion that the cosmos was a thing of symbolic and spiritual potency, a sacral arena for discovering knowledge and truth, another book like scripture, from which one could constantly and easily read off the things of God, was beginning to be replaced by a view that there was nothing rational or beautiful about nature at all; ideality was a thing of the mind. The previous Christian onto-theological synthesis was severed.

This nominalist notion of a separation between the idea and the real finds its later home in Descartes' description of the objective nature of ideas. If nature no longer conforms to reason, the mind's link to reality becomes much more tentative and fraught with misunderstandings and errors. The only way forward is to maintain a sense of certainty by fixing the mind upon truth governed by a more dependable model; in Descartes' view, a model of mathematical reasoning. But as perception of the world brought about by the senses became substituted by objective mathematical reasoning, the result was that a central mode of engagement with the world was marginalised and devalued. As Dupré comments, 'The point is not that perception provides absolute certainty – Descartes is, of course, right in asserting that it never does – but that it provides the only available way of contact with the physical world' (1993: 85). It was left to the French philosopher, Blaise Pascal (1623–62), to discern a more balanced approach in asserting that it is important to know when to doubt, when to affirm and when to allow oneself to be governed by the heart (Dupré, 1993: 86).

Both Taylor and Fergus Kerr agree that the legacy of Descartes was to have an overriding and lasting influence on the cultural social and religious trajectories of modernity (Taylor, 1992; Kerr,

1989). Cartesian influence was largely responsible for many of the modern conceptions of the self which became tightly centred around an unbridgeable gap between the body and the soul and which were to have such devastating consequences for many later social and religious practices. In the Cartesian world the only thing which is certain is the 'I'. According to Kerr, Descartes' philosophy was to 'break with his inherited ideas – for example, "that I was nourished, that I moved about, and that I engaged in sense-perception and thinking;" For Descartes, "I am, then, in the strict sense only a thing that thinks; that is, I am a mind, or intelligence, or intellect, or reason, . . . a thinking thing" (quoted in Kerr, 1989: 4). Thus, a person can now peel off 'everything, my previous beliefs, my senses, my body, my confidence, even that the external world really exists, and I shall find, in the end, that I am essentially a thinking thing' (Kerr, 1989: 4). The consequences of this under-standing of personhood for previously held notions about individual and social embodiment were overriding.

Descartes strove to master a definitive and absolute conception of reality (Kerr, 1989: 23). The Cartesian searcher of truth cease-lessly attempts to extricate him/herself from any bias whatsoever, so that a pure and unadulterated conception of reality might be attained. As Kerr contends, 'To want the absolute conception of reality is to aim at a description of things as they would be in our absence' (1989: 24). This in turn meant that 'The drive for objec-tivity, then brought with it the uncanny thought that the only perfect depiction of any reality would have to be from nobody's point of view – or, if there is any difference, from God's' (1989: 24). This notion will be considered in more detail later when I outline the work of Bauman.

Descartes' attempt at securing an objective knowledge entailed a corresponding suspicion and doubt about any previously given and accepted truths about the world since these might turn out to be flawed. In the *Second Meditation* Descartes explains his position: 'properly speaking, we perceive bodies only by the understanding which is in us, and not by the imagination, or the senses, and that we do not perceive them through seeing or touching them, but only because we conceive them in thought' (Descartes, 1983). Taylor argues that this way of seeing the world calls for a remarkable change of direction since, 'it also does violence to our ordinary, embodied way of experiencing.... To bring this whole domain of sensations and sensible properties to clarity means to grasp it as an external observer would, tracing the causal connection between states of the world or my body, described in primary properties, and the "ideas" they occasion in my mind' (1992: 146).

The gathering of evidence began to be the guarantee of accurate knowledge. In order to avoid any premodern lapses into error, Descartes' method was based on a precisional scrutiny of all those claims made on the mind for certainty and truth. The various representations that appear before the mind, have to be arranged, ordered and fitted into a logically prescribed construction. There is no longer any preconceived set pattern that may be followed. The pattern has to be invented. Thinking, therefore, becomes likened to a process of gathering and ordering. The mind must make a constant effort to substantiate any claims to truth that might appear and these have to be justified before they can be a part of any newly emerging pattern. As Taylor comments, 'Thinking which is such a construction or gathering is rightly designated *cogitare* with its etymological links to notions of gathering and ordering' (1992: 145).

Any earlier medieval understanding of the importance of ritual, the body and the senses in locating truth about the world is replaced by a disembodied notion of thinking. The world and the body become objectivated, separated off from the *cogitare,* the central arena of truth. A disengaged perspective now comes to dominate. To grasp the nature of reality means discovering how the universe works mechanically, how it functions, how sometimes it breaks down. It is now possible to get hold of and grasp the once unknown universe, since the individual, unconnected and disengaged from its workings, can allow a cool hard look to take place. By this process, full knowledge will gradually, eventually, arrive. The endeavour also entails a similarly detached look at the self, as it becomes separated from the world it inhabits.

Taylor argues that this process of objectivity had enormous consequences for later understandings of the world. The construction and manipulation of the order of the universe was to be one of its most influential legacies. The previous notion of a submission of the self to a God-given order or providence started to collapse and reason began to substitute the senses and the body as the means by which the individual could eventually experience order, pattern and meaning. What developed was a new understanding of the self which consisted in its unconnected distance from the constructed order itself created. 'Self-mastery consists in our lives being shaped by the orders that our reasoning capacity constructs', and as the cosmos became neutralised it was 'no longer seen as the embodiment of meaningful order which can define the good for us' (Taylor, 1992: 7).

Taylor suggests that in the light of this new understanding of the self, rationality became defined procedurally, not substantively. A profound shift occurred between the idea of 'discovered' or 'found' orders and 'constructed' orders. Contrasting St Augustine's method to Descartes', he concludes that whereas the former's emphasis on internalisation always resulted in the individual's acceptance of a lack of self-sufficiency in the face of God, for the adherent of Cartesian philosophy, the right method involved a self-legitimating search for certainty which had no need of anything external to its cognitive self. I may now discover accurate knowledge about myself and the world by the powers of my own self-legitimating reasoning, without any recourse to God whatsoever. God, for Descartes, is simply an inference, outside the world, emerging out of my own self-validating attempts at certainty, as I locate error and dispel ambiguity.

The most disturbing consequence of this type of self-mastery, is the occurrence of an attitude of instrumental control towards the universe. This approach sees no value in the norms given by tradition and convention. It creates its own norms, identifies them and in the process, defines that which is abnormal. In this new understanding of discovering the truth about the world, the individual is no longer prepared to be bound by the indeterminate complexities of a premodern cosmos. There inevitably emerges a need to conquer (with all the mental capacity possible), the imprecision and unknowability of the world. It may even dislodge us from experiencing ourselves and the world in the most 'normal' everyday kind of ways, as a process of disengagement occurs whereby our most personal experiences become objectified, as if they were secondary ones. We begin to engage in a series of reflective processes to understand personal experience itself. Taylor concludes that because of this tendency, the modern conception of reason is always procedural. We are never called to be *contemplators* of order, but constructionists of a picture of things following the canons of rational thinking.

Pope John Paul II has identified some of these unfortunate and harmful legacies of Cartesian thinking (1994). He argues that one of the greatest anthropological shifts in philosophy occurred after Descartes, since he directed the use of reason away from the view that it was a means of finding God, towards an acceptance that reason is a conscious and self-sufficient thing, able to scrutinise perfectly and then construct the order and truth of the world. Reason, in other words, becomes an end in itself. Whereas Aquinas' theology led to a God of autonomous existence, Descartes', by making subjective consciousness absolute, moved towards pure consciousness of the Absolute and in so doing, the Absolute became autonomous thought rather than autonomous existence (Pope John Paul II, 1994: 51).

Rationalism promised a world that would be self-sufficient, a world which had two major consequences for belief in God. First, that a person was supposed to live by reason alone as if God did not exist; and second, that even if God did exist, he was banished from the world, since it was an unverifiable concept. There simply would never be enough evidence within the Cartesian model to establish God's existence. (It was the Deists who were to become the most forceful exponents of this position.) As a consequence of all this, soteriological roles were to become severely altered – the world no longer had any need of the divine. God's love for the world became redundant, as man's self-sufficiency became ever more pronounced in the name of progress. For David Lyon, this shift reflects a central thrust within modernity and is described as a move from providence to progress, from a God-centred medieval view of the world to a belief in the self-sufficiency of reason to promote progress: 'The wresting of reason from medievalism and tradition prompted many to believe that further and more rapid advance was within human powers to achieve... But by emphasising the role of reason, and downplaying divine intervention the seeds were sown for a secular variant of Providence, the idea of Progress' (1994: 5).

Pope John Paul II has also argued that any such attempts to try and free man from the mysteries of human existence were bound to fail. The world can never be freed from the mysteries of suffering and death. Nor can it ever escape the 'precariousness' that the entire world is subject to, as St Paul had declared in chapter 14 of his letter to the Romans. The world which appears under this Cartesian epistemological regime degenerates into a source for ruin, or becomes a testimony to the folly of self-sufficiency. The papal view is clear: 'This world which appears to be a great workshop in which knowledge is developed by man, which appears as progress and civilisation, as a modern means of communications, as a structure of democratic freedoms without limitations, this world is not capable of making man happy' (Pope John Paul II, 1994: 56).

Gellner sees similar dangers in Cartesian philosophy. Descartes' attempt to create what he calls a 'culture-free', 'Robinson Crusoe' stance in the pursuit of certainty, was problematic from the start (Gellner, 1992a: 14). During modernity's attempts at the rationalisation of everyday life, 'custom and example' were to be given no place and everything had to be discovered anew with clear eyes. Custom and example were indeed the enemies Descartes had set his whole enterprise on, for they suggested a secretive and clandestine knowledge of things only available to the initiated. For Gellner, such bulwarks of the premodern world could no longer be seen as essential, resting as they did on a sacred and privileged background. Previously, in the premodern age, knowledge had been discovered by validators who were able to perceive and recognise sacred evidence, but now such methods had to be abandoned in favour of independent, rationally investigated evidence. Or as Gellner puts it,

> A vision of the world is not allowed to dictate rules of evidence, with privileged sources, which then confirm the vision itself. One clear and distinct and self-justifying idea dominates: namely, that anything which is in conflict with independently, symmetrically established evidence, cannot be true (1992a: 146–47).

The one thing that disturbed Descartes above anything else was the possibility of making an error.

David Hume's contention that the senses are the most reliable means through which we come to know the world was always anathema to Descartes, since the most valuable contents of the mind could never have passed through the senses. A Cartesian world was to become characterised by a constant search for the tiniest dot of evidence in order to substantiate claims to truth. Gellner adds that even Marx had held a belief in the providential care of the world. In the world envisioned by Marx, one had at least to live and be engaged in its historical and social processes, in order to know and understand it. It was never possible to stand outside the world and tell it where to go. There was, 'No towering above the social process... we can trust revolutionary practice, his version of the Holy Ghost,' concludes Gellner (1992a: 158). Conversely, the Promethean aspiration of Descartes set the tone and agenda for the making of the modern world, which would in turn lead to the construction of the self as a 'cosmic exile', a phrase aptly used by Gellner, to describe the absolute disengagement of that self from the world that accompanied its rise. It is to some of the more alarming and unsettling consequences of this construction of the self in the modern world that I now turn in my next chapter.

3

MODERNITY AND DISEMBODIMENT

Inevitably, the influence of Protestant individualism and Cartesian dualism was to have its effects on how religion came to be perceived and practised during the modern period. The legacy of much of the reformed understanding of religion, coupled with the 'new' philosophy of Descartes, became gradually embedded in modern consciousness and was to have overriding consequences for the future understanding and organisation of religious, cultural and social life. The increased significance that was placed upon the exercise of instrumental reason as the primary means for discovering and consolidating what was true, meant that the kind of attention and status given previously to ritual embodiment and somatic experience attenuated. This chapter seeks to address the impact that this disembodied and deritualised approach to knowledge, meaning-construction and truth exercised on western culture. I focus primarily on two critics of modernity: Zygmunt Bauman and Michel Foucault. In discussing their analyses – and briefly those of other leading writers – of some of the central ideas and cultural repercussions associated with modernity, I suggest how influential and all-pervasive the notion of disembodiment became, as the process of ritual devaluation advanced.

The Work of Zygmunt Bauman

The central core of Bauman's argument is that modernity consti-tuted a process of gradual deanimation of nature and disenchantment of the world; a condition that he claims postmodernity aims to reverse (Bauman, 1991, 1992a, 1992b; Flanagan, 1996). Much of his discussion highlights the catastrophic effects of the strategies employed by instrumental reason and modernity's relentless urge to design and order the whole of existence. The human attempts to structure the world becomes the central motif in Bauman's work, a tension witnessed most visibly in the ongoing confrontation between reason and ambiguity. In this sense he is a key figure in demonstrating not only some of the central features of the modern period, but also the harmful consequences for a disenchanted culture which had come to disregard the importance of ritual tradition and somatic experience by replacing them with the tool of instrumental reason. As Flanagan comments, such a concern about despiritualisation returns 'to an ambition at the heart of Weber's worries over disenchantment and the calculation, which Simmel saw as coming to characterise the tragedy of culture' (1996: 215).

Bauman learned the limitations of structuralism from Lévi-Strauss. What fascinated him was the modern ceaseless urge to structure everything, the constant attempt to find *the* social structure, the belief that there was, or could be in the future, some definite, final, consensus to the underlying structure of everything; that ambivalence could be eliminated. Ambiguity for Bauman is the opposite of classification. It entails the possibility of assigning an object or an event to more than one category. It is a problem about the dysfunction of language, since it denies that things can be easily set apart, segregated, named, that the world consists of discreet entities, to be neatly apportioned. To classify is to give the world a structure, to reduce the probable, to behave as if events were not random. It strives for order and consistency in the face of the complexity and randomness of events and situations in everyday life (Bauman, 1991). It is, says Bauman, the ideal of classification to arrange things into a sort of 'commodious filing cabinet that contains all the items that the world contains – but confines each and every item within a separate place of its own' (1991: 2).

Disorder and anxiety occur when some of the linguistic tools of classification become strained or redundant and problems occur when this filing cabinet of knowledge is shown not to be able to classify every event in this way. The irony is that the more one pursues this activity, the more ambivalence is revealed to be an inextricable part of its pursuit. The more one attempts to classify everything, the more one is confronted by the impossibility of such a task. Ambivalence becomes 'the side-product of the labour of classification' (1991: 3) and its struggle is both self-destructive and propelling, urging one on to pursue that which is unrealisable.

According to Bauman, modernity endeavoured to order and classify the world to excess. It was a self-conscious flight away from the chaos, contingency and transparency of the world. Religion, ritual and magic were to be abandoned forever (Thomas, 1991).

This was one of the most significant tasks that modernity set itself. But it did much more than this; it allied this enterprise to a process of reflexivity upon this sought-after order. In the process, the discovery of the non-naturalness of order resulted in the acceptance of the Hobbesian view that order had to be individually and reflexively constructed. This is not to suggest, naively, that the premodern was complacent about such order, but rather that modernity became, as Bauman puts it, 'saturated by the "without us", a deluge feeling' (1991: 7). The enterprise of modernity did not attempt to discover the order lying behind any interruptions of chaos, but instead designed what would otherwise not have been there. That is, it invented the task of designing, rather than serenely accepting the given order of the world which had been consolidated by ritual practices for generations.

The created order was no longer acknowledged as something gifted and given, but as a set of phenomena which was in need of being 'understood' so that it could be controlled and tamed. The autonomy of the world devised by the autonomy of reason became an object of human investigation rather than a mirror reflection of divine creative love. Scriptural authority concerning the nature of the world was to be substituted by scientific and mathematical authority as a process of disenchantment occurred. Ward comments about this shift: 'The created order takes on an autonomy, governed by mathematical configurations and geometrical relations. It becomes a timeless construct, a machine to be interpreted according to the laws of mechanics.... an accumulation of entities owned or waiting to be owned, property to be arranged, labelled, evaluated (according to the market and demand) and exchanged' (1997: xx). Ironically, Galileo and Descartes, in spite of their Catholic formation, were to be highly influential in tempting others along this road which would eventually lead to the logic of atheism.

The consequences were enormously significant: since nature now was something in need of mastery, domination, subjugation, it was also in need of being remade. Order was a thing to be manufactured from the ruins of recalcitrant nature. But this remaking had consequences for those at the mercy of the designers, since those with power set about the task with unwavering efficiency. The existence was modern in so far as it was administered by resourceful and sovereign agencies who commanded the right to administer existence itself and lay aside chaos as the left-over that escapes definition (Bauman, 1987, 1991). But if classification was to be the task ahead, then there were bound to be those who had no place within its confines, who could not be allocated a role, those beyond classification, who still held on to notions that the body might have something to teach us. Modernity became concerned to fill in all the blank spots of the *compleat mappa mundi* and intolerance came to characterise those involved in the process. If modernity were intent on a march forward in the name of progress, it was an obsessive and futile endeavour, borne out of the frustration to frame the unframeable, to circumvent and yet simultaneously, map the space of modernity. This impossible task was set by the *foci imaginarii* of absolute truth, and the consequent hostility towards the Other who rebelled against this focus during modernity. Whether we use the image of Richard Rorty's as the walk towards an ever-receding horizon or the storm of Walter Benjamin who sees walkers propelled into a future to which their backs are turned while the pile of debris before grows skyward before them, the present is always as a result of such activity undermined (Bauman, 1991).

Anxiety and restlessness, became the products of this futile journey since a Sisyphean-like war is waged on the countless local fields that refuse to be constructed out of this falsely ordained order, in the so-called name of progress. Bauman writes that this is the supreme folly of the dream of modernity: to suggest that the fragmentation of the world (itself caused by the ordering process) is easily made whole again. As the attempt to solve the problem of the fragmentary nature of unclassified territory increased (due to its own attempts to drive the relative into the ideology of autarchy), the problems became larger and more diverse. Such devices are always moves away from what is considered to be the abhorrence of ambiguity. But as Bauman writes, 'more ambivalence was the ultimate product of modern, fragmented drives to order. Problems were created by problem-solving, since these became the efforts to suppress the "endemic relativity of autonomy"' (1991: 14).

The dream of the Enlightenment was that humanity could be free from all those constraints and anxieties which had hitherto enslaved it, but its attempt to rationalise human existence resulted in a reductionism which betrayed the grounds on which that project was based. The so-called triumph of instrumental reason ended in attempts to classify ceaselessly. Everything had to be specified, mapped out, systematically made sense of. Plans were formulated against any attempts to evade this Kafkaesque world of manipulative, bureaucratic scrutiny. Whether this misguided epistemological approach was partly responsible for the worst atrocities of the twentieth century, or whether a less damning approach can be argued for, is a matter for debate. As Harvey notes, 'Which position we take depends upon how we explain the "dark side" of our recent history and the degree to which we attribute it to the defects of Enlightenment Reason rather than to a lack of proper application' (1990: 14). Certainly for Bauman, this 'dark side' was largely the result of the blind application of instrumental reason.

In *Modernity and the Holocaust* Bauman reserves his most pressing indictment of the social repercussions of bureaucratic efficiency and classification when matched with an ideologically obsessed power elite. Here the devastating impact of the 'gardening' state is revealed in all its harmful effects. The Hobbesian dream of the civilisation of the barbaric is revealed as the etiological myth of modernity. A malign construction emerged from the distrust of nature, out of a predetermined logic which set as its task the establishment of a perfect social order, a wish for an ideal life and a perfect arrangement of human conditions. According to Bauman the Nazi programme fits well with Weber's description of modern administration: precision, speed, unity, strict subordination, discretion. The eradication of any hindrances to this operation are seen to be creative not destructive, since it conceives as harmful anything that gets in its way. Bauman never suggests that the occurrence of the Holocaust was determined by the bureaucratic efficiency of modernity. But he does concur that the rules of instrumental efficiency are singularly incapable of preventing such phenomena. In other words, there is nothing in those rules which disqualifies the Holocaust-style methods of social engineering as improper or indeed the actions they serve as irrational. In such a climate of bureaucracy there well might be located the breeding-ground for the conception of the idea (1989).

By accident of history, the Jewish experience had a special significance for understanding the logic of modern culture. Bauman shows that the perpetrators of the Holocaust were 'normal' people and that those enlisted into the Nazi organisation were neither unusually sadistic nor abnormally fanatical. But he claims that the SS administration transformed them into perpetrators of the most heinous of crimes. The use of rationality at the expense of all other criteria of action, and particularly the tendency to subordinate the use of violence to rational calculus, is one of the most disturbing lessons the Holocaust teaches. The choice of physical extermination as the right means was simply a product of routine bureaucratic procedure. The department in the SS headquarters in charge of the destruction of European Jews was called the 'Section of Administration and Economy'. Ethical blindness is the worst corollary of this type of efficiency. Terrorism and torture are no longer instruments of wayward passion but become the instruments of political rationality. This is partly realised by the process of distantiation, the spatial removal of those who administer killings. Most bureaucrats composed memoranda, drew up blueprints, talked on the telephone; became capable of destroying a whole people by sitting at their desks. The Other as a bureaucratic number, as a file in the system, does not belong to the Other I know – the second belongs within the realm of morality, while the first is located firmly outside it. It is not surprising to discover that Bauman regards Levinas' work on the 'Other' to be some of the most inspiring of the twentieth century (Bauman, 1992b: 40–48; Critchley, 1994; Hand, 1992).

In *Ambivalence and Modernity* Bauman pursues the thesis of the Other with particular reference to the stranger. The evil of Nazism was simply one example of the 'deviation-free society' that modernity (trapped in its post-Enlightenment hubris and self-confidence) would produce. Bauman shows that German National Socialism was only one example, pushed all the way to its ultimate fateful conclusion – a most natural development, one might say, of that modern spirit which crushes any recalcitrant reality which comes in its path of classification. The Other or enemy became dehumanised, beyond redemption, categorised as non-human. As a result, an asymmetrical process comes into being, as individuals delineate who are to be their friends and who their enemies. But, in the process, the relationship between friends and enemies becomes more problematic. One defines the Other, is a reflection of the opposite of the one to the Other: 'Being a friend and being a enemy, are the two modalities in which the Other may be recognised as another subject, construed as a subject like myself, admitted into the self's own world' (Bauman, 1991: 54). The stranger is much more of a threat than any socially constructed enemy. She or he is the one who threatens sociation itself, who comes and ' "calls the bluff" of the friends/enemy dichotomy, who stays in that space where the map cannot locate her' (1991: 55), one of those 'undecidables', who might be friend or enemy or contain an element of both. Neither inside nor outside, her real potency and potential danger is located in this underdetermination.

The hermeneutic problems set up by the stranger destabilise situations, making neat classification a flawed thing. The major obstacles are not simply those who are unclassified at a certain stage in the process, but those who will perhaps never be: 'They do not question just this one opposition here and now: they question oppositions as such, the very principle of the opposition, the plausibility of dichotomy it suggests and feasibility of separation it demands. They unmask the brittle artificiality of division' (Bauman, 1991: 58–59). Not only does this stranger unsettle the moral reasoning of that world, but it significantly undermines its spatial ordering in the process, exposing falsehood and fragility. Like Jesus before Pilate, the modern, hegemonic world wants to differentiate categorically between friends and enemies, between those who are for and those who are against: 'If you set him free, you are no friend of Caesar's' shout the crowd – the stranger's irredeemable sin is 'his simultaneous assault on several crucial oppositions instrumental in the incessant effort of ordering' (Bauman, 1991: 60). Quoting Douglas, Bauman reinforces his position: 'any given culture must confront events which seem to defy its assumptions... It cannot ignore the anomalies which its scheme produces, except at the risk of forfeiting confidence' (1991: 6). The advent of modernity administers the social removal and upholds the legal consequences for the stranger, the Other who cannot be categorised. Nevertheless, such strategies simply reveal the mounting neuroses of the classifiers. The victims, by being who they are – the ambivalent strangers – who do no harm to anyone, present the most pressing of oppositions and incur, innocently, the most cruel of penalties.

The notion of 'antinomies' in liturgy discussed by Flanagan (1990) is appropriate here. Antinomies are 'contradictions that cannot be resolved through reason' and proceed 'on the basis of double knowledge. By knowing what is opposite, one proceeds to understand what is worth affirming' (1990: 72). This knowing through contradiction is part of the apophatic tradition and points to what is beyond knowing by reason alone. Liturgy and rite allow antinomies to emerge: 'The enactment of liturgy involves handling dualisms, or polarities of meaning or attributes... Antinomies which arise in liturgy need to go beyond the form, or social frame of the rite' (1990: 73–74; Turner, 1995), but they always allow some frame to be set before God to mirror the holy. Following Vagagini, Flanagan writes that liturgies are able to handle signs which make known a hidden reality, but at the same time offer a kind of obstacle to this knowledge since it can never be perfectly transparent and fully understood (1990: 76); antinomies 'seem to fracture the glass, but they also permit glimpses of the holy' (1990: 74). Rites present the social legislator with the same kind of difficulty that strangers present to classifiers: their very indeterminacy and contradictory nature become problematic for the process of *mathesis*.

Bauman argues that the question of the subject or élite possessing the knowledge borne of a reasoning propensity becomes crucial in the war against that which needs to be ordered, controlled and made sense of. The iron cage of bureaucratic rationality, most strongly criticised by Weber, is always *someone's* ordering, *a* subject's rules, to which others must obey. And that ordering becomes intolerant, even of the most minute of ambiguities, the most harmless of things that cannot be regulated or classified. Postmodernity's unmasking of the myth of representation partly addresses this dilemma. Modernity's insistence on social order meant that it depended on so little. At one time that order depended on religion to preserve a 'sacred canopy' under which stable meanings could be maintained. Now, under the relentless surge of secular, bureaucratic efficiency,

> A hair, literally a hair, lying where it shouldn't, can separate order from disorder. Everything that does not belong where it is is hostile. Even the tiniest thing is disturbing: a man of total order would have to scour his realm with a microscope and even then a remnant of potential nervousness will remain in him (Bauman, 1992b: 113).

Death and Deritualisation

Bauman's social analysis of the legacy of Enlightenment thinking centres then, upon this crucial dialectic between reason and its arch enemy, ambivalence. In *Mortality, Immortality and Other Life Strategies*, he argues 'Human culture is, on the one hand, a gigantic (and spectacularly successful) ongoing effort to give meaning to human life; on the other hand, it is an obstinate (and somewhat less successful) effort to suppress the awareness of the irreparably surrogate, and brittle character of such meaning' (1992: 8). Death is the subject and central event around which this brittleness is most clearly shown in Bauman's argument. In contrast to the meaning system and community context in which death occurred during the Middle Ages, modernity has no strategies of dealing with this phenomenon; death emerges as the ultimate defeat of reason. Unlike death in the medieval period which was a natural and visible part of everyday social living, modern culture has no Church that the majority of people call upon to make sense of life's meaning through the administration of rituals. Phillipe Ariès' account of medieval death emphasises its community and ritual underpinning: 'the shutters were closed in the bedroom of the dying man, candles were lit, holy water was sprinkled; the house filled with grave and whispering neighbours, relatives and friends' (1981: 559). Although fear and superstition surrounded the process of illness and death, for the most part they were contained by the rituals of the Church (Bossy, 1985).

The Protestant Reformation did its best to rid the Church of such ritual undertakings. The Requiem Mass was abolished and prayers for the dead discontinued, although such endeavours were far from straightforward or easily accepted. To a large extent, Protestantism increased the problems associated with death, since as a result of the reforms there were no longer any social or ecclesiastical arrangements in place to deal with its occurrence. As Shilling and Mellor note, 'While religious orders and ritual structures sought to "contain" the terror of death in medieval Catholicism, Protestants were left *alone* with the task of interpreting and investing these events with meaning' (1997: 120). And as Berger rightly comments, 'Insofar as the knowledge of death cannot be avoided in any society, legitimations of the reality of the social world *in the face of death* are decisive requirements in any society. The importance of religion in any legitimations is obvious' (1990: 43–44).

In contrast, a process of privatisation towards death occurred during modernity (Bauman, 1991, Mellor, 1993). Bauman argues that death itself slices through and makes a mockery of much of the foundation the modern world had constructed for itself, resting as it did so confidently on instrumental reason. We can never know what death is like. It is the ultimate mystery. But reason, in search of security and precision, has always to face the Other of death, and in the process is confronted by its own fatuous power to understand and rationalise such an occurrence. The individual who attempts to imagine her/his own death, is forced to admit that this is simply a spectator-like experience. Death is the 'scandal', the 'ultimate humiliation of reason' (Bauman, 1992b: 15). It saps the trust in reason and in this sense, the horror of death is the horror of not understanding, of not comprehending that which cannot be tamed by reason. If reason promised choice, then death denied that choice. Death cannot be avoided. It therefore either becomes a felt anticipation or a sorrowful loss.

People deceive in its presence. Many humans behave as if death were not going to happen. This is a remarkable triumph of the will over reason, since reason knows that death cannot be avoided and will come, eventually, to everyone.

A turning away from death, therefore, constitutes the social means of discovering a way to live with death. No longer contained within a community, or the supernatural and ritual framework of the Middle Ages, reason's inability in the modern period to find an answer to death results in the social construction of the disbelief of death. Bauman argues that this can only be self-sustaining as long as it is not too closely inspected, too closely examined. Culture constructs the means of debilitating the gnawing, unsettling of death. Social arrangements are lodged in between life and death and 'societies are arrangements that permit humans to live with weaknesses that would otherwise render life impossible' (1992b: 17). The most crucial of such arrangements are those which conceal the 'potentially poisonous effects of its unconcealed known presence' (1992b: 18). Knowing that we know about the fact of death is part of the process of living in a society with a language that attempts to understand and get hold of the uncertain, but it also constitutes part of that self-same society where attempts are made to repair the damage that has sometimes been done, where ambivalence finds a gap in the otherwise carefully plotted and mapped-out routine of daily life, or where the contingency of life, with a scare, breaks through to the surface, as if to say, don't forget me.

If Hegel suggested that history is what man does with death, then it was the task of culture to 'solidify the contingent, to entrench the rootless, to give the powerless an impression of power, to hide uncontrived absurdity behind contrived meanings' (Bauman, 1992b: 22–23). Culture becomes the counter-mnemotechnic device to forget that of which we are most aware. Even if the body becomes the site for the socially constructed fight against the knowability of death, this battle fares no better than that waged on society, since it too becomes a 'monster of ambivalence: half-friend, half-enemy' (Bauman, 1992b: 36) being both the object and means of the struggle. Even if culture declares a war of attrition on death and ambivalence, it is doomed from the start, since it becomes intent on cutting the 'ambivalent human predicament into a multitude of logically and pragmatically unequivocal situations' (Bauman, 1992b: 38). The social consequences can be grave. For survival's sake, a war is pitched on those who threaten survival. National identities become entrenched, as tribal patriotism 'transmutes individual unselfishness into national egoism' (Bauman, 1992: 39). Universalism becomes the tool of exclusion. With left-overs out of the way, an inner circle is left who continue the fight against those outside the camp who need either to be destroyed, converted or possibly allowed in, but on asymmetrical terms.

Bauman's analysis of premodern religious attempts to deal with the contingent nature of the world may appear somewhat romantic and, at times, blatantly untrue, but it does give some indication of the radical shift in approaches towards dealing with the existential questions and problems which inevitably emerged in the two periods. He suggests there was a premodern timeless world in which 'the timelessness of the religious message chimed well with the stagnant, self-repetitive life of routine' (1992b: 91). The form of that world was not open to challenge, the concept of its order a non-existent thing, since it was only modernity which called it that, 'having eaten the tree of the unexpected and the unfamiliar... looking back at what was no more, and with poorly concealed wistful nostalgia' (1992b: 91). Any disasters, like the plague, were simply a 'ripple on the eternal sea, temporary disturbance, a momentary departure from the place things have been, and should be again' (1992b: 91). With modernity, came the task of imposing meaning on a world which at times seemed to despair of ever finding it. Before this period, religion did not seek to attach meaning to the world's affairs, since life just was: 'as the rest of the world, which only when prodded out of its self-sameness would become an object of anxiety-fed scrutiny' (1992b: 92). Religion was the acceptance of the world as it was and how it was lived, 'One does not demand that the obvious should justify itself' (1992b: 92). Modernity, on the other hand, made the meaning of life a daily task, a chore to be done, a search to be commenced. Once the questions began to be asked, the enterprise became a human one, endowed with a secular mission, born of free-will, to make sense of the seemingly meaningless, as the interruptions to the routine of ordinary life loomed large. The ordering and meaning of the world was now in the hands of individuals.

Roman Catholic Power and Sacrifice

Although Bauman never explicitly refers to Catholicism, his critique of religion in the premodern world sheds some light on the role liturgy had assumed before the reforms of the 1960s.

Essentially, the exercise of worship was in the hands of bishops and priests, those ordained with supernatural power to perform the rites of the Church and consisted of ritualised performances enacted within the context of the history of redemption. The rites of the Church saw to it that the things of God pervaded the whole of the social realm, that worshippers were able to offer praise to their Creator, have their sins forgiven and be allowed to prepare for a good death (Bradley, 1995; Duffy, 1992). There was no imposing of new meaning onto a liturgy with each performance, (for example, by a group responsible for its preparation). It was simply an annual cycle of priestly-led repetitive acts of salvation, with the most important being a bloody act of sacrifical ritual – the Mass. But crucially, the order and meaning of the world was maintained by such an annual cycle of salvific rites.

The sacrifical cult, conducted by the priestly office, set in place by the authority of apostolic succession, was also responsible for securing a clear understanding of social organisation inside and outside the Church. Ecclesiastical power and influence were never regarded as simply being in the hands of 'ordinary' men. It rested fundamentally on a belief in the supernatural basis of hierarchy, through which bishops and priests had been given authority to act, not as ordinary human beings, but as chosen participants in a divine plan (Jay, 1992: 112). Even the writers of the document on the Church, *Lumen Gentium,* at the Second Vatican Council, who had been so insistent on modernising the Church, did not fail to state this: bishops and priests are commissioned to be instrumental in the continuation of a divine plan destined to last until the end of the world. Just as the apostles were endowed by Christ with a special outpouring of the Holy Spirit, so this gift is transmitted down the ages through episcopal consecration (*LG,* chapter 3, paragraph 21). Bishops and priests preside 'in God's stead over the flock of which they are the shepherds in that they are teachers of doctrine, ministers of the sacred worship and holders of office in government' (*LG,* chapter 3, paragraph 20).

As the above indicates, the Roman Catholic Church's hierarchy has never been analogous to a secular social structure or hierarchy (Jay, 1992). The power given to certain men in the Church sanctifies them to use that power in the service of salvation. Priests have always been regarded as *intermediaries* between God and man, who with divine sanction given at ordination, exercise special powers. The kind of world they liturgically re-enact is one modelled on the kingdom, a supernatural reality which can never

be 'invented' by men or women themselves. Such an understanding of authorised ritual power is distinctively different from
the secular power based on instrumental control Bauman speaks
about as characterising modernity.

However, a change in the sacrificial role of the priest occurred
after the reforms. The sacrificial function of the priest was less
emphasised at the Second Vatican Council. Indeed, one of the
central criticisms of the changes to the liturgy given by Archbishop
Lefebvre (excommunicated in 1988) rested upon the notion of
the priest who alone was able to offer the 'sacrifice' of the Mass.
For Lefebvre, the reforms, by their insistence on lay participation
and communal assembly, diminished the priestly office and
undermined the sacrificial power of the Mass. In a sermon given at
an ordination, he emphasised the unique role of the Catholic
priest as being marked with a 'sacerdotal character that unites you
to... the priesthood of our Lord Jesus Christ in a very special way,
a participation which the faithful cannot have' (quoted in Jay,
1992: 121). The shift of power away from the sacrificial role of the
priest in favour of the involvement of the laity after the Second
Vatican Council reflected attempts to establish a far greater
democratisation of worship. The unique sacrificial role of the
priest was beginning to be eroded.

The Oppressive Taming of Nature

In Chapter 4 of *Legislators and Interpreters* Bauman uses the
metaphor of the gardener to describe the task of modernity, in
contrast to that of the gamekeeper in the premodern world. The
gamekeeper was, by nature, a religious person, modestly content
to ensure that the plants and animals self-reproduce and happy to
trust the resourcefulness of the trustees: gamekeepers are not
great believers in the capacity of humans to administer their own
life. They do not fashion and pattern the ways of nature to their
own ends, but rather are content to accept the modest claims of
humanity in the face of Nature and the Providence of God. The
shift from a traditional way of doing things to a self-conscious task
was due not only to the invention of this gardening-like activity.
but had been set off by the 'incapacity of the wild culture to sustain
its own balance... by the disturbing disequilibrium between the
volume of gamekeepers' demands and the productive capability of
their trustees' (Bauman, 1987: 52). The new legislators secured
the boundaries and erected the fences against the irrational and

passion-filled appetites of the lower and uneducated populace. Bauman uses again the word 'brittleness' to describe the destabilising effect that the interruptions and ambiguities in the daily round of life released, the feeling that things 'fall apart at the centre'. The very discovery of principles (now seemingly fragile) on which human life was based quaked under the force of uncertainty and contingency. Things began to occur which were not anticipated. Religious worship seemed to offer no remedy.

One overriding consequence of this split between nature and the social order was that a social contract had to be put in place, a means for regulating the terror of ambiguity and uncertainty that modernity had discovered and now set about taming and classifying. The legislator as the design-drawing despot, emerged as the hero of this new social order that had to be drawn up (Bauman, 1987). Reason fought its war against the wayward passions of man, against the illiterate and uneducated, against those localised communities that were regulated by their own sense of time, place and destiny. There was a plot to be turned over by this new-found efficiency of the gardening state. The orderly society, the world of better men, the designated spaces of civilisation, were to be managed in the most efficient (and intolerant) of ways.

In *Mortality, Immortality and Other Life Strategies* Bauman exposes the Faustian man in all his brutal and subtle power, epitomised in the constitution of the national state. His chapter entitled 'The Selfish Species' contains the most radical exposé of modernity's gardening proclivity. Here power-assisted universality was to become the goal of modernity's erasure of the diverse and different. Uniformity was to reign as an indication of social order and success. There was a 'call for unconditional and uncontested subordination to the power of the supra-communal state, which had now been juxtaposed, as the epitome of universality, to communally based parochiality' (1992b: 98). Such conquests were described as conquests of liberation. Now the imparting of beliefs, constructed and disguised as education, was coolly administered. Identities had to be forged out of the bureaucratisation of this national state, which left little room for disagreement. Meaning was to be given as a gift to those who were in need. Thus started the formation of the masses, and the imposed monopoly of an education by the experts, the élite, the masters of reason. The Renaissance 'chain of being' with its divisions and sub-divisions, was being replaced by an amorphous group of the masses defined by the élite. Reason waged a war on superstition (Thomas, 1991).

For Bauman, like many other postmodern writers, the
Enlightenment had produced the signs of a totalitarian state,
oppressive and divisive. The élite now held sway on what constituted meaning. It was *their* meaning, *their* methods, either entailing
the close control of conduct backed up by confinement, so vividly
described by Foucault (1984), or by legitimisation. This entailed
the organisation of collective repression by the representation of
order as order itself. Thus the rise of nationalism emerged, being
the most effective and collective form of political organisation. In
the process, the bid for territory ensued. As Bauman writes,
'Drawing the boundary between the natives and the aliens,
between the prospective nation and its enemies, was an inseparable part of the self-assertion of the national élite' (1992b: 106).
He has no hesitation in calling nationalism the racism of the intellectuals (1992b: 109). Vigilance then became the ever-present task
of nationalism, lest someone promised to unsettle that universal-
ising it so desperately needed for its own survival. Ambiguity and
the stranger were its most disturbing and unsettling components,
and in its pursuit of its goal it 'prompts feverish defence of the soil
and frantic blood-testing, it creates the state of permanent tension
it claims to relieve' (1992b: 113). Its strength depends on the
connecting role it plays in the promotion and perpetuation of
the social order which it so carefully defines. Friends (as opposed
to enemies) are artificially constructed into an imagined
community of national commonality. Nationalism redefines
friends as natives. It engages in the propaganda of so-called shared
values and attitudes; it promotes joint historical memories. It
preaches a sermon of common fate and common destiny.
Nationalism becomes 'the church' which forces the prospective
flock to practise the cult.

Personal Repercussions

Bauman also focuses his attention on some of the personal and
psychological repercussions of this type of will to dominate. The
social consequences were the inevitable result of the emergence of
a conditioned, modern spirit that suffered from its own neurotic
struggle to free itself from the unanswerability of life. One of
the worst legacies of the Enlightenment myth was that it left the
individual alone, anxious and selfish. That condition was hatched
by the anxious yearnings to understand and get hold of the world
in all its contingency and unexpectedness. The painful price

humanity paid for the comforts of modernity was the discovery of the absurdity and loneliness of being (1991: 48–50). It became an existence without a script written in advance, a stage set for actors whose action could never be foretold. The Second Vatican Council likewise spoke of modern man's plight as one of ceaseless yearning, questioning and selecting by setting this struggle within a divine context: 'Torn by a welter of anxieties he is compelled to choose between and repudiate some among them', believing answers can be found to such questioning by 'human effort alone' (*Gaudium et Spes,* Preface, paragraph 10).

Bauman discusses how the site for transcendence came to be understood to reside in the human partnership of love: 'It is now the partner in love that is expected to offer the space for transcendence, to be the transcendence. My own self... is to acquire a vicarious immortality by sundering its private bond and being set free' (1992b: 28). It might then gain a new, unbound and more credible existence within the trans-individual 'universe of two' (1992b: 28). But this false dream becomes equally brittle, since 'my stakes in immortality have been invested in another mortal creature, and this latter fact cannot be concealed for long by even the most passionate deification of the partner' (1992b: 29). Other attempts to stem the surge of anxious thoughts and yearnings are located in the promise of a better future, but the modern mode denies the past its ultimate meaning – given authority and hands over the right to assign meanings to an unknown and uncertain future. This is a foolish task since, 'It is precisely the endemic inconclusivity of effort' (1991: 10) that produces restlessness. Modernity becomes obsessive because it, 'never gets enough... its ambitions frustrated' (1991: 10).The worst tragedy of all is that,

> modernity becomes branded with a contradiction it cannot wash off: it divides when dreaming of unification... since in the attempt of power-assisted action to universalise, the carrying power can never reach beyond its own carrying capacity and as a result, only secures new divisions and separations (1991: 112).

It is not difficult to see why Bauman regards Emmanuel Levinas as the greatest moral philosopher of the twentieth century, and how his own depiction of modernity manifests the absence of the type of moral responsibility Levinas envisages as the only true morality. Ethics is not about being with each other in a reciprocating sociality of sameness, where one engages only with those whom one can understand or feel some connection with. Ethical

responsibility is about being for the Other. Ethics does not rest on
rationality but precedes it. Addressing the alterity of the Other, in
all its difference, constitutes ethical responsibility. Meaning is
borne out of this move towards the Other in all its ambivalence
and indefinability. This calls for 'an abdication of sovereignty in
the face of the Other, responsibility for the Other stops the
meaningless, rumbling clamour... This concern fills the emptiness
of contingency' (Bauman, 1992b: 42; Hand, 1992).

Through modernity's sieve of social order, this move towards the
Other is regressive. However, it has done its job well since that
better ethics, which precedes sociality, is disturbingly absent.
Bauman quotes from Levinas' thesis:

> It is extremely important to know if society in the current sense of the
> term is the result of the limitation of the principle that men are
> predators of one another, or if to the contrary it results from the
> limitation of the principle that men are for one another. Does
> the social, with its institutions, universal forms and laws, result from
> limiting the consequences of the war between men, or from limiting
> the infinity which opens in the ethical relationship of man to man
> (1992b: 48).

Unfortunately, modernity's social manipulation of this 'infinity' is
based on, 'the existence which is not being for' (1992b: 49). But the
space that modernity relentlessly attempts to fill reflects a false
dream. Lifelong exertion of this kind can do nothing but create
more uncertainty. Modernity has ushered in a new slavery. Life is
now a lonely pursuit. The inalienable response of the individual
is reduced to a lonely voice facing a lonely death. Caustically Bauman
concludes: 'Unless I do something to change all this: to force others
to be for me as staunchly as I refused to be for them' (1992b: 50).

This is the telling paradox. The social forms and manipulations
of modernity only extend the existential anguish (created, for
example, by the sequestration of death) and the refusal to be for
the Other. Sociality makes a pariah of the self since it cannot be for
others, only for those who are a reflection of its own self in relation
to the Other. In modernity's futile endeavour to locate ethical
action within an inner circle, demarcated by mathematical
reasoning, nation from nation, friend from foe, stranger from
native, me from you, modernity sinks into an ideology of preten-
tious, but highly dangerous, social practices. Conversely, for
Levinas (and indeed for Bauman), it is the answerability to the
Other, the 'pre-ontological and pre-intellectual relationship which
already contains the "for": I being for the other', that makes one

an individual (1992b: 42).This is a journey to the unknown, like Abraham who leaves his fatherhood in search of the unknown land. Death, for Levinas, is the experience of something which is absolutely Other. For Heidegger there was a rationale to death, since we are beings who achieve authenticity in its presence. But as Loughlin suggests, 'Levinas opposes an ontological subjectivity which "reduces everything to itself", in favour of an ethical subjectivity which "kneels before the other sacrificing its own liberty to the primordial call of the other"' (Loughlin, 1994: 22). This is not the call borne of Reason, or a relationship of mutual reciprocity. Neither is it the Kantian dictate of universal reason nor a Heideggerian definition of Being. It is a command that falls upon the individual, a slap in the face of reason, reflecting an almost biblical urgency of call (Loughlin, 1994).

The Work of Michel Foucault

Foucault's writings, like Bauman's, have been highly influential in evaluating some of the central personal, social, cultural and political developments that have taken place during modernity. I choose his work, in particular, because it identifies the process of psychologisation which was to become established in the modern period and which was to run counter to the collective and embodied routes to securing meaning and self-identity during the premodern world. I focus on his analysis of the shift from an emphasis on the role of embodiment in premodern times to the emphasis on 'mindful bodies' in the modern period. By this I mean Foucault's belief that the body became substituted for the mind as the *locus* for discursive power. I do this mostly with reference to his writings on penal reform. I also show that his social analysis has had considerable influence in identifying important developments within modernity, not least in the field of contemporary surveillance strategies, in order to shed light on some of the more contentious forms and effects of disembodiment which have arisen in the modern period. Foucault successfully identified a significant strand in modernity by revealing that social life became no longer shaped by a fully embodied experience of the world, but was largely determined by powerful discourses based on non-bodily discursive analyses. The only feature of the body which did survive was the eye, but this too, I show, was separated from the body of the flesh to become, in many instances, the abstracted gaze of watchfulness.

A modern reaction to Foucault's graphic description of penal torture and pain in the opening of his work, *Discipline and Punish* might be one of gratitude that such procedures no longer take place. By the end of the book, however, the reader's attitude to such procedures is likely to have been changed. Foucault presents us with this opportunity by building up, chapter by chapter, the transitional signs of a system of punishment that characterises the modern period. This shift is described in terms of a move from the importance of the symbolically tortured body in penal legis-lation, to one which incorporates an investigation into the intricate workings of the mind; from a discourse about bodily punishment to one suggesting how the mind might affect the actions of the person who commits a crime; from a discourse about the estab-lishment of the authority of the sovereign to one about examining and diagnosing, from a psychological perspective, certain types of behaviour with reference to new forms of criminal classification; indeed, from looking at earlier bodily punishments of crime to analysing how 'criminality' became an objective, diagnosable mode of abnormal behaviour. In summary, I highlight the process of psychologisation and normalisation which was to govern and dominate the modern period.

Foucault did not witness a gradual emergence of this new type of discourse. On the contrary, he is at pains to point out that at certain periods in history, distinctive forms of discourse occur without necessarily involving any connecting systematic progression. He uses the word 'episteme' to describe this concept, which is an *a priori* set of rules which conditions certain discourses to develop. As McNay notes, it allows 'different objects and different themes to be spoken at one time but not at another' (1994: 52). But this never becomes an epistemological enquiry in itself, since 'epistemes' occur without regard to subject–object relations and are always anterior to such. Foucault's genealogy of prisons shows that there is no sense of evolutionary progress in their emergence at all. For this reason alone, Foucault might be associated with those other postmodern thinkers who decry the notion of 'progress' after the Enlightenment, and who see only one type of knowledge being replaced by another in history, not necessarily any more rational, constructive or more helpful than the previous. Foucault suggests that the modern system is to be viewed as a transitory one, which will be substituted by another in the future. Mark Poster makes the same point: 'The genealogy of prisons reveals that the modern system is first, finite and second, without exclusive right to rationality' (1990: 96). And 'the appeal to reason, the promise of a more rational world, that is implicit in Marx, is lacking in Foucault' (1990: 97). Previous penal systems are not necessarily any better nor any worse in Foucault's writing. Any attempt to legitimate present organisations by contrasting them (unfairly) with previous systems is ill-founded: 'The display of the difference of the past avoids the danger of dismissing it [as barbarian] and thereby legitimating the present... as a superior and unsurpassable world' (Poster, 1990: 98).

Nevertheless, the attempt to make more rational and psychological sense of criminal offences in the modern period did result in a radical reorientation towards understanding the importance of the mind (although he does reserve a chapter in *Discipline and Punish* to analyse the rise of the 'docile body' as a consequence of, and in relation to, such practices). Psychological knowledge of the criminal became crucial in understanding the crime itself and in turn was to become associated with the accumulation of power for those who diagnosed and spoke about such understandings. Previously the body had been the *locus* of attention for punishment, and regarded as a public means and spectacle of ritual torture. The legislative pursuit of the body as a viable form of ritual, penal practice or 'an element in the liturgy of punishment' meant meeting two demands: first, 'it is intended, either by the scar it leaves on the body, or by the spectacle that accompanies it, to brand the victim with infamy... torture does not reconcile'; and second, 'it traces around, or rather on the very body of the condemned man, signs that must not be effaced... public torture and execution must be spectacular, it must be seen by all almost as its triumph' (Foucault, 1991: 34).

At the Enlightenment radical reforms concerning such torture emerged. Punishment was no longer a matter of the body but based upon the psychological make-up of the offender, with the intention of reforming and reconciling. Not a regressive move one might suggest. But, for Foucault, such attention given to the mind of the criminal was inextricably linked to notions of power. As Merquior writes, 'the prime concern of penal authority became the mind, not the body, of the criminal' (1991: 89) and psychological knowledge took over the role of casuistic jurisprudence. Barry Smart makes this same point:

> Foucault has argued that the shift of exercise of power (punishment) to the 'soul' or 'knowable man' conceptualised in terms of psyche, subjectivity, personality, consciousness, and individuality was a product

of the emergence of new forms of power and concomitant new forms of knowledge. The inference here is not that of a liberating process in which the body is released from the tyranny of power, but rather of a fundamental and positive transformation involving the emergence of a new technology of power, discipline, and the production through the exercise of this new form of power, of a new reality and knowledge, that of the individual (1989: 109).

As Foucault himself states, 'But what was now beginning to emerge was a modulation that referred to the defendant himself, to his nature, to his way of life and his attitude of mind' (1991: 99). In this new system, power was exercised; indeed, a whole system of power was invested.

A similar exercise of power occurred when madness came to be diagnosed as a pathological condition rather than a form of unreason. What happened was that a *discourse about* madness was established, creating a divisive and discriminating category. The 'illness' became objectified by new pathological discourses about the condition. As a result, 'rational reason puts "unreason" under a pathological curse fraught with ethical overtones' (Merquior, 1991: 23). A monologue of reason about madness unfolds, rather than a dialogue between reason and unreason; the medical gaze began to exercise its own discriminating power. Foucault contends that in the modern period punishment began to make use of representation as a mechanism for the exercise of social power. A rational articulation of the causes of crime began to replace the earlier corporeal realities on which power was exercised. Foucault writes, 'what must be maximised is the representation of the penalty, not its corporeal reality' (1991: 95). What came to characterise modern forms, therefore, was surveillance in the pursuit of justice. Above all, no crime committed must escape the gaze of those whose task it was to dispense justice. The power of rationalisation and surveillance replaced the power of ritual. The judge no longer used ritual forms, but common reason, and putting to one side the old model, adopted the new model of empirical research (1991: 96–98).

The Renaissance doctrine of acquiring knowledge through the discovery of resemblances (for example, by science and magic existing complementarily) was to be substituted for representation. The mathematisation of reality meant that a new mode of knowledge developed, which proceeded from the notion that individuals have clearly formed *a priori* concepts of material things which can exist independently of those things. As Pickstock notes, 'an object can now be defined independently of a material thing, and in indifference to materiality and spirituality, whereas for Aquinas our mode of grasping any being is always conditioned by our grasp of the material thing. In consequence, the object is now defined on the basis of the concept, as *representation*' (1998: 130). Bacon and Descartes untiringly sought certainty through exactitude and order with *mathesis* and *taxonomia* becoming dominant ways of pursuing knowledge. Blaise Pascal had issued a warning at the start of modern philosophy that Descartes' overestimation of reason and his efforts to construct a universal science based on mathematics was skewed in its rejection of the will, feeling, imagination, disposition, emotions and passions (Kung, 1995), but his concern was relatively uninfluential.

Foucault identifies that during modernity this process to gain exact knowledge (and thereby exercise power) rested also on an investigation into the psychological and internal workings of the person; knowledge of the inner person was underway. The concept of 'criminality' established by psychological knowledge, rather than the action or punishable body of the criminal became the object of penal intervention. The openly visible, externally marked criminal body, was to be substituted by a new method of investigation – a carefully worked out mapping of the mind of the offender. Consequently, a classified taxonomy of crimes and punishments began to be established. Knowledge was accumulated of the repetition of crimes – the possible reasons behind the committing of the crime sought: 'Now through the repetition of the crime, what one was aiming at was not the author of an act defined by law, but the delinquent subject himself, a certain will that manifested his intrinsically criminal behaviour' (1991: 100). Acts of crime became objectified within the discourse of criminality as well as being the object of investigative intervention. This process is not unlike Foucault's description of the classification of madness in *Madness and Civilisation* and his description of the development of houses of confinement. A process of medicalisation of madness occurred and as McNay contends: 'The introduction of a notion of responsibility into the treatment of madness led to a subtle change in the techniques of treatment from overt repression to a more covert form of authority which manifests itself through continuous surveillance and judgement' (1994: 23).

This move from the body to the mind also indicated a shift in power which was to have implications for present-day understandings of the exercise of power. This is fundamentally what

Foucault became interested in. Not that one cultural system was necessarily any better or worse than another, but different systems displayed different forms of power and domination which needed to be understood if knowledge of the power struggles in contemporary society were to be accurate. As Poster suggests of Foucault, 'he attempts to extract from the complexity of the past, certain lives of struggle because, he thinks, they can have an impact on the way we think about structures of domination in the present' (1984: 100). The 'episteme' of the modern age, released new forms of power. The application of power no longer resided in the ritual punishment of the body but in 'the mind or rather a play of representations and signs circulating discreetly but necessarily and evidently in the minds of all. It is no longer the body, but the soul, said Mably' (Foucault, 1991: 101).

Normalisation

Along with judgement and diagnosis, came the construction of normalisation. The criminal was to be set against certain classifications of criminal behaviour, according to specific criteria. Parallel with the objectification of crimes and criminals occurred a definition of the 'abnormal' individual, the deviant criminal who had been judged unworthy by an orderly society. The *homo criminalis* became an object of study in this newly emerging field of knowledge. The mind, not the body, became the surface for the inscription of power, the recipe for the exercise of domination, with semiology as its most lethal tool. A new process of submitting the body was performed through the control of ideas and which surrounded the subject of the new knowledge called 'criminality'; a more effective means than the ritual anatomy of torture and execution was sought. If formerly slaves were kept down by iron chains then, in the modern period, ideas become the means of political domination and slavery, suggests Foucault.

This, of course, was to echo other strands and developments in modernity, which we have already noted. Merquior contextualises this technique of discipline within the most dominant features of the modern period:

> The web of discipline aims at generalising the *homo docilis* required by 'rational', efficient, 'technical' society; an obedient, hard-working, conscience-ridden, useful creature, pliable to all modern tactics of production and welfare. And ultimately the main way to achieve

docility is the moral pressure of continuous comparison between good and bad citizens, young or adult: discipline thrives on 'normalizing judgement' (1991: 94).

Correspondingly, Foucault's description of prison and normalisation extends to other fields. Modern society is shot through with powerful disciplinary strategies ensuring the continued power of the dominant group. Control becomes exercised through the process of watchful normalisation:

> In a modern penal regime... the prisoner is subjected to surveillance arising not only from the requirements of physical constraint but also from a set of 'assessing, diagnostic, prognostic' and normative knowledges, such as criminology, psychology, medicine, etc. These knowledges produce the pathologized subject of the delinquent which in turn make it possible to police low-level criminality (1994: 94).

One chapter in *Discipline and Punish* 'The Gentle Way in Punishment' traces the practice of instructing and reforming the criminal. Attention is now given to the criminal much more than the crime, to 'the potential danger that lies hidden in an individual and which is manifested in his observed everyday conduct' (1991: 126). Psychological screening developed alongside an encouragement for the criminal to 'go inside himself and rediscover in the depths of his conscience the voice of good' (1991: 122). Isolation became necessary and induced a 'terrible shock' which provided a perfect opportunity for the individual to locate the abnormality within him/her in the most intense of ways.

However, the body was not to disappear altogether in the modern period, simply to be used in a new, politicised manner. Merquior notes that 'Foucault is explicit about it: his aim was to tell the political history of the body' (1991: 99). This process in turn leads to Foucault's indictment of the prison systems where a new 'docile body' was to emerge: 'The human body was entering a machinery of power that explores it, breaks it down and rearranges it' (1991: 138) and this was not simply with reference to the criminal body. The regulation of the body became apparent whereby the 'supervision of the smallest fragment of life and of the body... occurs' (1991: 140). This gives Foucault his cue to link other forms of institutional power to the prison system: the school, the barracks, the mental asylum. As Smart argues, 'It was in the course of the eighteenth century that discipline – the new methods of observation, recording, calculation, regulation, and training to which the body had long been subjected in monasteries, armies, and workshops – became a general formula for domination (1989: 110). Disciplinary operations came to control a manipulated docile body by means of an investigation into the mind. Panopticism becomes the central image in this disciplinary mode, through which the normalising gaze 'assures the automatic functioning of power' (Foucault, 1991: 201).

Panopticism

James Miller claims that Foucault's analysis of panopticism was central to *Discipline and Punish*. 'The neologism itself, which designated the modern "physics of power" that replaced the crude "mnemotechnics" of torture was inspired by Jeremy Bentham and his book *Panopticon*. Foucault himself wrote that Bentham's architectural idea offered him, "the diagram of a mechanism of power reduced to its ideal form"' (quoted in Miller, 1994: 222), and 'it mapped out the specific anatomy of modern power that Foucault called "discipline"' (Miller, 1994: 222). Foucault explained in an interview in 1978 how, 'I tried to show precisely how the idea of a technology of individuals, a certain type of power, was exercised over individuals in order to tame them, shape them, and guide their conduct' (quoted in Miller, 1994: 222). Other institutions, school, army, factories, were to be regulated in the same manner – docile bodies were being produced by the strict disciplinary routine and gaze of those in power. This then became a mechanism for regulation and surveillance through the whole of the social body, a means for the exercise of power across all social spheres. As Smart writes, 'A panoptic mechanism may be deployed in a whole variety of contexts where a multiplicity of individuals are located (eg. hospitals, schools, prisons, factories, and workshops), its effect being to make possible an improvement in the quantity, quality, intensity, and efficacy of the exercise of power' (1989: 111).

The spread of 'panopticism' throughout the social body is itself allied with a general amplification of power which does not curb or limit social forces, but encourages their enhancement. Foucault argues in his last chapter of *Discipline and Punish*, that this would entail an investigation without limit, involving meticulous and ever more analytical observation, a judgement that would create a file that was never closed. Extending Frederich Nietzsche's argument in *Beyond Good and Evil*, Foucault attempts to demonstrate how modernity took over the role of Christianity in disciplining the body. The will to know, the drive to investigate the offender and at the same time to persuade the individual to investigate him/herself through self-examination and regulation (a role previously assigned to the confessional) becomes central in Foucault's discussion.

In isolation the convict is able to discover much more acutely what is in his own conscience, the cell being the supreme site for self-examination: 'the cell confronts the convict with himself; he is forced to listen to his conscience' (Foucault, 1991: 123). The prison system became a method where 'no crime committed must escape the gaze of those whose task it is to dispense justice' (1991: 96). This is transmuted into a most effective form of self-disciplinary power whereby the individual begins to internalise the objective gaze of surveillance. The normalising gaze of the panopticon was to become the perfect disciplinary apparatus; it was now possible for a single gaze to see everything constantly. But what made surveillance even more oppressive was the asymmetrical arrangements involved. As Foucault writes,

> to arrange things that the surveillance is permanent in its effects, even if it is discontinuous in its action; that the perfection of power should tend to render its actual exercise unnecessary; that this architectural apparatus should be a machine for creating and sustaining a power relation independent of the person who exercises it; in short that the inmates should be caught up in a power relation of which they are themselves the bearers (1991: 201).

The use of space, isolation and surveillance became significant tools in the process. As McNay comments, 'The emergent prison regimes of the eighteenth century are the principal site where methods for the "political investment" of the body are developed and refined. Order is ensured in such regimes by the control of space with strategies such as the separation of individuals, the homogenisation of physical being and activity and the installation of permanent and intense forms of surveillance' (1994: 93).

A good example of such an arrangement is the prison chapel at Lincoln Castle, England. This Pentonville or Separate System Prison was built in 1845/6 and is the only surviving original example of such a penal system; it was built to support and reinforce the system of silence and separation. Twice daily, chapel services would be conducted when each prisoner would be herded into separate dividing pews to listen to the prison chaplain sermonise on the effects of sinful behaviour. It was considered that solitude and silence were favourable conditions for reflection and might lead to repentance. From the pulpit the preacher could see each prisoner but no prisoner could see another prisoner. Sermons were often on the theme of seeing: God's seeing of the individual's crime and the preacher's seeing of each prisoner. Prisoners awaiting execution would sit together in one row at the back of the chapel, since they were past redemption and could not be saved under the system. Many prisoners went insane as a result of such isolationist penal procedures. The most public demonstration of state power was no longer the scaffold, but Bentham's panopticon.

However, it is by no means clear that Foucault's description of normalising power is to be construed in every case as repressive. Disciplinary power is written about as having a positive force at times. In *The History of Sexuality, Volume I* Foucault argues that emerging modern discourses on sexuality are also discourses about new forms of power, 'Sexuality is not the most intractable element in power relations, but rather one of those endowed with the greatest instrumentality: useful for the greatest number of manoeuvres and capable of serving as a point of support, as a linchpin, for the most varied strategies' (1984: 69). Foucault develops in his history a non-essentialist view of sexuality. Sexuality and sexual perversion are produced; discourse about sex is a historical construct more influential in the modern period than the soul since we demand of sex that it tell us the truth about ourselves. Although discourses (for example, on perversion) might be sometimes a means of social control, they nevertheless speak on their own behalf and have their own voice. Power is established and operates through this construction of sexual discourse. Jonathan Dollimore writes, 'Foucault's perversion is not an innate desire socially repressed, but an identity and a category which are socially produced to enable power to gain a purchase within, and through, the realm of the psychosexual' (1992: 226–27).

Foucault was concerned to show how subjects are constructed through different agencies of power. Self-understanding often comes about in relation to external authority figures (for example, the confessor or the psychoanalyst). Such powerful figures construct within the subjects themselves an identity in relation to such power: 'the goal of my work during the last twenty years has not been to analyse the phenomena of power, nor to elaborate the foundations of such analysis. My objective, instead, has been to create a history of the different modes by which, in our culture, human beings are made subjects' (quoted in Rabinow, 1991: 7). Paul Rabinow claims that Foucault is primarily concerned with isolating those techniques through which the person initiates an active self-formation, but the word 'subject' can have two meanings: either that a subject is subject to someone else by control or, that he or she is tied to his/her own identity (Rabinow, 1991). Foucault's central concern in his writings about sexuality, therefore, is not the practice of sexuality, but how discourses about such practices are set up. As in the medical and criminal field, modernity seized upon sexuality as a thing to be scrutinised, a process which Merquior describes as 'anatomopolitics – a politics of the body – in conjunction with a biopolitics – the planning of the population' (1991: 121). Foucault wanted to emphasise the emergence of the constructed subject in relation to such discourses about sexuality. Therefore, going along with the psychiatrisation of insanity and the diagnosis of criminality was a corresponding self-awareness of the individual as a subject of sexual practices.

Foucault has not escaped criticism for his survey of penal reform and his analysis of the docile body. While his emphasis is often on the disciplinary mode of power, there is at times an uneasy and unclear relationship between that mode and elements of positive social power which are released. Foucault also fails to distinguish at times between the myriad types of institutions and how variations in disciplinary procedures reflect their differences. Another omission is Foucault's failure to account for any resistance that might accrue due to disciplinary procedure. His description is too one-sided, forever focusing on the official representatives of the institutions and rarely on those who are disciplined. This often leads to an overemphasis on the impact of such disciplinary measures. This point is taken up by Shilling when describing Foucault's account of the body:

> The body is affected by discourse, but we get little sense of the body reacting back and affecting discourse. Even when Foucault makes the occasional reference to the body putting up resistances to power and dominant discourses, he cannot say what it is about the body that resists (1993: 81).

Another criticism centres around the construction of the person in relation to the concept of the body. Foucault's analysis that certain types of power upon the body 'produce discourses about

the self which are self-regulatory (for example, the notion of the
confessional in *The History of Sexuality* which produces self-policing
subjects), suggests that subjects are easily constructed through
bodily disciplinary measures and that individuals are bereft of
autonomous, self-activated actions and thoughts' (Shilling, 1993:
81). Too great an emphasis is placed on the effects of a corporeal-
centred disciplinary power at the expense of a critique of how
other forms of power, for example, legal definitions of the person
might add to the construction of the modern individual (McNay,
1994).

   Shilling's criticism about the materiality of the body in
Foucault is also persuasive: 'Foucault's epistemological view of the
body means that it *disappears* as a material or biological
phenomenon. The biological, physical or material body can
never be grasped by the Foucauldian approach as its existence is
permanently deferred behind the grids of meaning imposed by
discourse' (1993: 80). This amounts to a 'disembodied' analysis
even when Foucault refers to the body itself. The body is clearly
there as a topic for discussion but 'is absent as a focus of investigation' (1993: 80). One partial reason for this, as I have
suggested throughout this chapter, is Foucault's primary concern
about the mind and its overriding influence on the body. It is
very much a 'mindful' body. This is what Foucault is arguing for,
as Shilling concedes: 'Once the body is contained within modern
disciplinary systems, it is the mind which takes over as the
location for discursive power' (1993: 80). In no sense does
Foucault ever suggest that the body is able to shape and influence
knowledge. It is always left to the mind through its construction
of varied discourses to do this. That is why Dews can write that,
'Without some theory which makes the corporeal more than a
tabula rasa, it is impossible to reckon the costs imposed by "an
infinitesimal power over the active body"' (quoted in Shilling,
1993: 80).

   The influences of Foucault on understanding some of the
central features of modernity is unquestionable. The purpose
of this next section is to examine these influences with
particular reference to the development of precise non-bodily
practices in modernity and to locate this shift from the
premodern to the modern. I attempt this with particular
reference to the rise of the modern 'surveillance society' and
the deployment and application of Foucault's 'gaze' in
contemporary society.

Disembodied Surveillance

Lyon claims that Foucault's contribution to the rise of surveillance theory is highly significant and can be summarised succinctly:

> Modern societies have developed rational means of ordering society that effectively dispense with traditional methods like brutal public punishment. Rather than relying on external controls and constraints, modern social institutions employ a range of disciplinary practices which ensure that life continues in a regularised, patterned way (1994a: 7).

Giddens similarly suggests that modern surveillance is an important means of establishing power (1985). But what Foucault failed to address was the rise of electronic surveillance and the subsequent impact of information technology on the classification of personhood, normality and forms of social power. In contrast, Lyotard, in his seminal work on postmodernity (1984) argued that the postmodern condition, if failing any longer to respond to metanarratives, seemed to be relying on those apparently certain foundations of computer accuracy and technology. Poster (1990) similarly suggests that what essentially characterises postmodernity is a new mode of information, gathered through surveillance techniques and strategies based on power. Questions of personal identity became at stake: for example, the databases which build up information about individual selves may have a tenuous relation to the 'real self' which is experienced in social relations. Lyon also sees some of these dangers in terms of 'constraint by classification' entailing important questions of justice and fairness which must be raised when people's everyday activities are monitored and their habits, commitments and preferences classified by would-be omniscient organisations (1994: 81–157). Fears arise particularly when such surveillance attempts to classify those things which resist such procedures.

What I want to suggest here is that such surveillance strategies are significantly different and 'modern' due to another central feature, often overlooked in discussions of surveillance theory: the notable absence of the body in such practices. One characteristic of Foucault's panopticon is the absence of the sight of the watching body in the process of surveillance. The inmate internalises the fear of the gaze since he/she imagines that an all-seeing, watchful eye is ever-present, but never sees such an eye. The body behind the surveillance operation is never located. Just as any modern surveillance video watch sets up the fear of surveillance, in the mind, without recourse to a seen physical body, so too did the panopticon. 'Manpower' is replaced by non-bodily electronic power. This is clearly demonstrated in the numerous advances in new technologies of teaching where non-bodily teaching strategies replace the bodily presence of tutors.

If, therefore, Foucault identified a shift in the site for domination from the body to the mind or soul, then clearly electronic surveillance has developed and exaggerated this division, producing a radical change in social practices with concomitant repercussions in personal, social and political spheres. The non-bodily, unseen operation of modern electronic surveillance has three important consequences. First, the asymmetrical gaze is likely to produce uncertainty; one can never be sure who (if there is such a who), one is being watched or classified by. There is literally *no body*, and *nobody* to which one may relate. (This is not to suggest naively that the body is easily deciphered for meaning, but it does raise the question of the construction of meaning and knowledge through non-bodily operations.) As Lyon comments, the only certainty 'resides in the system, and, one might add, with the inspector, the one "in the know"' (1994a: 65). Second, modernity ushers in a unique form of mental isolationism; the Foucauldian premodern crowd watching the public torture is substituted by a deliberate policy of separation: 'Each individual has his own place; and each place is separate' (Foucault, 1991: 143). Sometimes prison chapel services were conducted by holding them in a central position above the inspection lodge, without the need to remove prisoners from their separate cells. The bodily collectivity of the group was replaced by an atomised, non-relational seclusion. Third, questions of personal identity arise. Previously, it was usual to give personal data only to those who could be trusted and with whom one had some personal relationship, perhaps the doctor or the priest. Now this is replaced by the anonymous, non-bodily presence of the data collector. As Lyon argues, 'personal data, in a world characterised by face-to-face relations, tends to be limited to voluntary disclosure to chosen confidants within relations of trust' (1994a: 194). What electronic, non-bodily communication does is to objectify those relations with astonishing results. Similar issues in the medical field arise with reference to the ethics of non-bodily means of human reproduction, particularly with reference to modern IVF treatment.

Bentham's panopticon arrangement was itself based on a parody of the Christian God. Taking a line from Psalm 139 to make his point: 'Thou art about my path, and about my bed; and spiest out all my ways' (quoted in Lyon, 1994a: 206), his invective against a

God with omniscience and an all-seeing nature was to become embedded in his new secularised ideology. Indeed, the dystopic ideal of Bentham had far-reaching effects, witnessed most acutely in the rise of electronic surveillance where the all-seeing eye or the gaze of modernity was to become central in new forms of technology. This is hardly surprising since its roots lie in Enlightenment thinking; knowledge during the seventeenth century became organised around seeing in a previously unknown and important way. It was the age of the ocular when the dominant sense of seeing was first in the hierarchy of the senses. What was seen became submissive, defenceless to classification, with knowledge no longer being achieved through the bodily relationships of persons.

Lyon identifies this crucial shift by suggesting that electronic surveillance carries this Enlightenment motif into the late twentieth and early twenty-first centuries by its reduction of persons to data-images (1994a: 83–85). Within such a system, the data-image is distanced from the person and from forms of accountability and responsibility; this distancing effect of such technology may produce extremely negative results. The non-bodily accumulation and distancing of the collection of data and the insistence on controlled gathering of asymmetrical infor-mation means that modern forms of surveillance become impersonal and dangerously abstract. The gaze all too easily slips into a mode of domination. Such strategies of control in the modern period are part of the inevitable consequences of a culture which sees ritual largely in terms of magic or superstition and attempts to exercise its own secular power upon the world having acknowledged that God is dead. As Driver has reminded us (1991), religious ritual always relies on a supernatural presence or power to be effective and bring about what it signifies. With the demise of ritual, such a presence became substituted by secular powers, based largely upon psychological manipulation and invasive strategies of *mathesis*.

Summing up, it has been my intention here to present the central features of Foucault's idea of power with particular reference to the 'mindful body' and to suggest that his views represent a significant change in understanding how knowledge, meaning and self-identity became constructed in the modern period. For Foucault, the mind rather than the body began to dominate the site for discursive power; the role of the body was reduced to an essentially passive and inert appendix. Ritual became redundant. Foucault's analysis of the body in the modern

period, therefore, becomes focused on its reduction and manipulation by disciplinary regulatory powers. Modernity produced
docile bodies, controlled by discourses centred around psychological prescriptions. In this important sense, Foucault, despite his
critics, has identified a major shift in epistemological enquiry and
drawn helpful attention to the process of psychologisation which
developed in modern western society.

The Mind Replacing the Body

Other social theorists have highlighted some of the cultural and
personal effects of devaluing somatic and ritual experience in the
process of giving sole epistemological regard to cognitive apprehension and reason. Seidler's work (1991, 1994a, 1994b) on the rise
of the modern period is not dissimilar in tone and emphasis to
Bauman's (1993, 1994). He speaks of the need to 'recover the self'
after the impact of the Protestant Reformation and the legacy of
Descartes, arguing that the division between the mind and the body
became highly influential as the Enlightenment concept of the
'rational man' took hold. Such a radical break between the mind
and body was to revolutionise understandings about human nature
and personhood. The concern for science and reason invaded
almost every aspect of individual and social existence combined with
a strong sense that society had to be radically reorganised on a
rational basis for people to be able to discover meaning in their
everyday lives. Although Seidler does pay some attention to the
negative influence of Kant's categorical imperative (which he claims
reduced the conducting of moral reasoning independently of
people's natures), his most trenchant criticism is reserved for Luther
due to his emphasis on the negative and sinful nature of the body and
the need for human beings to rise above its corrupting influence.
Within the period of the Enlightenment it became important for
individuals to prove themselves in the eyes of God, in a constant
battle of legitimation of their own self-worth. This, he contends,
reflected a distinctively Protestant attention to the notion that
somehow people's 'natures' were rotten and useless (1994a: 66).

As I have already discussed, the decline in ritual activity during
modernity can be partly paralleled to this rise of instrumental
reason as the basis for discovering truth and eliminating doubt.
The suspicion the Reformers held for ritual practices became
allied in the modern period to a view that self-identity had nothing
to do with collective ritual gatherings; instead it consisted

essentially in cognitive self-criticism and individual acts of submission to God. Rituals which claimed to confer grace or win merit were curtailed, since the most effective manner in which salvation could be assured was by the preaching and reception of the word of God and a humble acceptance of one's own worthlessness before God. Catholic ritual implied 'popery' and superstition and Masses were frequently associated with 'sorcerous witchcraft' (Cameron, 1991; Thompson, 1991).

There was no clearly defined awareness of 'the individual' even in relation to God during the Middle Ages. (Fromm, 1995: 35). Each person's identity was inextricably tied to a social role within a strong ecclesiastical, even if somewhat hierarchical structure (Duffy, 1992; Swanson, 1995; Fromm, 1995). Fromm writes that awareness of one's individual self, of others, and of the world as separate entities, had not yet fully developed (1995: 35–36). In traditional societies a strong sense of corporate identity underpinned by ritual expression was common. Richard Fenn maintains that the extraordinary achievements of highly ritualised societies are apparent, especially in relation to their establishment of a strong sense of collective identity and in their ability to continue the past to the future (Fenn, 1987, 1992, 1997). In traditional societies the past can always be brought into the future. The life and self-identity of the community revolved around such rites. In the premodern world to live 'outside the camp' or the community and still retain a sense of self-identity was not possible.

Individual Doubt

The Protestant Reformers attempted to free the person from submissive responsibilities towards authoritarian collective bonds, especially those secured through somatic experience. A person must become free from any authority except God. Inevitably this entailed a much more lonely and individual quest (Seidler, 1994a, 1994b). Luther's legacy of the inevitable doubt which sprung from this insistence on a person's powerlessness and rottenness was only assuaged by a quest for certainty. Like Descartes, Luther sought certainty, but in the latter's case by submitting to a power greater than himself, not through the process of *mathesis*. But such attempts at relieving anxiety and doubt were never fully realised by Luther who had fits of anxiety and uncertainty until his death (Fromm, 1995: 66). If the Reformers had as their intent the undermining of ritual practices based on their 'new' theology and upon their concern to rid the Church of any abuses or corruptions, then they were soon to discover that what they considered to be a route to freedom away from the burden of spiritual authorities was also a route towards anxious and lonely feelings of individual worthlessness and insignificance (Fromm, 1995: 68).

Giddens work points to some of the unsettling cultural effects in the light of the devaluation of ritual in the modern period. His examination of the construction of the self in what he terms the 'post-traditional age' is tied to an analysis of the repression of key existential questions and hinges partially on the demise of ritual. He argues that 'we tend now to counterpoise fate and the openness of future events' (1991: 111–12), a process radically different from the ancient idea of fate which always suggested that the future was in some way settled. However, this opening up to a possible problematic future invariably involves the operation of risk, with 'fateful moments' becoming highly significant for the individual or the group. These occur when individuals are 'called upon to take decisions that are particularly consequential for their ambitions, or more generally for their future lives' (1992: 112). At these moments in traditional societies the advice of the oracle would be sought or divine powers negotiated. What often happens at such times is that the 'protective cocoon' of ontological security is broken (1992: 14). This might be seen as a liminal phase of unstructured and potentially frightening proportions and without the support of ritual to contextualise and give meaning to such times, other ways of coping are required. What may occur in the light of this shift is a deflection of some of the unsettling consequences that thinking in terms of risk inevitably carries. In other words, the reality of the difficulty is repressed or ignored. Expert systems to focus on the reconstruction of the self also occur at such disruptive times to lend some meaning and consolation.

For Giddens, such measures do not always solve the problem. Ontological security is immensely fragile at such moments and the deeply rooted issues which lie at the base of such times of existential doubt might be ushered nervously aside or even ignored completely. He discusses how human beings face the prospect of being completely overwhelmed during such periods by anxieties about meaningfulness and what is 'real' in the world. Traditional societies often contained ritual practices to assuage such unsettling times,

Traditional ritual, as well as religious belief, connected individual action to moral frameworks and to elemental questions about human existence. The loss of ritual is also a loss of involvement with such frameworks, however ambiguously they might have been experienced and however much they were bound up with traditional religious discourse (1992: 204).

A parallel evolution of reflexivity occurs with the demise of ritual expression. This process of reflexivity does not stop short of the modern gods of science and technology either. Science's monopoly on rationality is itself frequently questioned and its previous claims to objective investigation seen to be built on a 'house of cards' (Giddens, 1992). Competing intellectual claims vie for acceptance. Further problems ensue in a 'risk society' when those who profit and those who suffer from the consequences clash. What emerges is another pool of anxiety.

A notion that things have constantly to be revised and reconstituted in the light of new thinking characterises this emergence of reflexivity. The order of the world is no longer accepted as being 'given', but must be constantly constructed. Giddens acknowledges that the gap opened up by ritual's decline is never filled by self-constructed reflexive techniques and that the kind of reliable knowledge that was envisaged by rationalist assumptions and positivistic science is never achieved. Restless wandering characterises this modern condition (Bauman, 1992b; Flanagan, 1996a). This 'depthless culture' (Jameson, 1991) is exacerbated by the cultural fragmentation which comes from commodity consumption and reformulations of the body as an object of consumerist desire (Baudrillard, 1993; Boyle, 1995; Featherstone, 1991; Shilling, 1993).

Throughout this chapter I have identified some of the dominant assumptions involved in the shifting relationship and status accorded to the body and the mind in the modern period and traced some of the cultural and political consequences which occurred in relation to them. I suggested how these reformulations were intrinsically associated with the demise of the importance attached to ritual expression and the rise of more cognitive approaches to meaning and knowledge-construction. I now go on to discuss how such assumptions began to infiltrate much liturgical and theological thinking in the modern period and were to become major influences on the reforms of the liturgy at the Second Vatican Council.

4

MODERNITY AND LITURGICAL REFORM

In the previous chapter I outlined the process of rationality and psychologisation which was to occur during modernity and the extent to which the mind replaced the body as the site for knowledge, identity and meaning-construction. I also traced the corresponding rise in individuation and reflexivity, as the communal and ritual mechanisms for validating religious under-standings of the world and the self became eroded and dismantled. I now consider how specifically religious beliefs and practices were affected by such wider civilising developments of the age. This prepares the ground for any later discussion about the dominant influences on the reform of the liturgy at the Second Vatican Council.

The purpose of this chapter, therefore, is twofold: first, to plot the influence of disembodied and cognitivist approaches to knowledge on liturgical theory and practice as they emerged during the eighteenth, nineteenth and twentieth centuries; and second, to suggest that what was to characterise much Roman Catholic theology during this period was a similar attention towards a disembodied, psychological and cognitive approach to religion and the sacred. I argue how the scepticism towards more objective, communal and ritualised models of religion which accompanied the rise of Protestantism and its secular heir modernity, began to feature in many forms of Roman Catholic worship and theology and to trigger off different conceptualisa-tions of the Christian faith. Within this shift, I outline particularly how subjective experience and cognitive understanding began to dominate the manner in which the Christian religion itself came to be viewed and finally why the changes in the liturgy were to prove so problematic.

The Importance of Subjective Experience

Before discussing this mutation of meaning associated with worship in the modern period, it is important to remind ourselves of some of the more general shifts in religious self-understanding which occurred as the Enlightenment project took hold. Inevitably, as more individualised understandings of religion progressed, the status accorded to subjective experience increased correspondingly. What a person thought and felt as a unique individual assumed much greater importance. Colin Campbell's work (1987) on the relationship between Protestantism and hedonism points to this change by taking as one example the procedure of admittance into the Puritans. He shows how, originally, individuals who wished to become members were simply expected to search inside themselves for signs of God's grace. However, in New England and Britain this developed by 1640 into a public recital of the manner in which God's grace had been bestowed upon them. Of such measures Campbell argues that what is of particular importance is the way in which personal, subjective experience is being used as a crucial test of religious worth. As this transition to a far more individualised form of Christianity occurred, it became common for individuals to plot their inner religious journeys, frequently checking their descriptions for guarantees of the operation of God's grace and signs of 'election' within their own souls (Mellor and Shilling, 1997: 56–58). A personalised struggle between faith and doubt inevitably started to characterise such developments (Campbell, 1987: 129).

Campbell discusses the eighteenth century in relation to the emergence of a more 'abstracted self'. He argues how the disenchantment of the world which accompanied the Enlightenment project entailed a process of 'de-emotionalization' (1987: 72). By this he means that in the premodern world emotions were inherent in various aspects of the natural world. After the 'disenchantment' of nature in the modern period, reality became regarded as something wholly neutral and impersonal. As a result, emotions came to reside 'within' rather than 'without' individuals. This had significant reprecussions for understandings of self-identity and self-awareness. As Campbell states, 'the disenchantment of the world, and the consequent introjection of the power of agency and emotion into the being of man, was closely linked to the growth of self-consciousness' (1987: 72). This, in turn, led to a much more 'self-conscious' person, separated from any external agencies, always prepared to negotiate and at times dominate its own relationship to the external world. The self was beginning to become abstracted from the material world and associated with its own inner powers and creative potential. The self was no longer a constituent member of a divinely created natural order. The 'modern' person would now look dispassionately and at a distance at the 'object-ness' of the world.

Pickstock plots how an intensification of subjective piety within religious practice occurred in relation to the demise of ritual activity, quoting Erasmus as being the person responsible for the deritualising of the peace as early as the sixteenth century (1998: 47). This in turn led to the growth of a secularised form of ritual as mannerly and civil behaviour increased; the peace that had once been established and 'given' through ritual activity was being replaced by polite ways of doing things, unconnected to the purifying of the self. The medieval notion of ritual saw no difference between outer behaviour and inner motive or social ritual and personal sentiments. Asad's description of the practice of the Rule of St Benedict in the early Middle Ages demonstrates how even activities like calligraphy became rites, whose function was to discipline the self into the ways of Christ. The sacrament of confession gives one example, as does the cultivation of 'tears of desire for heaven' (Asad, 1993: 64) of how inner emotions and externalised rites were never separate during the medieval period. As Asad writes, 'the compunction for one's sins had to accompany the desire for virtue, the ability to weep became at once the sign of the genuineness of that compunction and the progress attained by that desire' (1993: 64). In contrast, the early modern period broke down the intrinsic interrelationship between public behaviour and private thoughts or feelings as life in the court circle became saturated with the notion of representation, which divorced appearance from reality. The pursuit of power and the association of symbolic action with ideological motives then came to be a real possibility. In referring to Bacon's text, 'Of Simulation and Dissimulation' (a text investigating how representational behaviour is often associated with the attainment of power), Asad concludes how 'it is only here, in the hidden exercise of strategic power, that symbolic behaviour becomes what I think one may now call ideological' (1993: 66).

The emergence of Quaker worship during the seventeenth century cut any association with 'the spirit' of medieval liturgy, since there were no clergy, no preaching, no choirs or organs and its practice was largely bereft of all ceremonial (White, 1989: 135; 1990). The emphasis given to the resources of the inner self separated it from any medieval devotion apart from its regard for mysticism and the possibility of a direct encounter with God (White, 1989: 136). The influence of Wesleyan Methodism, allied to the growth of Romanticism, was also to provide further definition to the importance of subjective experience by its overriding emphasis on the creative individual and its claim that each soul was unique in God's eyes. Its acknowledgement of the importance of each individual's personal drama of conversion and salvation and its advocacy of the fruits of personal expression was responsible for a new religious attention to the emotional and inner self. Unlike the Puritans, John Wesley saw no compulsion to reflect this need for conversion within liturgy – he omitted the rite of confirmation from his prayer book (White, 1989: 156).

Later Romantics were to claim that what lay at the centre of the human person was the unconscious mind, the primary source from which the imagination was fed. This is not to say that the earlier Counter-Reformation was not wholly resistant to such moves towards greater self-scrutiny and reflexivity. Both Protestantism and the Counter-Reformation encouraged a purification of external rituals as the practice of examining one's conscience became an essential part of the path to moral virtue (Cameron, 1991). Indeed, the Catholic Church itself had begun to rationalise its organisation and to postulate how communities should operate. The Council of Trent placed considerable stress on a more discursive knowledge and understanding of religious truth, while still endorsing the importance of ritual expression.

The Work of Pierre Guéranger

Within the liturgical field an important figure was to emerge in the nineteenth century who would attempt to counter the cultural effects of this rise of modern individualism – the French Benedictine monk, Dom Pierre Guéranger. As a keen ultramontanist, Guéranger has been associated with his attack on the localisation of rites and an insensitivity to pastoral needs (Davies, 1978: 216), but Chandlee speaks for the majority of commentators when he writes that Guéranger's work at the Abbey of Solesmes was

a springboard for a revival by the Benedictines of their traditional concern for liturgy which eventually placed the monks among the pioneers of the Liturgical Movement, and it spurred an investigation

into the origins and history of the liturgy in which such scholars as
Cabrol and Batiffol provided the foundation for present-day liturgical
study (Davies, 1978: 216; see Flanagan, 1991; Nichols, 1996).

It was from the Middle Ages that Guéranger and his contem-
poraries claimed an ideal and sought refuge: 'Le moyen age
des Églises d'Occident a produit, dans le genre liturgique, des
sequences d'une rare beaute; un de nos premiers soins sera
d'initier les fideles qui nous liront a ces sources si pures de
tendresse et de vie' (Guéranger, 1995: 18). Here was to be found
the golden age of Christian worship and its reflection in an orderly
society (Readt, 1997). Guéranger constantly reasserted the
importance of ritual within worship, applying his arguments to
the regeneration of European society which, he claimed, had
become increasingly fragmented and divisive. Rites would restore,
as they had within the medieval Church, a sense of collective
responsibility and were an anodyne against the individualism of
the nineteenth century. William Franklin's research (1976) into
the work of Guéranger emphasises two things – his concern about
individualism and his belief in the unifying power of liturgy. As a
seminarian he had read Lamennais' *Essai sur l'indifference en matiere
de religion* which argued that individualism was the major source of
the social disorder experienced in nineteenth-century France. He
had also been deeply influenced by Chateaubriand's *Genie du
Christianisme* which discussed how the celebration of the Mass was
the most effective solace and support for people in a confused and
uncertain age. Guéranger's essays on liturgy began to pour out of
Solesmes, reflecting his concern about the collapse of European
civilisation. This was blamed squarely on the rise of modern
individualism which he said resulted in the advent of a sense of
anomie (Franklin, 1976). Individualism could be altered and transformed by the unifying beauty of collective worship; the increase
in secularisation which was disturbing the social order could only
be stemmed by a renewal and belief in the power of ritualised
liturgy. Worship was the answer to cultural decay. The Church's
ritual is the 'mysterious means of communication between heaven
and earth' (Franklin, 1976: 154) and the means *par excellence* of
uniting the people of God.

Guéranger claimed that one of the most effective ways that
liturgy could confront the social problems of early and mid-
nineteenth-century France was by the restoration of its former
dignity, secured through an attention to a prescribed rite which
released a sense of the sacredness of adoration. Truth is best

embodied in signs and gestures (Readt, 1997). As Flanagan points out (1991: 326), Guéranger's interest in the gothic style of liturgy reflected his understanding that Christianity needed to represent the sacredness of mystery in its liturgy. Aidan Nichols also writes of Guéranger's work, 'It is by acceptance through faith of our composition into a supernatural unity through a pre-existing rite that community is engendered, not by the devising of new or adapted rites that have the creation of community as their immediate end' (1996: 42). Guéranger's book *L'Église ou la Société de la Louange Divine* is about how this unity of the members of the Church is achieved by a liturgical communication between heaven and earth.

In 1833 when Guéranger went to live at Solesmes his influence on parish liturgy began to spread throughout France. Franklin writes,

> He was urging parish priests to consider that it is chiefly by what they themselves do in church that the people are educated in the meaning of the redemption, not by what congregations read silently or hear in vigorous sermons. Through initiation into the significance of rite, parishes would come to learn the meaning of the whole of life in the light of the Church's sacred actions. Here would be seen the true meaning of 'community': the common work of worship, the one food of the eucharist, the subordination of the self before the universal (1976: 154–55).

Guéranger's liturgical work was never an attempt to divorce the prayer of the Church from the cultural problems which had arisen in early to mid-nineteenth-century France. What he wanted was a return to the 'unselfconscious coherence' (Anderson, 1991:16) that had characterised the 'imagined communities' of the Middle Ages. As Nichols rightly puts it, the question Guéranger attempted to answer was 'How is a Christian community to be re-created?' (1996: 41–42). But an emphasis on the subordination of the self in favour of collective regeneration was clearly at odds with the increased attention being given at the time to more self-referential and subjective approaches to religion by both secular and Church authorities (Flanagan, 1991).

Indeed, Guéranger was to argue quite differently about the nature of worship from many who were to become associated with the Liturgical Movement itself as it unfolded at the start of the twentieth century. Ritual was not an anachronistic practice without application to contemporary concerns; it was the means towards renewal and unification within the Church and larger society. Guéranger's second conviction, however, was centred around the need for liturgy to be intelligible and understandable, and in this regard his writing was cognisant with many of the liturgical ideas which were to prove influential as the Liturgical Movement took shape and advanced. What Guéranger believed would restore a sense of community was a comprehension of the liturgy: 'It can heal and save the world, but only on the condition that it be understood' (quoted in Franklin, 1976: 156). Indeed, this was one of Guéranger's major concerns – that the congregation may participate intelligibly in the prayer of the Church as fully as possible: 'We have endeavoured to give, to such of the laity as do not understand the Latin, the means of uniting in the closest possible manner with everything that the priest says and does at the altar' (quoted in Franklin, 1976: 156). In this regard, Guéranger prefigures a common concern of the Liturgical Movement itself in his insistence on participation established through understanding.

From Ritual Expression to Personal Experience and Intelligibility

The nineteenth century was not bereft of other important European figures who contributed to a revitalisation and reawakening of the Christian liturgy: Pusey in England, Grundtvig in Denmark, Möher and Loehe in Germany. They all encouraged an interest in liturgy as the source of the Church's life and ministry against the backdrop of a modern culture which had attempted to sap dry any notion that truth might reside or be discovered in collective liturgical practices centred around embodied experience. Guéranger's influence at the Abbey of Solesmes quickly became a symbol of liturgical renewal and splendour and was to influence the establishment of other monasteries such as Bueron in France, Mont-César in Belgium and Maria Laach in Germany.

Key liturgical events at the turn of the twentieth century reflected the emphases liturgical theory and practice were to take up to and beyond the Second Vatican Council.[1] For example, in 1903 Pope

---

[1] There were exceptions. The planning of the new Roman Catholic Westminster Cathedral at the beginning of the twentieth century reflects much earlier attitudes towards worship. As Richards notes: 'The liturgy itself was not a problem; it was taken for granted that everyone knew what Catholic worship was' (1979: 2). What figured in the debate was the architectural magnificence of the building which would give glory to God. This

Pius X issued a *Motu Proprio* on church music in which members of the Church were encouraged to be actively engaged, followed by a call for congregations to receive Communion on a more regular basis. The Conference at Malines in 1909 advocated the liturgy as the supreme means for the instruction of the faithful and called for a translation of the Roman missal into the vernacular. In Britain, George Tyrrell, a key representative of the Catholic Modernist revival in the first decade of the twentieth century, argued in favour of human experience being given more cognisance in any formulation of liturgical theology and in his *Lex Orandi* of 1903, he signalled a new approach to liturgical revival which he said would engage the many (rather than the few) in acts of worship (Daly, 1980). By advocating inner subjective experience as the basis of Christian worship and identifying ritual with anachronistic practices, the seeds were sown for later developments: 'The archaic language, music, and ritual has by lapse of time acquired a value, originally lacking to it, which now appeals to the historic and aesthetic sense of the cultured few; but what of the cultured many?' wrote George Tyrrell (quoted in Crichton, Winstone and Ainslie, 1979: 9). A turning point in liturgical understanding had arrived.

This denial by Tyrrell of the intrinsic importance of ritual is in contrast to Guéranger's earlier insistence on the formal and organic nature of worship, but the British influence was to prefigure much of the thinking of the European Liturgical Movement itself. Tyrrell's devaluation of the importance of ritual was significant since it associated such ritualised models with the past rather than the future:

> the understanding of liturgy as ceremonial, with its aesthetic appeal or with its evocation in feudal terms of the Catholic order of the past, however appropriate it may have been to the mood and social conditions of the day, was not a sufficient expression of the mind of the Church to provide lasting satisfaction of human needs (quoted in Crichton, Winstone and Ainslie, 1979: 10).

---

did not entail forgetting the poor, however, who were to be given due regard and attention. The liturgy had to be a magnificent performance which according to Cardinal Vaughan would 'announce the glad tidings of redemption in Our Saviour's precious Blood; to offer, without price, the exhaustless treasures of the daily sacrifice; and to give to many a weary soul the peace and hope that silently distil under the unceasing melody of the Church's liturgy of prayer and praise' (quoted in Crichton, Winstone and Ainslie, 1979: 6).

A new understanding concerning the nature of liturgy emerged in the wake of such evaluations, as the revitalisation of the liturgy began to be seen predominantly in terms of personal participation and comprehension rather than ritual form and aesthetic coherence. Clearly the modern period's attention to cognitivism and individualism was beginning to infiltrate understandings of what liturgy was essentially about. What was widely being accepted was that a much more subjective and personalised approach to worship would secure a renewal of the Church for the future.

Such early twentieth-century influences on the later Roman Catholic reform of the liturgy should not blind us, however, to previous 'civilising' influences. Nichols' trenchant critique (1996) of the Roman Catholic reforms of the 1960s owes much to the legacy of the Enlightenment period as a whole which, he argues, can be compared to much contemporary liturgy. He takes Trapp's suggestion that the keynotes of the eighteenth century were a utilitarian philosophical infrastructure in which happiness or usefulness is the key to truth, an emphasis on anthropocentrism, a predominance of ethical values over strictly religious ones, a downplaying of the notion of special revelation in favour of religion within the limits of reason and aesthetics, and an ideal of noble simplicity, *edle Einfalt,* all of which resulted in a liturgy, 'as sober and cold as classicism, because it was carried along by intellect and not by the totality of life' (quoted in Nichols, 1996: 22). *Qua* Trapp he comments that this produced three main strands in the liturgical domain: a demand for the simplification of the liturgy, an emphasis on the socially useful and community-building character of liturgy and an insistence on intelligibility which would edify morally those who worshipped.

Trapp's work traces the strong anti-devotionalism which occurred in the Catholic Church during the eighteenth century. Its opposition to sodalities, processions, pilgrimages and devotions (for example, the rosary and benediction) was highly influential although he concedes that these might have been justified by a desire to achieve more unity with Protestants. The Synod of Pistoia of 1786 had proposed changes, including that there should only be one altar per church, one Mass each Sunday, that Latin should be opposed and that devotion to the Sacred Heart should be downplayed. Such proposals were not granted but reflect the thinking that was common at the time. Trapp argues that such reforms are diametrically different from the reforms in the interwar years, a position which Nichols challenges preferring to argue that such cultural traits were highly influential on modern reforms. As Nichols writes, 'What we, over half a century after Trapp, may note in our turn, however, is that the approach to liturgy that apparently predominates today is much more reminiscent of the Enlightenment as he describes it than of the interwar liturgical movement he presents as its foil' (1996: 28). Nichols is convinced that the modern reforms reflected the imperfect attitudes of the European Enlightenment. He quotes two further examples: the freedom given to parish priests in eighteenth-century Germany to modify individual celebrations of the liturgy and the unwarranted fixation on the fourth century and before when liturgy exhibited a 'noble simplicity'. The more moderate representatives of the Enlightenment faced a question about liturgy which still echoes down to the present day: Is the liturgy primarily latreutic and concerned with the adoration of God or essentially didactic and concerned with the education of the community?

The Emergence of the Reforms

There were other important events in the lead up to the Roman Catholic liturgical reforms. In England the Society of St Gregory, established in 1929, emphasised the need to make liturgy more personally meaningful by more direct active participation of the congregation. Although the actual words 'active participation' do not appear in the four aims of the Society, the theme is implicit in the phrase 'congregational worship' (Crichton, Winstone and Ainslie, 1979). Dom Bernard McElligott, who originally called the meeting which led to the formation of the Society, stressed the importance of lay participation and began to organise missions on liturgy in parishes during which he spoke about the principles of active participation. The Society became one of the main forces for the education of lay people in the meaning and instruction of the liturgy, with summer schools being organised as well as the publication of a quarterly magazine, 'Music and Liturgy'. Many of the liturgical reforms of Vatican II had been well rehearsed in articles written in the Society's publications. The key note of the Society can be summed up in a sentence by Dom Laurence Bevenot: 'Until 1942 it had been assumed that the significance of the liturgy did not need explaining' (Crichton, Winstone and Ainslie, 1979: 43). The Society was soon to correct this omission.

The move to a more comprehensible, subjective and meaningful liturgy during the first half of the twentieth century became apparent in the production and revision of liturgical texts. For example, in 1915 Adrian Fortesque's popular edition of the Roman missal was published in English, in which only the 'Propers' of the Ordinary and the Canon were given in Latin. On the Continent in the early 1920s, the dialogue Mass had been launched under the influence of Lambert Beauduin, whereby the congregation and servers would answer the celebrant and in which the *Gloria,* Creed, and *Sanctus* were recited in harmony with the priest. In 1922 the Congregation of Rites gave formal approval to this development. The strides towards a vernacular rite were further enhanced by the formation of the English Liturgy Society in 1942 which put forward arguments for the regular and widespread use of the vernacular in liturgy. The *Centre de Pastorale Liturgique* founded in Paris in 1943 emphasised the importance of addressing pastoral needs within liturgy. Its publication, 'Maison-Dieu', conferences for priests and influential Congresses made it one of the main focuses for pastoral liturgy in France. In America, too, under the leadership of Dom Virgil Michel, St John's Abbey, Collegeville, Minnesota, became a centre of excellence for liturgical discussion. Its periodical 'Orate Frates', now known as 'Worship' published influential articles on the new directions liturgy was taking.

A more definite shape to the twentieth-century renewal of the liturgy, however, came about through the work of the Sacred Congregation of Rites and in 1946, Fr Loew, the Vice-Realtor General of the historical section, gave an outline around which any future reforms of the Roman Catholic liturgy might take place. This took two years to complete, followed by the formation of a commission for liturgical reform which met for the first time on 22 June 1948. For twelve years the commission gathered and worked in secrecy, possibly because of the fear of Rome or because they might have believed that their deliberations were too technical for public debate. The fruits of its work were the restoration of the *Triduum* Easter liturgy in 1951 and in 1955 the acknowledgement of principles of reform for a revision of the whole of the Easter Week liturgy, including the Divine Office (Emsley, 1998: 105).

The specifically liturgical encyclical *Mediator Dei* of 1947 gave further encouragement to a renewal of the worshipping life of the Church. Although there was a warning given against those who tried to disregard the traditional content and shape of the liturgy, this was counterbalanced by a stronger admonishment against those who attempted to hinder any new developments. Theodor Klauser comments on this encyclical that it 'gave special praise to those who had pledged themselves to a renewal of liturgical life, but at the same time issued a warning that many of them were too anxious for innovations and for this reason raised a series of warning signals' (1969: 22–23). Chandlee also writes of this encyclical, 'This document has been regarded by some as the charter of the liturgical movement, and as an endorsement of it' (1972: 219). In essence, the Pope had now expressed the view that the faithful should be able to participate fully in the liturgy with understanding and that they should take an active part in the services – lay participation and comprehension were to be the building blocks for a reformed liturgy. Louis Bouyer's *Life and Liturgy* (1956) was an attempt to put into practice the spirit and recommendations of this document.

The next event of importance was the International Congress for Pastoral Liturgy which convened in Assisi in 1956, followed by the Conference for Liturgy and Missions held in 1959 in Nijmegen. Both attempted to spell out in detail some of the implications of the changes emerging in the liturgical life of the Church. The theme for the Assisi Congress was again the pastoral nature of the liturgy. Two important lectures were given. The first 'The Pastoral Idea in the History of the Liturgy' by Fr Jungmann and the second, 'The Pastoral Value of the Word of God in the Sacred Liturgy'. These lectures contained principles which were to be set down later in the Constitution of the Liturgy in 1963. The problems associated with the use of the vernacular and the reform of the Divine Office were also discussed at Assisi.

The Liturgical Movement must also be seen within the wider reforming movements of the Roman Catholic Church. Adrian Hastings refers to the Liturgical Movement as one example (along with others, for example, biblical scholarship, the need for Catholics to participate in democratic politics), which was to produce a 'profoundly altered consciousness within the more wide-awake parts of the church by the later years of Pius XII's reign. The post-medieval, ultramontane model was not proving workable in either intellectual or social terms' (1991: 3). Chandlee suggests that the Movement 'sought to reach ordinary church people rather than the theologian or the intellectual' (1972: 217). Jungmann endorses the presuppositions of the liturgical renewal because, as a result, worship is no longer a 'beautiful spectacle in

which the wondering people are to admire venerable tradition'
but one in which 'the priest himself should vividly realise what a
properly celebrated divine service entails and can mean' (1964:
27–28). Consequently, he has no qualms about suggesting that an
act of worship is the best of catechetical lessons for the Christian
people.

The Liturgical Movement, too, may be seen as an important part
of the Ecumenical Movement. The Anglican liturgical scholars Dix,
Ratcliffe, Shepherd and Davies had considerable influence on
Roman Catholic thinking about liturgical renewal. Within the
Reformed tradition it is also important to acknowledge the work of
Eugene Bersier in Paris and the achievements of the Church
Service Society in Scotland. The liturgy of the Church of South
India is also significant for its influence on much of the liturgical
revision in the Protestant Church and the reforms sanctioned at the
Second Vatican Council. The work of Guéranger might also
be paralleled to the work of those individuals involved in
the Tractarian Movement within Anglicanism at the end of
the nineteenth century since both stress the centrality and
importance of the Eucharist in worship. Spurred on by the publication in 1935 of Herbert's book *Liturgy and Society*, significant
moves developed to restore the celebration of the Eucharist as the
norm of Anglican parish liturgical life. Herbert writes in his Preface,

> I write as an Anglican. This book was originally intended to be a treatise
> on the principles of Christian worship, inspired to a large extent by the
> Liturgical Movement in the Roman Catholic Church, which, in seeking
> to reintroduce the Catholic laity to the treasures of the liturgy, has
> found itself possessed of a key to unlock many doors, and engaged in
> an ever-widening circle of interests and activities (1935: 6–7).

The Roman Catholic Reform

As a result of these influences, the most wide-ranging renewal of
the Roman Catholic liturgy was to emerge from attention being
given to a pastorally based liturgy centred around the active
participation of the congregation. The 1963 Constitution on the
Sacred Liturgy, *Sacrosanctum Concilium*, encouraged the view that
participation was the aim to be considered above all else in liturgical reform. This reflected a renewed pastoral concern instigated
at the start of the Liturgical Movement itself. Archbishop Bugnini
(the *peritus* for the Conciliar Commission 1962–64 and the
secretary of the Concilium for the Constitution of the Liturgy

1964–69) emphasised that the 'The liturgical movement was an effort to unite rites and content, for its aim was to restore as fully as possible the expressiveness and sanctifying power of the liturgy and to bring the faithful back to full participation and understanding' (1990: 6). Bugnini lists active participation as one of the guiding principles of the Constitution which is both a right and a duty of the faithful who have been baptised into a royal priesthood: 'The full and active participation of all the people has been a special concern in the reform and promotion of the liturgy, for the liturgy is the primary and indispensable source from which the faithful can derive the true Christian spirit' (1990: 41). This participation (since it is concerned with the sanctification of human beings) entails understanding and the opportunity for the liturgy to be shared by each member of the Church.

On 25 January 1959 Pope John XXIII announced that a Second Vatican Council was to take place on 6 June 1960. Cardinal Cicognani was appointed President of the Preparatory Commission on Liturgy, a group of sixty-five members and consultants and thirty advisors. The appointees were to plan for the most wide-ranging reform the Catholic Church was to witness since the Council of Trent and to prepare for some of the most crucial changes to the worshipping life of the Church. The Constitution on the Liturgy promulgated in 1963 was the first document issued because of its supreme importance and the satisfactory nature of the preparation involved, a preparation, some might argue, spanning four hundred years.

Theological Roots: Roman Catholic Modernism

Let us now consider some of the major theological influences at the time of the Liturgical Movement. Roman Catholic Modernism, a movement of thought beginning around 1890 and ending in 1907, was to have considerable influence on later twentieth-century theology. Although officially condemned by the encyclical *Pascendi dominici gregis*, it was concerned with renewing and understanding theology within the 'modern' context brought about by the cultural and philosophical changes prevalent in the late nineteenth and early twentieth centuries. Ranchetti argues that the movement 'wished to restore Catholicism as a doctrine of truth' and 'to free it from the limitations imposed by outdated philosophies, insufficient historical knowledge, and an uncritical acceptance of centuries-old scientific discoveries; and to allow it to

take advantage of the discoveries of more modern science and
philosophy' (1969: vii–viii). Reardon suggests 'Towards the
century's end... it was... obvious to catholic scholars, awake now
to the nature and extent of modern Protestant research in the
field of the Bible and early Christianity, that the narrowly tradi-
tionalist standpoint upon these matters, rigidly upheld in the
seminaries, was likely to involve all catholic teaching and apolo-
getic in increasing discredit' (170: 13). Condemned as a heresy of
'agnosticism' by Pope Pius X, the movement petered out, but was
a significant turning-point in Roman Catholic thinking and
provides an insight into Catholic debates about the role of
individual experience, the nature of truth and the experience
of faith at the turn of the century. It also sheds light on some of
the central issues which were to emerge in the era leading up to
the Second Vatican Council and beyond.

The Modernists were intent on moving away from the stran-
glehold neo-scholasticism and, in particular, Thomist philosophy
had exercised on notions of religious truth since the thirteenth
century. Under the reign of Pope Leo XIII it was felt that a new
and much needed more liberal approach was possible and to be
welcomed. Loyal to the Church which they served (many were
ordained priests), and yet insistent that change was necessary, men
such as Alfred Loisy, George Tyrrell, Maurice Blondel, Lucien
Laberthonnière and Friedrich Von Hugel, began to articulate
approaches to religious faith which they believed reflected the
findings of modern scholarship (including their implications for
biblical exegesis) within a legitimate, if significantly altered,
Catholic orthodoxy. Some were officially condemned, while others
narrowly escaped criticism.

Key themes emerged in their publications during this period.
One emphasis throughout all their writings centred on the
importance of personal experience and action for theological
understanding. For George Tyrrell, the Anglo-Irish Jesuit priest,
Christian truth was founded on religious experience and articu-
lated in symbols and rituals. In the past, neo-scholastic
intellectualism had been formulated without any regard to human
historical experience and had dominated theological thinking for
too long. It was a weak substitute for life and action, the source of
real religious vision and insight. Tyrrell writes:

> Concurrently with this transformation of revelation into a revealed
> theology there arises a parallel and dependent perversion of the notion
> of faith into that of theological orthodoxy. Faith is now an intellectual

assent in this revealed theology as deriving directly from the Divine
intellect; it is no longer the adhesion of the whole man, heart, mind,
and soul, to the Divine Spirit within – primarily a spirit of life and love,
and thereby a guide or beacon leading the mind gradually to a fuller
instinctive apprehension of the religious truth implicit in the inspira-
tions of grace (quoted in Reardon, 1970: 116–17).

A clearly defined scholastic formulation of truth, open to the
faculty of reason and objectively unchangeable was rejected in
favour of a notion of ongoing revelation – partially and gradually
developed, incomplete, primarily discoverable in human
experience and action. Maurice Blondel, a lay representative, went
further, arguing that human action and experience were the
primary means which led to transcendence. But as Flanagan
reminds us about Blondel's link between theology and action,
'Finding God involves the application of discipline to the social, to
its structure, by sticking to the letter, to rituals that specify for...
the *act of faith* should inspire *faith in acts*' (Flanagan, 1996: 161).
Rejecting Aristotle and Descartes, Blondel wrote that 'Truth is no
longer *adequatio rei et intellectus* and one no longer lives on "clear
ideas." But there remains the truth, and the truth which remains is
living and active; it is *adequatio mentis et vitae*' (quoted in Daly,
1980: 31). John Macquarrie writes of the Modernists on this point,
'Revelation, they maintained, is not an imperfectible deposit of
truth, descended from heaven, as it were, and expressible in
propositions to which intellectual assent may be given... Religious
truth is the kind of truth that must be lived' (1981: 181).

Blondel's chief work was *L'Action*. He argued that without an
acknowledgement of the supernatural our understanding of reality
was incomplete. It was in the will to act and in the act itself that the
individual encountered a reality which prevented any degeneration
into nihilism. Our actions push us to accept that our life is of a
divine origin. His theology wrestled with new formulations of what
the 'supernatural' meant in relation to concrete human actions
and as Davis points out, although 'Blondel recognised clearly that
the life of grace and our supernatural destiny were beyond human
power. At the same time he claimed that his method of
immanence... uncovered a necessity or demand for a supernatural destiny' (1994: 9). He discussed how there is a sacrifice
involved in acknowledging that our actions point to something
more meaningful than we realise. John Milbank writes of Blondel's
position, 'in every action there is present an implicit faith that a
new and "correct" synthesis will be discovered, and that this self-

grounded norm is somehow more than arbitrary' (1990: 214). For
Blondel there is nothing supernatural over and against us, separate
from our 'pure nature'; the only thing 'over' us is our action, since
every action secretly refers to Christ. The aspiration of the will goes
beyond what is understood and each action invites and offers an
openness to Being and an encounter with a true meaning.

On this point, it seemed as if Blondel was compromising an
understanding of the 'supernatural' which had been prevalent
since the Middle Ages. The 'supernatural' had always been
described as being beyond the scope of the exigencies of human
beings; it was never conceived as being part of, or in some sense,
embedded in human action. The gratuity of grace appeared in
danger and a metaphysics of historical humanity, contrary to
orthodox teaching, appeared as one possible interpretation of the
Modernist position. Blondel's work, however, was always sure to
reconcile the notion of the free gift of grace within his method of
immanence.

Nevertheless, Blondel demonstrates the beginnings of a new
theology to emerge later during the twentieth century which
focused attention on *praxis* in relation to the 'supernatural'. For
Milbank, Blondel was one of the most important theologians of
the twentieth century, since he was able to free himself from the
restrictions of medieval realism, with its insistence and division
between 'pure nature' and the 'supernatural' and could offer a
more balanced position, insisting that it is primarily through
action that we become most receptive to the beyond. Milbank
congratulates what he terms this 'supernatural pragmatism' (1993,
97: 218). Davis is not so sure that Blondel was as anti-metaphysical
as Milbank seems to think (1994: 13).

It is fair to say that the Modernists argued that the supernatural
was not a separate divine 'thing' deposited upon human nature.
Such a view would include a separatist understanding of truth,
dividing the worlds of the spirit or supernatural and human
nature, thought and action. As Blondel states,

> it was no doubt right to distinguish and discriminate between them,
> but it was wrong to separate, isolate and even set them in opposition to
> one another. In fact, human action seemed to me to be the point on
> which the powers of Nature, the light of the understanding, the
> strength of the will and even, the benefits of grace converge – not
> indeed to merge into one another, as still less to fight and destroy each
> other, but to combine their efforts and bring about the magnificant
> unity of our destiny (quoted in Reardon, 1970: 196).

Laberthonnière, too, was keen to emphasise that his method of immanence was designed to locate the supernatural within notions of the undivided person. Scholastic apologetics mistakenly formulated a notion of two truths – the supernatural and the natural. This dualism renders 'the God of religion' as a 'power commanding us from on high, arbitrarily, as slaves are commanded'. Being a Christian 'does not mean adding supernatural thoughts and acts to natural thoughts and acts; it means imparting a supernatural character to all our thoughts and acts. It is, as it were, a raising of our entire being to a new power' (quoted in Reardon, 1970: 107). The Modernists were also significantly influenced by the work of Pascal. Daly argues that, 'The Modernists in general, and the Blondelians in particular, insisted in trying to reintroduce the Pascalian vision into the mainstream of catholic theology. For doing so, they were condemned as "immanentist"' (1980: 25). Their focus for an understanding of truth was centred on the heart not reason and in this they shared company with the thinking of other influential eighteenth and in particular nineteenth-century religious thinkers – Kierkegaard, Coleridge and Newman. Intuition was an authentic personal experience enabling the person to grasp the true significance of any religious claim.

However, of all the Modernists, it was Tyrrell who was the most forthright and the most decisive. He argued that scholasticism was inadequate since it identified revelation simply as a body of propositions to be absorbed; lived experience should be at the centre of theological reflection. Tyrrell's understanding of revelation entailed rejecting propositions and concepts in favour of religious experience, using language to express the experience simply as an aid towards understanding and accepting that the kingdom of God is non-theoretical and comprises of a form of truth which is mysterious, independent of those truths used for its illustration. Throughout his life, Tyrrell remained committed to the idea that Christian revelation is always directed to the heart or will, while accepting that the affective power of Catholic symbolism in rites and texts was the most effective means of communicating the gospel. Laberthonnière's writings also stressed the importance of individual experience. It is within the individual that knowledge of truth comes to reside, 'The knowledge we have of what is without is relative to the knowledge we have of ourselves; and the knowledge we have of ourselves is relative to what we are' (quoted in Reardon, 1970: 196).

The protests which followed such writings were often rooted in
arguments about transcendence and immanence. The Modernists
seemed to their opponents to be echoing strongly Kantian influences and as Daly suggests, 'Since it was the philosophy of
Immanual Kant which seemed to give strongest critical support to
the drive towards "subjectivism" implicit in Luther's doctrine of
faith, Kant rapidly became the *bête noir* of Roman Catholic apologetics' (1980: 8). Essentially, the fear was that the Modernists were
simply on a wayward path of subjectivism and therefore wholly
susceptible to the vagaries of personal, self-composed beliefs. They
had been too influenced by liberal Protestantism. The objectivity
of revealed religion, taught faithfully by the Church, based upon
Thomist philosophy, was under attack. The Church's view of revelation, knowable by reason, was in no need of challenge. God's
truth had been revealed and could be clearly discerned. The objectivity of such truth was not susceptible to the shallow transience of
modern culture. As Daly comments on the dominant Roman
Catholic approach at the time,

> The scholastic conception of revelation is ontological and absolute.
> Scholasticism sees revelation as 'a communication of the Truth made
> *directly* and externally by God to men, on matters which men would not
> otherwise have been able to know' and treats this communication as
> immutable (1980: 193).

The Modernists, in contrast, appealed to those who believed
that revelation was an ongoing, evolving matter. Theological truths
are relatively true they maintained and as Loisy wrote in *L'Évangile
et l'Église*:

> It is not indispensable to the authority of belief that it should be rigor-
> ously unchangeable in its intellectual form and its verbal expression.
> Such immutability is not compatible with the nature of human intelli-
> gence. Our most certain knowledge in the domains of nature and of
> science is always movement, always relative, always perfectible (quoted
> in Reardon, 1970: 85).

Tyrrell, likewise, in his attack on medievalism, demonstrated his
dissatisfaction with any notion that revelation was fixed and
complete:

> The difference is that whereas the Medievalist regards the expression
> of Catholicism, formed by the synthesis between faith and the general
> culture of the thirteenth century, as primitive and as practically final
> and exhaustive, the Modernist denies the possibility of such finality and
> holds that the task is unending just because the process of culture is
> unending (quoted in Reardon, 1970: 165).

There were differences in the emphases given by individual Modernist writers. For example, the major split between Blondel and Laberthonnière was that the former safeguarded the gratuity of divine revelation, while the latter seemed to give complete weight to the vital forces immanent in humanity when considering religious creativity in human experience. The Christian religion, said Laberthonnière, unlike Greek idealism, was based on realism, whereby individual Christians are able to share in eternity by 'our action and by our very being. Eternity is not outside time, as that which was before time and will be after' (quoted in Reardon, 1970: 99).

After the encyclical *Pascendi*, Pope Pius X insisted that an oath be taken by clerics prior to their reception of the subdiaconate and also by those appointed as preachers, confessors, canons, seminary professors and religious superiors. Articles 1/4/5 of the oath echo the issues which I have dealt with here and highlight the serious concerns of the Church at this time: the first – that God can be known and proved to exist by arguments of natural reason, the fourth – that there exists a constant deposit of faith, so that the avowal that dogmas change from one generation to the next and with a different meaning from that taught by the Church is heretical. And the fifth – that faith involves a real assent of the intellect to truth revealed from an external source, rather than a blind and inherent sense brought to the surface of human consciousness by a morally ordered will. The oath was rescinded in 1967.

The charges against the Modernists were largely unsubstantiated. Accusations about agnosticism and 'vital immanence' were not conceded by any of the writers. But what was significant in most of the condemnation was the underlying rebuttal of any notions of subjectivism or the use of experience as the basis for revelation. Condemnation criticised any 'sense' or religious consciousness as being equal to the expositions of revelation as taught by the Church. Daly writes that

> When the Modernists were accused (as they frequently were, of capitulating to the protestantism) their accusers had in mind not this or that doctrine of the Reformers but the general drive towards individual, personalised, subjective response which seemed to the scholastic mind to be so erratic and capricious as to be incapable of receiving the stamp of certifiable divine authority (1980: 7).

Desiré Joseph Mercier's attack was couched in similar terms: Modernism, he claimed 'consists essentially in maintaining that the devout soul should draw the object and motive of its faith from itself, and itself alone' (quoted in Macquarrie, 1981: 281).

In spite of such condemnations, an important development emerged as a result of the Modernist movement focusing upon the notion of 'integralism'. This is the view that in everyday humanity there is no such thing as 'pure nature', since every person has been worked upon by divine grace and therefore it is impossible to separate analytically the 'natural' and 'supernatural' elements in human existence. Later liberation theologians would respond to such suggestions and argue that this inevitably entailed that it was no longer possible to differentiate so-called 'spiritual' concerns from social and political concerns. Gutièrrez quotes Blondel as the seminal figure in this move from orthodoxy to orthopraxis when arguing for a change of direction in theological thinking: 'Maurice Blondel, moving away from an empty and fruitless spirituality and attempting to make philosophical speculation more concrete and alive, presented it as a critical reflection on action. This reflection attempts to understand the internal logic of an action through which man seeks fulfilment by constantly transcending himself' (quoted in Hodgson and King, 1985: 391).

But what was remarkable about the movement was that within half a century the mistrust of personal experience as the basis for understanding revelation was wiped away. It became obvious that the anti-Modernist purge could not prevent the Catholic Church from being influenced by the cultural and intellectual attitudes which pervaded Northern Europe. The Modernist Movement serves as an example of how modern European culture had influenced much Roman Catholic thinking. Despite the official condemnation, the Roman Catholic Church was at a turning-point in its history. During Pope Pius XII's reign, glaring paradoxes began to be seen: more open biblical scholarship, the beginnings of a lay apostolate, alongside attempts to silence Congar and Teilhard de Chardin and the denunciation of dangerous new ideas in the 1950 encyclical *Humani Generis* (Hastings, 1991: 2–4). The intellectual basis of ultramontanism was no longer credible as new historical methods and biblical scholarship swept away any resistance to change. The promulgation of *Dei Verbum* at the Second Vatican Council in November 1965 was symbolic of the change of direction which had occurred since the 'crisis' of Modernism. Here was a document which strongly encouraged

Catholics to see revelation not in prepositional terms, but as the dynamic operation of the Holy Spirit. Such a positioning of subjective experience at the heart of its formulation meant that a variety of personal responses would inevitably emerge.

Besides the strong secular influences and assumptions which pervaded liturgical revision, theological speculations and innovations during the twentieth century were inevitably to prove another major interlocking strand and concern. The attention of much twentieth-century Roman Catholic theology towards the importance of subjective experience reflected the modern emphasis on the role of the inner self and the turn to 'within' for discovering a sense of the sacred, a characteristic that Paul Heelas has identified as reflecting the more general process of detraditionalisation during the modern period (1996; Vanhoozer, 1997).[2] Sennett argues that the psychic life had become so precious in the modern world that each person's self became his/her principal burden (1986: 4).

Harvie Ferguson's account of the religious transformation in the west recognises this direction, characterising modern theological concerns as being primarily based on an existentialist model and a search for becoming authentically human. The religious quest, he argues, was identical to the secular one in that 'The modern search for the authentically human has become identical with the religious demand for salvation' (1992: 185). The modern world's search for happiness is 'marked above all by the dissolution of distinctions once held to be unambiguously natural' (1992: 185). The secular and religious search for an authentic self rests itself on understanding and scrutinising the self. In the process, 'Human subjectivity acquires foundational status; the doctrine of God becomes an implication of some aspect of being human,' writes Vanhoozer (1997: 159). Ferguson's account encapsulates this anthropocentric thrust of much twentieth-century theology.

The central characteristic of modern theology for Ferguson and other commentators (Gunton, 1997) has been this emphasis

---

[2] Outside Catholicism similar attention to the impact of the modern world on theology and liturgy was being focused. For example, in 1968 the Assembly of the World Council of Churches considered a document entitled 'Worship of God in a Secular Age'. There were mixed reactions to this. But what became a repeated claim within the debate was that worship must acquire new meaning and relevance in relation to the contemporary world.

placed upon the nature of the individual. Such anthropological concerns allies the modern theologian with the 'secular critic of human self-estrangement' (1992: 199). Secular and theological anthropology are overlapping philosophies, since in both 'the aim is the liberation of the human being from the "misrelation" of his corrupted nature' (1992: 199). 'Pascal's "hidden God" reveals Himself in the urge towards human self-expression' (1992: 199). Quoting Kierkegaard's notion of man as a synthesis of infinite and finite, Ferguson argues that the 'condition of modern living has revealed that both poles of this synthesis, the finite and the infinite' are contained within 'the purely human' (1992: 200):

> The purely human, therefore, is a religious phenomenon, and religion is a wholly human phenomenon. Thus while the experience of the modern world can be described as the secularisation of older forms of religiosity, it can with equal validity and greater pathos be characterised by the consecration of the profane world (1992: 200).

It would be fruitless to claim either Man or God as the ultimate ground of the other, since for both 'the body becomes a potentially whole, but actually fragmented, form of Being' (1992: 200). What Ferguson points to here is that the search for a legitimate theology inevitably entailed an investigation into the mystery and complexity which constituted the human person. But by beginning theology by turning to the subject, it seems that one mystery – God, is simply exchanged for another – Man (Gunton, 1997: 159).

Twentieth-Century French Roman Catholic Theology

During the mid-twentieth century it was particularly in France that a new wave of Catholic intellectuals began to make their mark on the direction European theology would take. Men such as Marie-Dominique Chenu, Yves Congar and Henri de Lubac, attempted to develop a theology which would build bridges between the Church, the world and human experience. The Dominican Chenu attempted to show how the Church and the world were not enemies but partners in a search for meaning and happiness. Along with his colleague, Congar at *le Saulchoir,* he became committed to an emphasis on contemporary experience as the foundation and starting-point for theological investigation. Congar claimed that his mission was 'to rotate the Catholic church through a few degrees on its own axis' (quoted in McSweeney, 1981: 102). His writings reflected a desire for lay people to be more involved in the life of the Church and in his most famous work, *Lay People in the Church,* he argued how lay participation in liturgy, missionary and administrative duties had been severely lacking (Congar, 1965; Nichols, 1989). De Lubac was similarly influential during the 1940s and 1950s and his interest in Communism and atheism, discussed in his writings, attempted to reconcile religious and non-religious ideologies working towards a more just society. Teilhard de Chardin was another key figure at the time whose work on the interface between biology, evolution and divine providence became an important aspect of the modern debate about the relationship between science and religion (King, 1996).

Bill McSweeney sums up the impact these new theological approaches had on the reformed liturgy: 'The newly emerging theology marked a shift of emphasis from Christ's divinity to his humanity; from the Church as institution of salvation to the Church as community; from the objective to the subjective aspect of liturgy; from God's transcendence and otherness to his presence among men' (1981: 112). Roman Catholic worship was now beginning to reflect this more anthropocentric emphasis. It was more concerned with the existential and ontological status of the worshipper as a site for pastoral support and less centred on its latreutic nature. This far more subjective and personalist approach to worship based on the relevance the liturgy would have for the individual minds and the psychological welfare of the worshippers, reflected a dominant trend in theological thinking which was to pervade the second half of the twentieth century. Helping individuals to understand themselves was beginning to be a central aim and task of liturgy.

Subjective Experience and the New Theology

This far more subjective approach has been referred to as 'doing theology backwards' (McSweeney, 1981: 113), and is characterised by starting with human experience rather than with speculative theology. There were some institutional warnings given about the dangers inherent in such a theology. For example, in 1950 Pope Pius XII issued his encyclical *Humani Generis* in which he criticised those teachings which were threatening the doctrines of the Catholic Church and accused recent theological trends which encouraged any whittling away of the traditional meaning of doctrines and the view that the whole world was capable of continual evolution without God's assistance. The *Catechism of the Catholic Church* quotes the encyclical under the heading, 'The knowledge of God according to the Church' (1994: 16–17). The text was a warning to those theologians who believed they could discover the things of God by autonomous reason alone. But such publications did not prevent the force and impact that alternative approaches to theology were to have on the life of the Church.

John McDade's account of Roman Catholic theology in the second half of the twentieth century identifies the central features of this alternative method. One characteristic is the prominence given to human history as the *locus revelationis*.[3] The Church witnesses to the things of God situated in the things of Man. Classic doctrinal truths are rediscovered to have an anthropological and metaphysical significance. He writes, 'The new stage on which post-conciliar theology is to speak is set unambiguously in the middle of human history and experience' (Hastings, 1991: 423). Karl Rahner's words in 1974 on the core dimension of Christian theology, echoes this emphasis: 'the divinization of the world through the Spirit of God occurs when the mystery of man becomes the agenda for the location of the mystery of Christ in modern theology' (Hastings, 1991: 424). McDade quotes Jean Calvin about the impossibility of acknowledging Man or God as the ultimate ground of the other: 'Our wisdom in so far as it ought to be deemed true and solid wisdom, consists almost entirely of two parts: the knowledge of God and of ourselves. But as these are connected together by many ties, it is not easy to determine which of the two precedes and gives birth to the other' (Hastings, 1991: 426). The guardian of the separations between God and man, Church and world had been the Vatican, but the new theology of the 1950s and 1960s began to blur such distinctions.[4] The same

---

[3] Lindbeck sees the new theology of the Church envisioned in the conciliar documents as a treble venture: it is a sign and witness to the new age, not only by its words (the worship and preaching which constitute its *leitourgia*), but also by its secular service of the world (*diakonia*), and by the quality of its communal life (*koinonia*) (1970: 5). Socio-economic co-ordinates could not be ignored if theology is to be rooted in human history.

[4] The anti-modernist reaction of Pope Pius X, characterised by an ecclesiology emphasising the radical otherness of the Church, was replaced at the Second Vatican Council by the concept of a faltering, pilgrim Church, rooted in history and carrying with it responsibilities to respond to the

tendency was clearly evident in the writings of French and German existentialists after the Second World War. Gregory Baum, a leading exponent of this approach, echoes this new approach: 'The contemporary theologian will ask the question... whether a careful description of human life might not reveal that man is open to the supernatural... Is it possible, the theologian will ask, to discern the supernatural or the divine in the finite actions of man?' (quoted in McSweeney, 1981: 182).

The theology of the Second Vatican Council reflected to some degree these intellectual strands. With the promulgation of *Dei Verbum* at the Second Vatican Council, Catholics were encouraged to see revelation not in propositional but in personal terms. As anthropological rather than ecclesial paradigms came to dominate understandings of revelation, the centrality of human experience advocated by the Modernists became widely accepted. One of the most important movements in theology which was to emerge in the 1960s – liberation theology – reflected this move as a focus on

---

secular world, in its variety and complexity. At the turn of the twentieth century, after the long pontificate of Pius X Pope Leo XIII had signalled a new approach and theology indicating an openness to the world which was to be more definitively proclaimed at the Second Vatican Council. The two central questions which had dominated Catholic debate in the nineteenth century were the structure of power in the Church, epitomised in the impact of ultramontanism and the social question of the distribution of wealth and income. The Modernists were solely interested in the former. The most significant response of the Catholic Church to the plight of workers and the need for justice in working conditions and wages came during this pontificate with the publication *Rerum Novarum* in 1891. But it is worth noting that Leo's espousal and restoration of Thomist theology and philosophy was an attempt to rid the world of all those social ills which had come about due to the secular and political philosophy of the Enlightenment. Leo was intent on combating the evil of socialism and the way to do it, he believed, was to reinstate Thomist orthodoxy. But clearly the post-medieval ultramontane model was pushed aside to reveal a church identified as the people of God, struggling to understand itself and the world of which it was a part. McDonagh points to the pastoral nature of *Gaudium et Spes:* 'the main contribution of the document was seen to be a Christian doctrine of humanity or a Christian anthropology. Its emergence involved a pastoral sensitivity, a loving awareness of humanity in all its actual condition and a loving sense of the responsibility to it' (Hastings, 1991: 98). It showed a remarkable openness to the world and built on earlier social encyclicals and on the previous theological writings of Chenu, Congar and Rahner.

the anthropological took precedence over the ecclesiastical. The human person, understood within a political and social context, must become theology's primary concern.

The Work of Karl Rahner and Edward Schillebeeckx

It was Karl Rahner, above all other Roman Catholic theologians, who epitomised this new theological anthropology and attempted to describe how self-understanding coupled with involvement in the world would lead to a sense of transcendence. In *Foundations of Christian Faith* he writes,

> In the fact that man raises analytical questions about himself and opens himself to the unlimited horizons of such questioning, he has already transcended himself and every conceivable element of such an analysis or of an empirical reconstruction of himself. In doing this he is affirming himself as more than the sum of such analysable components of his reality (quoted in Hodgson and King, 1995: 168).

Man's transcendence is rooted in his experience of daily living in the world, and not in a reflective experience of a transcendent being, 'It is self-evident... that this transcendental experience of human transcendence is not the experience of some definite, particular objective thing which is experienced alongside other objects. It is rather a basic mode of being which is prior to and permeates every objective experience' (quoted in Hodgson and King, 1995: 172). Rahner emphasises that this experience occurs when there exists an openness to being as such and 'which is present precisely when a person experiences himself as involved in the multiplicity of cares and concerns and hopes of his everyday world' (quoted in Hodgson and King, 1995: 172).

Rahner understands grace as the reality of God's self-communication at the ground of an individual's human experience, a position that had moved well away from any neo-scholastic notion that grace was extrinsic and could not affect the consciousness of a person. Rahner places considerable stress on the importance of the historical and human experience of divine grace:

> Whenever man in his transcendence experiences himself as questioning, as quieted by the appearance of being, as open to something ineffable, he cannot understand himself as subject in the sense of an *absolute* subject, but only in the sense of one who receives being, ultimately only in the sense of grace (quoted in Hodgson and King, 1995: 172).

Rahner's theology is not unlike Edward Schillebeeckx's. Both stress that the most important interpretative framework for theology is human experience. For Schillebeeckx each person must endeavour to achieve what he terms the *'humanum'*, the human movement towards fulfilment and transcendence achieved through action. He writes that the individual has already answered this call to fulfilment by 'his human praxis, in a positive or a negative sense or by a nihilistic or sceptical attitude to life' (quoted in Schreiter, 1984: 61). Schillebeeckx argues that it is in the vicissitudes of concrete human living that glimpses of revelation occur: 'It seems to me undeniable that human life includes particular experiences which are signs or glimpses of an ultimate total meaning of human life' (1984: 1). Human historical experience is the condition for understanding Christian revelation and at the same time the answers given by revelation. The abundance of meaning which is contained in the meaning a man or woman has already discovered in the world is manifested in the light of revelation (1984: 63).

Von Balthasar's Critique

One of the sternest critic of Rahner's theology has been the Swiss theologian Hans Urs von Balthasar, whose contemplative theology is in stark contrast to Rahner's emphasis on self-reflection and self-questioning. In response to *aggiornamento* and the location of theology within the world, Balthasar writes,

> Indeed, it was not as though we were unaware that with an opening up to the world... a translation of the Christian message into a language understandable by the modern world, only half is done. The other half – of at least equal importance – is a reflection on the specifically Christian element itself, a purification, a deepening, a centring of its idea, which alone renders it capable of representing it, radiating it, translating it believably in the world (1982: 196).

His *magnum opus, The Glory of the Lord*, is concerned with the beauty and glory of God, but in trying

> to perceive God's own beauty and glory from the beauty of the manner of appearing, we must never simply equate the two – since we are to be transported *per hunc (Deum visibilem) in invisibilium amorem* – nor ought we to attempt to discover God's beauty by a mere causal inference from the beauty of God's epiphany, for such an inference would leave this epiphany behind (1982: 124).

According to Balthasar, the world was made to reflect this glory; theology therefore must always concern itself with an act of perception, *aisthesis,* and with the particular thing perceived, *aistheton.* Knowledge of the glory and splendour of God occurs not through a self-absorbing understanding of the self, but by a move away from the self,

> For what is at stake here is the movement effected by seeing what God has shown. This is a movement of the entire person, leading away from himself through the vision towards the invisible God, a movement, furthermore, which the word 'faith' describes only imperfectly... The transport of the soul, however, must here again be understood in a strictly theological way... as the movement of man's whole being away from himself and towards God through Christ, a movement founded on the divine light of grace in the mystery of Christ (1982: 121).

It is certainly not a 'psychological response to something beautiful in the worldly sense' (1982: 122).

We can now see the definitive points of departure between Rahner's and Balthasar's theology. In 1966 Balthasar's *Cordula oder Ernstfall* enunciated how what had been lost in much modern theology was an emphasis on the possibility of wonder and contemplative openness to a glorified Lord. Balthasar criticised the notion that salvation is a matter of 'hominisation' or as McDade puts it, 'At issue for Balthasar is Rahner's linear convergence of the dynamism of the human spirit and the corresponding shape of God's revelation, and his consequent treatment of Jesus as the undialectical fulfilment of human potentialities' (1991: 426). Balthasar has little patience with notions that human need has anything to do with christological understanding. Rowan Williams also points to what he believes is a key omission in Rahner's theology of the world in his discussion of the debate between the two theologians: 'The heart of the difference here seems to be that Rahner thinks of human frustration in terms of incompleteness, Balthasar in terms of tragedy.... the world is not a world of well-meaning agnostics but of totalitarian nightmares, of nuclear arsenals, labour camps, and torture chambers' (Riches, 1986: 32–33). The world is a far more complex thing for Balthasar than it is for Rahner. The conversation between a Christian and an anonymous Christian recorded in *Cordula* pinpoints this difference in a sharply ironic manner and as Williams suggests, 'Balthasar's harsh clear-sightedness is an important disturbance of any easy assumptions about "humanism" convergences in our world' (1986: 33). And 'If Rahner's Christ is an answer to the human question, a faintly but distinctly Tolstoyan figure, Balthasar's Christ remains a question to all human answers, and to all attempts at metaphysical or theological closure' (1986: 33–34).

In the light of the above, it is not difficult to see why a renewal of worship eventually proved so problematic. If, as I have argued, ritual action, as the basis of liturgy, is a highly stylised performance and consists in predictable stylistic repetition to maintain its form, then it follows that the subjective intentions of individual worshippers must always be subordinated to the objective world the liturgy endorses by its form. The distancing of a formalised drama of sacred action, free from any erratic interruptions emerging from the psyche of the worshipper ensures its stability and power. Liturgical rites are far removed from quotidian occurrences by their location in a space set apart, their limited duration and their stylised action and speech which always follows a predetermined order and arrangement. Pickstock writes that 'This deprioritisation of the psyche enables the polis to be stable, for the psyche is contingent, diffuse, irresolute, and demurring' (Bradshaw and Spinks, 1993: 124). *Contra* this model, what emerged during the 1960s was an emphasis on the pastoral nature of liturgy underpinned by a more personalist, anthropocentric and individualistic approach to worship. The secular and theological culture of the time had clearly encouraged this far more rationalist, classificatory and subjective approach to worship. The challenge (never signalled at the time by the Church reformers) was to meet the demands of pastoral liturgical sensitivity while preserving the liturgy of the Church as an objective ritual performance whose form, by its very nature, resisted alteration. It is not surprising that such a task proved increasingly difficult to achieve.

5

SACROSANCTUM CONCILIUM – A CRITICAL EVALUATION

I argued in the previous chapter that modernity's emphasis on the autonomy of the self and subsequent turn to the subject was reflected in the emphasis of the Modernist Movement and the emergence of much Roman Catholic theology in the second half of the twentieth century. This overriding concern to place theological anthropology at the core of the Church's response to the challenges of the modern period, was to feature as a key element underpinning the preliminary discussions and final publication of the conciliar documents. *Sacrosanctum Concilium* was the first of a series of documents at the Second Vatican Council to lay stress on a pastoral approach and sensitivity towards the existential condition of the individual in the modern period. This chapter outlines how the document on liturgy attempted to set out this approach in detail and includes a summary of some of the major critiques which have emerged in the light of this emphasis on a more pastoral, psychological and mentalist approach to Roman Catholic worship.

Although the Constitution on the Sacred Liturgy was careful to align its reforms in accordance with 'sound tradition', the overriding impression gained by reading the document is the importance placed on meeting the personal and individual needs of the 'people of God' in the modern world and of addressing the perceived pastoral responsibility which accrues from reading 'the signs of the times'. There was a widely held contention at the time of the Council that the Church itself was in need of a new lease of spiritual life and that a vigorous programme of revision was necessary if it was to meet the challenges of a socially fragmented culture. The conciliar document on the Church in the modern world, *Gaudium et Spes*, endorsed this approach in an unambiguous manner by its insistence that members of the Church have a responsibility to live out the values of the gospel within the context of the social and political arena of their time and by its careful analysis of the psychological condition of the modern individual. Christian liturgy was to be a crucial strand within this process of *aggiornamento* and to play a significant part in pastoral renewal. The Council considered that an urgent task at stake was to adapt those elements of the Church's worship which were in themselves 'subject to change' (*Sacrosanctum Concilium*, paragraph 21), an endeavour which was to become more problematic than first envisaged.

The document proclaimed that the liturgy was the most important dimension of the Church's life. It was the 'summit toward which the activity of the Church is directed; it is also the fount from which all her power flows' (*SC* paragraph 10). The liturgical 'action' of the Church, because it is the action of Christ himself, 'is a sacred one surpassing all others. No other action... can equal its efficacy' (*SC*, paragraph 7). Liturgy is fundamental, since during liturgical celebration, the Church comes together to re-enact the paschal mystery, where Christ becomes uniquely present, in the sacraments, in the person of the ordained minister, and especially under the eucharistic species. He is also encountered in the word which is heralded. Within this christological and biblical framework, liturgy must be regarded as 'an exercise of the priestly office of Jesus Christ' (*SC*, paragraph 7), as well as of his body, which is the Church. It brings about a foretaste of the heavenly liturgy 'celebrated in the holy city of Jerusalem toward which we journey as pilgrims' (*SC*, paragraph 8).

In the light of such statements, the assumption held by those responsible for the reforms at the time of the Council was that if the liturgy suffered in any way from being anachronistic and was unable to communicate the paschal mystery effectively, then changes were not only advisable but morally imperative. The Constitution emphasised the need to turn to a more psychological model of worship by its clear emphasis on the double purpose of liturgy: it was to be concerned both with the worship of God and with the sanctification of the person, achieved through 'signs perceptible to the senses' (*SC*, paragraph 7). It had the task of assuming a much more anthropocentric focus and sensitivity. The confused and alienated condition of 'modern man' spoken about in *Gaudium et Spes* could not go unaddressed for any longer without severe repercussions. The liturgy of the Church had an overwhelming responsibility to meet face on this modern cultural degeneration into anomie. Guéranger had argued the same in the nineteenth century.

This more existential emphasis reflected, as I discussed in the previous chapter, many of the positions which were being taken up in western theology as the twentieth century unfolded. The earlier rubricism and strict observance of the laws governing valid liturgical celebration, were considered stultifying and obsolete by the Council Fathers. Those who held responsibility as 'pastors of souls' must no longer simply go through the mechanics of liturgical law, as if repeating a standardised rite mindlessly, but 'it is their duty also to ensure that the faithful take part, fully aware of what they are doing, actively engaged in the rite and enriched by it' (*SC*, paragraph 11). This is why liturgists like Barauna claimed that earlier Roman Catholic worship had invariably been reduced to the mindless following of rules and could be characterised primarily by four things: rubricism, clericalism, passivity and excessive conservatism (1966: viii). The overriding concern at the Council for more active lay participation confirms Barauna's argument; the priest as ritual expert was no longer acknowledged as being central to Christian worship. The earlier theological emphasis on the importance of the active involvement of the laity in the Church, as advocated particularly by French theological writing in the 1950s, considerably influenced this move towards regarding much of the Tridentine liturgy as excessively clericalist, conservative and passive. A crucial turning-point had arrived in the history of Roman Catholic worship: the rubricism, repetition and conservative invariance needed to retain the form of a liturgical rite had been interpreted as 'mindless repetition' and lacking in pastoral awareness. The organic ritual form necessary for liturgy to function as a transformative rite was criticised at its very roots.

The new approach consisted in giving much more attention to conscious awareness and active participation by the congregation in the liturgy. This shift pervaded the entire document and became an encouragement to pastors to focus more on the pastoral and intelligible dimension of liturgy in services. Members of the Church should be facilitated to understand liturgical rites more easily, so that they may take part in them more fully. Active participation was to be 'the primary and indispensable source from which the faithful are to derive the true Christian spirit' (*SC*, paragraph 14). 'Full, active and conscious participation' must be the goal to which all members of the Church should strive and it is to be the particular responsibility of the ordained clergy to ensure that necessary instruction is given to maximise this pastoral intent' (*SC*, paragraph 14). The nature of liturgy had been radically reinterpreted by those responsible for the reforms and it was up to priests and seminarians to endorse and put such new theoretical approaches into practice.

Interviews with Priests

Since the Second Vatican Council instigated a radical change in consciousness towards liturgy, clear-cut goals had to be achieved if the reforms were to work effectively. As I mentioned in the Preface, Roman Catholic priests spoke to me about their reactions to the reforms in a series of interviews I conducted. I refer to two more here to demonstrate how the reforms were open to different interpretations and understandings. A long-serving priest, who had been ordained before the reforms, expressed his attitude by maintaining a delicate balance between the benefits the changes had brought about, with some sense of nostalgia for past practices. He understood the liturgy to be essentially 'the work of the people, this is what the word means, doesn't it? Worship is also our response to God, in Jesus Christ.' Both elements were important. He said that it was important to keep a ritual element, but before there were

> bells all the time. There was a warning bell for communion. This told the people where the priest was in the Mass. There was more of a routine before. But every minutiae about movement and gesture was strictly adhered to. I remember in May 1964, after saying Mass in Latin a professor of liturgy saying to me, 'This has to change, hasn't it?' Now all those genuflections have gone and I am pleased the Mass has been simplified.

> I remember going to Deanery conferences on the new liturgy in 1965–66. We were all thrilled at first. The liturgy was exciting. It was coming alive. And ecumenism was being discussed. The liturgy was now able to touch people where they were. At first it was a struggle with the people. They were not ready for the changes. There was no catechesis. There have been difficult times. There still are. Some still hanker after the Latin. There is still room for this. There is no need to lose this completely. There is now a greater need to take into consideration your group. The liturgy should adapt to a certain extent to meet people where they are. People don't always want to be involved. You can be involved simply by listening. The working-classes, however, have developed confidence by being encouraged to participate in the liturgy.

A second interview was conducted with a deacon six months prior to his ordination. He said,

> Liturgy is the celebration of the faith of the people and of individuals. It comes together as a community celebration. But the formal religious side of community is dropping off. It isn't happening in churches, it is happening somewhere else. If you have to start explaining what a ritual is, then it has lost its meaning. The church has got lots of rituals. Some people might understand them, and some people might not. If people don't understand them, there is obviously a need for preparing and helping people get behind what's happening. Some things might need teasing out. There may have been a time when things were more focused on the priest and the priest did lots of things. I don't really know, it was before my time. So now there is a move away from that, because the focus is not so much on the priest. There may have been a losing sight of some of the gestures, and the priests weren't prepared for the changes.

> A big thing that people keep going on about is catechesis, so that everybody knows what is going on. Catechesis depends on whatever stage you are at with the community you are working with. You don't want to overburden the liturgy, but it might be helpful just to give a little bit to illustrate what is happening, but you have to try and avoid overplaying that. There is a shift from a priest-centred activity which was largely observed by the rest of the people to a different dynamic and a different participation and so reflecting the congregation, its men and women. There is obviously now more flexibility than in the past where it was much more rubric conscious. I still think rubrics are important, provided you understand what they're meant to be used for. There is flexibility, but you have to be careful, it's not just your ritual. We are still working through changes and we still need catechesis.

The Process of Adaptation

The process of adaptation was crucial. The reformers recognised that any management of liturgical change on this scale would be no easy task. Change inevitably occurs slowly and is likely to be met with opposition. The exhortations to adaptation were to be implemented as naturally as possible and were to 'grow organically from forms already existing' (*SC*, paragraph 23). Warnings were given that any unofficial changes or indulgent innovations would be harmful to the intent of the Council: 'No other person may add, remove or change anything in the liturgy on his own authority' (*SC*, paragraph 22). Nevertheless, despite such reservations, it was accepted by the Church Council Fathers that in order to achieve a pastorally framed liturgy, more active participation and comprehension by the laity were indispensable. It is interesting to note that the one reference to symbolic bodily action is contextualised within a discussion about participation. Participation 'should be encouraged... by means of acclamations, responses... as well as actions, gestures and bodily attitudes' *(SC,* paragraph 30). Since the liturgy itself contained much instruction for the faithful, it should be used as such.

The overriding method recommended to achieve this was simplification and clarification; there must be a 'noble simplicity' (*SC,* paragraph 34) to the rites and they must be 'short, clear and unencumbered by useless repetitions' (*SC,* paragraph 34). The worship of God must occur within people's powers of comprehension and should 'normally not require much explanation' (*SC,* paragraph 34). This insistence is reflected in the abandonment of the Latin language. Services after the reforms were to use the vernacular, the most obvious sign that the Church was fully committed to comprehension and understanding of the rites, rather than the continuation of a liturgical tradition. The degree of uniformity which had characterised earlier practices was no longer essential since the Church had 'no wish to impose a rigid uniformity in matters which do not involve the faith or the good of the whole community' (*SC,* paragraph 37). The kind of standardisation of rites overseen by the Congregation of Rites established in 1588 during the Baroque period of the seventeenth century (and beyond), was recognised as being anachronistic and unnecessary. This influential Congregation which had drawn up a series of instructions on how the sacred actions of the liturgy were to be carried out, were printed in red (the rubrics), and was largely responsible for later liturgical scholars naming the seventeenth century the 'epoch of rubicism'. This is not to deny that earlier manuals on instructions for the performances of Mass had not been produced. For example, the Ordinal and Consuetudinary were introduced as early as the later twelfth century to offer guidance in such matters, but the Congregation of Rites was the first systematic attempt to oversee that such instructions were being followed carefully.

A renewed liturgy would also give increased attention to sacred scripture. A love for the word of God was encouraged among the clergy and laity and bible services were to be fostered. Many of the recommendations reflected the changes which earlier sixteenth-century Protestant Reformers had been keen to

introduce and put in place. White (1989: 37–57) suggests that
Luther's reforms were underpinned by a strong pastoral concern.
Removed from clericalism, the laity could be more actively
involved in worship. Ritual experts were no longer needed. The
sacrificial nature of the Mass was downplayed. The debate
concerning the significance of *sacrifice* in relation to the reform of
the celebration of the Mass reflected some of these more
Protestant emphases. There is no doubt that a conception of the
Mass as the Eucharist-*Convivium*, which had been originally put
forward by the liturgical commission underplayed its specifically
sacrifical character. The original draft of paragraph 47 in chapter
2 of the document on liturgy stated: 'Our divine saviour...
commanded his disciples to repeat this paschal meal (*Convivium*)
in memory of him, ... He desired that in this way his victory over
death and his triumph be made present...' After many protests
(particularly from Cardinal Bea who referred to the Council of
Trent's emphasis on the sacrifice of the Mass and Cardinal Browne
who quoted the words of St Thomas Aquinas on sacrifice), the text
was adapted to: 'Our Lord instituted the Eucharistic sacrifice of his
body and blood. He did this in order to perpetuate the sacrifice of
the cross throughout the centuries...' Le Pivain comments on
these amendments that 'This text makes clear that the Eucharistic
sacrifice defines the sacrament instituted by Christ at the Last
Supper, and that the Last Supper, and thus the Mass, have no
reality except in reference to the sacrifice of the cross...' (Le
Pivain, 1998: 158). However, the original text saw no need to stress
such a Eucharistic theology based on the importance of sacrifice.

Luther encouraged more frequent communion and inaug-
urated its reception at least once a week, including the precious
blood. Following Luther's lead, Protestant Reformers took it upon
themselves to give communion into the hands of the communi-
cants, a practice now common in Roman Catholic worship. The
vernacular also became important in reformed worship, since as
White writes, 'Although cautious at first, Luther soon realised that
little could change the role of the laity without putting the words
into a language the people understood' (White, 1989: 42). The
Protestant emphasis on preaching was another indication of the
importance attached to scripture. Luther saw no need whatsoever
to maintain a standardisation of rites (Maxwell, 1936).

The Protestant liturgical reforms on English soil had
encouraged in a similar manner a much less dramatic and
ceremonial rite. Cranmer criticised those who adhered to what he

considered to be a proliferation of medieval ceremonial in liturgy. In 1548 he banned the use of Candlemas candles, Ash Wednesday ashes and Palm Sunday palms and issued orders in the same year to alter drastically the ceremonies of Holy Week, including the banning of the setting up of Easter sepulchres on Maundy Thursday and the use of fire and holy water during the Holy Saturday ceremony. The Mass, too, was to be radically reformed, and became known as 'the Order of the Communion'. This new rite followed the traditional Latin until after the celebrant himself had communicated, then it broke into English followed by 'an exhortation to those present to be "partakers of the communion".' As Diarmott MacCulloch suggests in his biography of Cranmer (1996), the Communion began with an evangelical informality which must have seemed shocking after the use of traditional texts and liturgical actions. Cranmer's eucharistic theology itself became rooted in such liturgical changes centred around the word of God. The consecrated wafer had to be broken at least in two before distribution in order to reflect the Gospel narrative and was a way of undermining the symbolism of the Fraction of the priest's wafer which had been a crucial part of the Roman Mass.

The premodern world, as I suggested in Chapter 2, had emphasised the importance of somatic experience in Christian spirituality and worship because the meaning of the physical body was inextricably interwoven with the meaning of the social and ecclesiastical world it inhabited. These three worlds were sustained and nourished by the Eucharistic Body of Christ Himself and held significance in relation to a sacramental body. Such an understanding was never metaphorical but literal. As Ward points out, for Aquinas the historical could never be separated from the allegorical or spiritual senses (Ward, 1997: xx). All creation was from God and, while there existed obvious differences between heavenly and earthly bodies, these were never acknowledged as being unrelated, as Aquinas' doctrine of analogy demonstrates. It was in later debates surrounding the Eucharist between Catholics, Luther, Zwingli and Calvin, that a division of the literal from the metaphorical became a major source of dispute in theology (Ward, 1997: xx).

It is not surprising in the light of these reforms that the liturgical scholar Verheul can claim that there was considerable 'borrowing' of Protestant reforms in much of the Roman Catholic renewal:

> If we now follow the development of the contemporary liturgical reform movement in the Catholic Church, we arrive at the following

conclusion: the central Reformation demands, which the Counter-Reformation either failed to meet or ignore, are now the chief points in contemporary liturgical renewal (1987: 182).

George Lindbeck, an official Lutheran observer at the Council, has suggested that the Roman Catholic liturgical movement emancipated itself from its earlier ritualistic phase 'more completely than... the Protestant liturgical movement', and now 'its concerns are in most cases clearly "evangelical"... it works for greater simplicity, flexibility, informality, intelligibility, and, above all, active participation on the part of the congregation' (1970: 63). He argues there exists in recent Roman Catholic worship a much more 'personal-existential' aura. The Protestant insistence on 'the *pro me* of the Reformation and of Pietism, or what old Methodism would have called "heart experience"' (1970: 63) has dominated the reforms and their aftermath. This has been combined with a stress on the moral transformation of the individual and on social action with the result that liturgy is considered 'inauthentic' without a keen emphasis on such concerns. Liturgical transparency, simplicity and good preaching on the word of God would best achieve these aims.

Lindbeck is right to stress that the reformers at the Second Vatican Council envisaged simplicity, informality and participation as being central to the methods needed for liturgical adaptation. The Constitution, in claiming that a fogginess of purpose had crept into the celebration of the sacraments, argued that one of the primary purposes of the reforms was to revise the sacramental rites to ensure that the faithful might participate in them intelligently and easily (*SC*, paragraph 102–11). Throughout the liturgical year, too, the sacred seasons must reflect a form of worship which is suited to the conditions of modern times. The document encouraged a process of radical 'modernisation' of the liturgy which was considered essential if the Church was to fulfil its salvific duty. Earlier obscurantism must be abandoned in favour of a renewal which would adapt to the mentality of the times and which would endeavour to link pastoral effectiveness to liturgical celebration. The active participation of the faithful, fully conversant with the rites themselves, had to be encouraged if these aims were to be achieved. Rites had to be simplified and uniformity decreased to achieve this goal.

Critiques of the Reforms

Many liturgical writings after the publication of *Sacrosanctum Concilium* were keen to emphasise that the Constitution was exactly what the Church needed. Jungmann (1966) suggests that five emphases were to be particularly welcomed: the acceptance that the liturgy was not unchangeable, the decentralisation of the liturgy, the active participation of the laity, the pastoral character of worship and finally the limits and compromises involved. Vagagini points to the positive ecumenical spirit of the document with its call for communion under both kinds, its restoration of a central role to scripture in mainstream liturgy and its regard for invigorated preaching based on the word of God. He also welcomes the deathblow given to earlier prescriptiveness, particularly with regard to rubrical precision and insistence: 'There is no doubt that the Constitution gives the final blow to the prevalent excessively juridical and rubrical, even inflexible concept of the liturgy, which has been prevalent since the Council of Trent and the creation of the Congregation of Rites (1588)' (1966: 119). The reforms add a much-needed emphasis to the catechetical and pastoral nature of collective worship. He is pleased to see the didactic and pastoral character of the reforms prescribing simplicity and perspicacity in the rites, for only then can the 'new liturgy' become a living and vital experience.

Barauna is equally enthusiastic about the changes. He contends that the nature of the liturgy itself demands active participation: 'Liturgy as we knew it was full of words and symbols that were meaningful for the primitive Christian and for the medieval mind, but conveyed no meaning to the modern mind' (1966: 141). In a provocative statement he argues that the liturgy of the past had come to resemble 'a theatrical show, with lights, flowers, songs and boring ceremonies, inspired by Byzantine and medieval pomp, when it should have been a privileged meeting with God' (1966: 145). Jungmann echoes a similar tone about the reforms. Besides emphasising the aim of the Constitution to adapt liturgy to the needs of the time, he stresses its function of bringing unity to the Church and of bringing back the 'separated brethren'. He suggests that the secret to understanding the renewal can only occur within a framework of understanding the overall renewed ecclesiology sanctioned at the Second Vatican Council. Liturgy was simply part of a much bigger programme of ecclesial renewal and adaptation within the context of the economy of salvation (1966).

Other reactions and responses have touched on important considerations. Kevin Seasoltz welcomes in particular the Council's move away from what he regards as the harmful influence of nominalism, which had emphasised the validity of the sacraments to the detriment of other explanations. Consequently, 'the rubrics came to be interpreted simply as rigid norms for mere ceremonial, often devoid of theological significance' (1980: 204). He is delighted to see in the reforms an increased awareness of liturgy as celebration: 'the emphasis is not so much on validity as on meaningful celebrations of the paschal mystery of Christ' (1980: 204). Again rubrical slavery is seen as a disincentive to lively worship and 'ministers who blindly follow the ritual directives in the reformed liturgical books will run the risk of producing a new form of liturgical pageantry that might be externally correct but interiorly dead' (1980: 204).

Seasoltz suggests that the Constitution is based on the sound principle of 'personal consciousness and responsibility', and in this sense cannot be legislated for, since it is the 'free and loving response of the whole person to a loving God' (1980: 205). The liturgy is neither magic nor ceremony and can never be controlled by adherence to liturgical laws: 'When consciences have been developed and sound theological awareness has been deepened, it is best that Church law emphasise only the basic norms and principles' (1980: 205). He is equally convinced that the pastoral emphasis of the reforms is a beneficial one: 'No longer may ministers feel that they have done their duty if they have carried out the norms in the liturgical books; they must go beyond the norms, in the sense that they must bring the liturgy to life for people' (1980: 207). He wants the freedom given to priests at the Council reflected in the ensuing organisation of liturgies, what he terms 'opportunities for creativity within the liturgy' (1980: 207). In quoting Article 11 of the *General Instruction of the Roman Missal* he supports the view that the president may exercise creativity in introducing the liturgy of the day, the liturgy of the word, the eucharistic prayer, and in concluding the liturgy. The homily and the general intercessions allow flexibility for creative innovation. The texts provided in the Roman Missal for introducing the penitential rite, the Lord's Prayer, the kiss of peace and the Communion rite are also 'models or examples to be adapted to the needs of the diverse assemblies' (1980: 207). He concludes that 'many times the new rites explicitly sanction verbal creativity by the phrase *vel similibus verbis* "in these or similar words"' (1980:

207). His major hope is that the Church's liturgy, in the light of the Constitution's recommendations, may become a kind of internalised worship: 'The most profound change has to be that of the heart which takes in the Spirit offered by the Church in the celebration of the liturgy' (1980: 211). He sees no correlation between the following of a prescribed rite and the securing of ontological change.

Hubert Richards finds in the reforms a marvellous opportunity for scripture to come alive as it undergirds the liturgical celebrations of the Church: 'All the reforms it has listed – the vernacular, active participation, simplification, the stress on the homily, the multiplication and variation of the readings – are simply designed to make what was once a dead Word again the living Word of God' (1966: 51). For Burrett, the reforms have ushered in an overdue inclusiveness since they are able to emphasise that the liturgy was 'the people's community prayer and worship' (Crichton, 1966: 66). Liturgy is not meant to be simply for the benefit of those who have the time and capacity to study it deeply, nor is it to be the preserve of the few; it is the action of all God's holy people. He is pleased that various ceremonies which had once held some significance are now to be discontinued. He gives the example of the server holding up the priest's chasuble during the elevation. Originally, this action rested on the fact that the chasuble was once so heavy that any raising of the arms was difficult if someone did not lift the chasuble; such actions are no longer required.

Archbishop Bugnini has displayed equal enthusiasm for the reforms. In his exposition of the six principles involved in the liturgical reforms he draws particular attention to what he considers to be the most important elements for the future liturgical life of the Church (1990). The first principle, 'The liturgy as an exercise of the priestly office of Jesus Christ' (1990: 39–40), is crucial because by positioning the paschal mystery at the heart of worship, a real sense of 'celebration' can be expressed. Not dissimilar to Seasoltz's point noted earlier, he argues that

> Attention is no longer focused on the minimum required for the validity of liturgical actions nor simply on their outward form considered in isolation, but on the congregation which has gathered to hear and respond to God's word, share in the sacrament, remember the Lord Jesus, and give thanks to God the Father, by whose great mercy 'we have been reborn to a living hope through the resurrection of Jesus Christ from the dead' (1990: 40).

The second principle Bugnini calls attention to is the liturgy as the 'summit and fount of the Church's life'. Liturgy is the 'unifying centre of all the Church's activity' and is the 'sign that offers the truest and fullest image of the Church' (1990: 40). The third, 'full, active and conscious participation', acknowledges that 'the liturgy is the primary and indispensable source from which the faithful can derive the true Christian spirit' (1990: 41). The fourth empha-sises that the liturgy is the supreme manifestation of the Church, the 'sacrament of unity' (1990: 42) which belongs to the whole body of the Church. The fifth points to a radical shift from the view that 'worship in the Roman rite should always show perfect uniformity' (1990: 42). Since social, religious, cultic and psycho-logical factors have altered, there is a need to allow considerable flexibility within the rites of the Church. The sixth principle, however, states that 'sound tradition' and 'legitimate progress' must balance the innovations of the reforms and offers a more cautious note (1990: 44).

Other liturgical scholars have pointed to and developed key recommendations in the Constitution. For example, on the question of the cultural adaptation of worship, Chupungco argues that the Latin words *aptatio* and *accomodatio* may be reasonably translated as 'inculturation'. However, the use of the word *accomodatio* to replace *aptatio,* particularly in Chapter 3, demonstrates a certain reserve on the part of the reformers (1989: 25). He himself defines acculturation as 'the interaction between the Roman liturgy and the local culture. It consists of studying the cultural elements that can be assimilated and of establishing the method of assimilating them in accord with the intrinsic laws that govern both Christian worship and culture' (1989: 27). Inculturation is a more complete process, whereby, 'the texts and rites used in worship by the local church are so inserted in the framework of culture, that they absorb its thought, language, and ritual patterns' (1989: 29). The process is a subtle one, whereby 'the liturgy and culture are able to evolve through mutual insertion and absorption without damage to each other's identity' (1989: 31). The methods used for inculturation are all-important and based around two principles: the recognition of the immutable parts of a liturgy and the ability to distinguish the theological content of a rite from its liturgical form (1989: 40). Here we have one liturgist, perhaps unexpectedly in the light of his concern for liturgical adaptation, giving due cognisance to the laws governing ritual patterns and practices.

Aylred Shorter's argument (1988) about inculturation is that although many of the revisions made were for the benefit of different groups, locations and peoples, the Council did not envisage the creation of new rites. In the early days after the Council it was acknowledged by the Congregation responsible for *Sacrosanctum Concilium* that an extrinsic adaptation of the Roman rite by the choice of readings and prayers would be acceptable. But Shorter suggests this entailed more radical adaptation in mission lands, which amounted to acculturation, the insertion of elements from non-western countries into Roman rites. Originally it was stated that eucharistic prayers were not to be drawn up locally, but in fact many were.

Loss of the Sacred and Transcendent

Notwithstanding such positive endorsements, it is apparent that the reforms were regarded by many as a mixed blessing, if not by some as a complete betrayal of the worshipping tradition of the Roman Catholic Church. Many of the criticisms which have occurred reflected an anxiety about the loss of the transcendent and sacred in liturgy, in the light of its more deritualised anthropocentric concerns. The Roman rite which had existed in the Latin western tradition until the time of the Second Vatican Council, embedded within its highly ritualised structure a reconfiguration of time and space in relation to the eschaton. Liturgical time occupied a distended period before this eshcaton and the sacred spaces of ritual had assumed an analogical relationship to the heavenly realm. In contrast to this understanding, the document on liturgy was endorsed at the Council because it envisaged worship as being more in tune with the secular world. Such a move proved to be problematic because it failed to *challenge* the assumptions lying behind that world it so desperately wanted to include into its salvific framework. Ironically, the place to challenge such assumptions might well have been in the practice of liturgy itself.

During the medieval period the liturgy's relationship with 'culture' was never an issue because there was no separation between the two. Once the modern period began, liturgy had the task of persuading those 'outside', of the importance of the sacral world on which it rested. But there was no recognition at the reforms that there was any need to maintain any *distance* between the holy world and the secular world. In fact, the reverse occurred

as the secular colonising of time and space invaded the liturgical
realm. The replacing of a transcendent ordering of reality
maintained by apophatic reserve was substituted for an immanent
order resting on secular assumptions.

This is why Pickstock can argue that the reforms at the Second
Vatican Council were simply not radical enough (1998: 171). What
the Council needed to do was accept that any revision would have
to take into account the cultural and ethical nexus that liturgy had
been a part of for centuries. Since 'the Middle Ages was embedded
in a culture which was ritual in character' (1998: 170), and the
reforms failed to take into account the cultural assumptions lying
behind the texts, it resulted in a 'sinister conservatism' (1998:
171). The real task of reform would have been to 'challenge those
structures of the modern secular world which are wholly inimical
to liturgical purpose; those structures, indeed, which perpetuate a
separation of everyday life from liturgical enactment' (1998: 171).
As a result, the reforms were dangerously conservative because
they did not engage in any such revolutionary revisioning process
(1998: 171).

The loss of the sacred has gone hand in hand with the demise of
the priest's sacral authority, which had always rested upon the
Church's authority itself (Bourdieu, 1997). Bourdieu argues that
for ritual to function and be recognised as valid, it must operate
with symbols which demonstrate that the agent of the ritual does
not proceed with his own authority but 'in his capacity as a
delegate' (1997: 115). The rigorous, uniform performance of the
liturgy is important because it 'constitutes both the manifestation
and the counterpoint of the contract of delegation', and makes
the priest the holder of the means of salvation (1997: 115). The
Latin, priestly vestments and the consecrated places and objects
used, are important because they secure this delegation on behalf
of the Church itself, and reflect the conditions upon which
acceptance of these elements rests.

Social mechanisms operate to allow the complicity of those
involved in rites to remain stable. Bourdieu writes that for ritual to
be effective it must 'present itself and be perceived as legitimate'
(1997: 115). However, after the reforms, the conditions necessary
for the institution to operate effectively became eroded due to a
lack of liturgical uniformity. This had a devastating effect since,
'The crisis over the liturgy points to the crisis in the priesthood
(and the whole clerical field), which itself points to a general crisis
of religious belief' (1997: 116). The collapse of an entire set of

social relations is manifest in the erosion of the set of stylistic features and routinisation which had previously characterised a once uniform liturgy.

David Sanders analyses this aspect of the reforms in terms of how the 'human side' of worship became overemphasised and suggests that the objectivity of liturgy, which had underpinned much of the preconciliar worship, began to disappear. The result was that, 'personal eccentricities which reflect a secular and individualistic culture have intruded' (1995: 450). The leading English liturgist Rev. J. D. Crichton has become concerned about the ability of the reformed liturgy to maintain a sense of the sacred and has shifted in his position about the reforms since his earlier writings in the 1960s. He now observes that a 'loss of reverence' (1995: 453) has become part of much worship with a corresponding loss of the transcendence of God, the supreme object of worship. This is associated with more far-reaching consequences about forgetting what worship is actually about.

McSweeney, Archer and Kavanagh

In my view, the three most trenchant critics of the reforms (excluding Archbishop Lefebvre),[1] are McSweeney, Archer and Kavanagh. I now consider their positions in some detail in order to show how they represent and articulate some of the major concerns about the changes which were recommended at the Council.

McSweeney argues that the search for relevance during the 1960s is the key to understanding the new paradigm of the Church formulated at the Council and was to have positive but also considerable negative effects on postconciliar Roman Catholicism. The desire to make all things 'relevant' to members of the Church had significant repercussions on its liturgical theories and

---

[1] The most outspoken critic of the reforms was Archbishop Lefebvre, who in rebellion against the innovations at Vatican II, opened a seminary in Switzerland in 1968 dedicated to the abolition of the reforms and their accompanying theology. Lefebvre argued in his profession of faith on 21 November 1974 that the reforms continued to destroy the Church, to ruin its priesthood and to negate its emphasis on the sacrifice of the Mass and of the sacraments. The reforms arose out of liberalism and modernism and were poisoned by them; they arise from heresy and will end in heresy (McSweeney, 1981; Jay, 1992).

practices. The pursuit of relevance undermined the 'objective' character of worship which in turn bred the 'flexibility' of post-conciliar liturgy. Worship

> like dogma, has acquired a degree of elasticity which threatens its survival. The old belief in its objective character as an efficacious rite to which the members of the Church had to submit if they were to obtain the benefits made available to them depended upon a common understanding of the meaning of the Word of God of which the mass was the ritual expression (1981: 8).

This ritual expression has been eroded by a move towards a far more subjective experience during liturgy. In the new Catholicism, the Mass tends to become a therapy for the individual, its efficacy discussed in terms of its success in stimulating right feeling towards others.

McSweeney makes an incisive point here about the increased 'subjectification' of the liturgy, perceived by the Council Fathers as being the means towards a more pastorally effective liturgy. This move to relevance was not confined simply to the Roman Catholic tradition either. Outside Catholicism similar attention was being focused on the notion of relevance. Grace Davie's (1995) socio-logical account of religion in Britain during the 1960s reflects this distinctive turn towards relevance and the communication of meaning. In 1968 the Assembly of the World Council of Churches discussed how faith and worship must attempt to bridge the gap between the religious and secular worlds. The Church must offer a meaningful and relevant gospel to a culture which seems to have forgotten God.

Archer's attack on the reform of the liturgy is partly based upon his own experience as a Catholic priest working in Newcastle and his work has implications for both national and international developments. His argument in *The Two Catholic Churches: A Study in Oppression* rests on a loss of a sense of transcendence in worship and is discussed in relation to class. He contends that before the 1960s, the celebration of the Mass had been an opportunity for 'people to engage the sacred in their own fashion, providing for a whole range of religious demands and sensibilities and drawing people into space where there was evidently something more to life' (1986: 139). Its separation, difference and sacredness appealed to people of all social classes. But the new Mass has none of this. It has become 'neither one thing nor the other' (1986: 144). What occurred at the reforms was a radical disappearance and disengagement of all those familiarities of Catholic worship. The problem was these were replaced by nothing in particular, except a kind of secular vacuity: 'Nothing took their place. Disconcerted Catholics might have let the rosary beads slip from their fingers but they did not take up reciting the psalms' (1986: 32). He suggests that, 'The whole glittering army of Catholic symbolism had left the field' (1986: 133).

Archer discusses how the changes in the liturgy had considerable impact on Catholic consciousness after the reforms due to their emphasis on the intellectual and the cognitive dimensions of faith. Vatican II completed the work begun during the Counter-Reformation in order to produce, 'the consciously-committed catholic, articulate and with one's Catholicism properly internalised' (1986: 133). Paying close attention to the insistence on participation in the reforms, he argues that the reformed Mass was not to be a time for private devotion or individual prayer but rather collective celebration, but he scorns such moves by quoting Martin, 'A man or woman alone with God or just thinking or existing in *foro externo,* was becoming "an offence against the pressing demands of his fellow human being"' (1986: 135). The new Mass has lost all sense of occasion and with it a sense of the sacredness of space: 'Not only had it become in itself much less of a solemn withdrawal from the world. It no longer permitted individual withdrawal' (1986: 140). The reformed Mass reflected simply the passing fashions of the 1960s, and like so many other transient elements during that decade, was to have no permanent value.

The most debilitating aspect of the reforms for Archer was the fact that it appealed primarily to middle-class taste and left the working-classes struggling for inclusion and identity. Since the changes were characterised by the rational and intellectual impetus of the Counter-Reformation they 'cut off many of the ritual streams that had previously nourished Catholics and covered over many of the accumulated pools in which popular Catholicism had found its strength' (1986: 141). In his desire to compare the Counter-Reformation with the reforms of the 1960s, Archer here fails to recognise the deep sense of ritualism which pervaded the earlier Council. Nevertheless, his emphasis on a more rationalised and intellectual approach to liturgy which would appeal to the minds of worshippers is fair. He is keen to point out that the Reformers had been part of a remote intellectual world, far removed from the ordinary concerns and expectations of working-class Catholics. This is particularly ironic in the light of its professed pastoral intent. This was a grave mistake: at a moment in history when the Church sought to identify and respond to the pastoral needs of the Catholic community, the Council produced a document bereft of historical continuity and suited to the needs and aspirations of the middle-classes. It was natural, therefore, that 'what emerged should take the rational and aesthetically restrained form proper to intellectual conceptions of what was appropriate for universal use in an international church' (1986: 141). Archer also questions the theology and efficacy of the new rites themselves, which because of their insistence on congregational participation 'seemed to suggest that the communitarian assembly was either itself the source of grace or an essential prerequisite to its availability' (1986: 143). Ritual gestures were underplayed during the reforms and, as a consequence, the new liturgy which the reformers had tried to usher in failed and was no longer being trusted. He concludes 'In a time of ritual change, this trustworthiness could not be taken for granted through the measured words and gestures that had "always" been spoken and made, for these had disappeared: it had to be established afresh' (1986: 144). What happened in reality was that no such fresh establishment occurred.

Kavanagh's work is perhaps the best example of a sustained academic critique of the liturgical reforms based on a thorough analysis of the value and role of ritual in liturgy. Like his brother Benedictine Odo Casel, his entire position rests on an approach to ritualised liturgy as the pivot around which Christian living and belief exist. Liturgy precedes theological reasoning, it is the Church's faith in visible form and its expression, the arena within which theological reflection is done: The Church as *lex supplicandi* is the foundation for the constitution of a *lex credendi* (1992: 91–92). Using Augustine as his model, Kavanagh shows how Christians do not succumb to the grace of faith only to decide their options for worship at a later stage, but rather 'Augustine found himself being baptised and communicated at Ambrose's hands in the midst of those whose singing and Amens had helped bring him home' (1992: 98). But neither, one might add, does worship automatically produce belief, since this would entail a kind of liturgical pelagianism.

The criticism of postconciliar liturgy offered by Kavanagh moves on from this starting-point to an understanding of what ritual actually entails. If pre-Vatican II worship was characterised by a narrow insistence on the rubrics and the almost total separation between priest and people, then 'Some to-day argue that in post-conciliar liturgy this malaise has been replaced by another just as grave,... ignoring the rubrics of the reformed liturgy altogether in the expectation that relevance and good intentions dispense the worshipping assembly and its ministers from rubrical incumbrances' (1990a: 1). Kavanagh pinpoints the core of this malaise by suggesting that misunderstandingss arose due to a naivety concerning the nature of ritual itself. He balances the role and place of rubrical sensitivity with the concern at Vatican II to make the liturgy of the Church pastorally sensitive. His publication, *The Elements of Rite*, is precise on this matter and is an analysis of what gives such rubrics their *raison d'être*, power and value. A liturgical act is essentially a rite and a liturgy of Christians is nothing less than the way a redeemed world is performed through actions (1990a). The reason why such a definition of liturgy is unpopular today is that people no longer have a sense of rite as something creative and restorative, but rather view it as a stale act of repetition, the opposite of freedom and enlightenment.

This attitude and approach merely reflect the ceaseless modern search for an authentic self, devoid of all restraint or discipline from tradition and history. Consequently, subjectivism assumes a far greater prominence in worship. As Kavanagh puts it, 'Creativity of the Spontaneous Me variety condemns rite and symbol to lingering deaths by trivialisation, bemusing those who would communicate by rite and symbol to a point where they finally wander away in search of something which appears to be more stable and power-laden' (1992: 102). The operative word here for Kavanagh, is 'appears', for he believes that such searches are bound to fail. He does have some sympathy for those who suggest that some liturgy of the past became overburdened with rubrical precision, since he acknowledges that the liturgy at the close of the Middle Ages had become severely cumbersome and hypertrophied by ritual excess. There was simply more of it around than anyone could bear.

Ritual has also become misunderstood because of the slide into textual prominence in liturgy brought about by the renewed emphasis on the bible during the Reformation. The technology of printing had enormous effects on the style the liturgy was to adopt: 'A Presence which had formerly been experienced by most as a kind of enfolding embrace had now modulated into an abecedarian printout to which only the skill of literacy could give

complete access' (1992: 104). What occurred was that rite receded
in importance, as did the need and wish for a communal and
bodily re-enactment of redemption. This was replaced by the
congregation's reception of a didactic exposition of texts. Liturgy
had become partly instruction and a catechetical means of
educating those who had chosen to worship.

In contrast to such developments, Kavanagh's writing on liturgy
emphasises its unique symbolic and ambiguous nature. If the move
towards a more didactic approach entailed more explicit
exposition, then its ritual nature was bound to be undermined.
What occurred was a shift away from symbolic ritual and ambiguity
towards conceptual precision. Since the sixteenth century, the
attempt to use liturgy as an expression of doctrinal correctness and
orthodoxia had resulted in a diminution of liturgy as rite – it became
a means of *learning about* God, rather than an act of God. The
notion of liturgy as somehow re-enacting or literally acting out
God's story became unfamiliar and against the grain. Liturgy was
put in a category far removed from what it actually was meant to
do by its adaptation into a form of catechetical instruction. Liturgy
is not for altering as we wish, but rather serves the Word intimately
as an action of God.

This slide into doctrinal correctness and didactic instruction
had the result of taming the radically organic form of liturgy. It
substituted relevance for rite. In the past, ritual form had been
able to operate as a subversive force which, 'cracks open radical
values' (1992: 116). It was a performance more akin to the violent,
primitive and chaotic rather than the tame and mundane or the
human manipulation of a liturgical system. Kavanagh states that
Roman Catholics have allowed themselves 'to tame the lion of
Judah' (1992: 94). Rather than allowing the source of all life to
settle down and smash the false premises of much of our culture
and thinking, liturgy became 'civil religion filtered somewhat,
softened somewhat, by a generally benign middle-class liberalism'
(1992: 116) and was, as a result, in danger of being defensive,
inbred, and infertile. It was no longer brought into vigorous
interplay with the values of the gospel.

Kavanagh sees a subversive function to liturgy. It should aim
to bring the assembly to the edge of chaos. It has the power to
undercut and overthrow the very structures it uses itself. This
anti-structural nature of liturgy is the means by which new values
and social structures come into being. But this only happens when
liturgists adhere to operations embedded in its form, not by

relinquishing them. By tapping what Kavanagh calls the 'archaic', a power is released which can be channelled into a process of salvation for the life of the world. When liturgy becomes culturally tame it is indistinguishable from a meeting of the PTA or a political caucus. The political and social power of liturgy only resides in careful attention being attributed to the formal structures and qualities of rite (1992: 100–102).

Kavanagh argues that much in contemporary Catholic liturgy needs to reclaim this sense of a counter-cultural dynamic and insists on the importance which must be placed on worship as an assembly's preserve. It must contain a communitarian and even proletarian feel; in this regard he is not unlike Archer. But rituals are no ordinary social gatherings. The discipline of liturgy is able to uphold a distinctive and remarkable egalitarianism, what nineteenth-century liturgists would have called *gemeinschaft,* which carries with it a binding affiliation, a common identity, from within, as worshippers respond to the power of the rite as a unique social activity. Liturgy must maintain this sense of separateness from the quotidian and mundane. 'Political' liturgies come under fire since Kavanagh is critical of those services which develop a different form of politicised worship based on those cultural influences which the liturgy itself is meant to critique:

> many of the ideals and techniques are drawn into the worshipping group from outside cultures – something that may well implicate the Christian group in precisely those cultural elements it should wish to convert, such as political outrage and violence, social divisiveness, aggressive ideologies pushing for absolutized rights (1992: 159).

Such attempts at community create a sense of middle-class gentility and self-satisfaction, with the result that the liturgy becomes little more than a mere social gathering, losing all sense of its disruptive counterpoise. Liturgy is always *sub specie aeternitatis* and is never there to offer direct causal results on complex social issues.

Kavanagh reiterates throughout his writings his concern that worship must contain what he refers to as its 'normality' (1992: 163). Liturgy is able to be a powerful force of moral reawakening. Christian *orthodoxia* always regards the world as abnormal. The abnormal is caught sight of and restored through right worship. It enacts a world rendered normal by itself and 'In doing so, the assembly suffers greatly, as did its Lord, at the hands of systematic abnormality. It baptises into death; gives thanks over and itself

becomes a body broken and blood shed' (1992: 159). Such abnormality is not attained without a fight and that is why the ascetical
and monastic traditions have upheld (by discipline and ritual
regularity) a keen sense of this counter-cultural dimension to
liturgy. A true worshipping community learns to live in the
'normality' of the world and at odds with the 'abnormality' of
culture. If, as I am suggesting in this book, the ideas of the liturgical reforms absorbed too uncritically the dominant cultural
assumptions of modernity, then, along with Kavanagh, I contend
that modern liturgy has tended to increase rather than ameliorate
the 'abnormality' of the present culture.

The essence of Christian worship for Kavanagh is twofold: to
maintain a strong sense of communal unworthiness before God
and to develop a sense of gratitude at being freely and uncondi-
tionally raised up and forgiven by Christ. Any attempt to adapt the
Church's liturgy which entails a reduction in such emphases is
likely to fail. This is why liturgical theology must be doxological
and historical, recognising its festal, formal and ordered qualities.
It also requires a strong sense of the sonic, spatial and kinetic due
to its immersion in time and space, needing to be rooted in a disciplined reflection of the life-blood of the liturgical assembly; it is
only then inherently pastoral. It is eschatological, since it always
frames its action, both in the present and in the future, giving
simultaneously consolation and promise. What stands at the heart
of Christian worship is a presence which manifests itself in a
community of people who have no choice but to believe such
unsettling and deracinating things as 'here, on earth, we have no
abiding city'.

In summary, the overriding problem with the reforms for such
critics as Kavanagh, Archer and McSweeney resides in its lack of
attention to the ritual dimension of liturgy; its intellectualist and
cognitivist emphasis became its worst feature. Drawing from sociological and social anthropological insights their critiques are
associated with the extent and rapidity of the changes the
reformers insisted upon. Ritual patterns cannot be transformed
overnight, without a severe sense of dislocation and bewilderment
occurring. The problems left by the Second Vatican Council were
caused partly by the speed of the reforms themselves based on
mistaken presuppositions that reflect the worst of all the reforms'
weaknesses: 'the almost total absence of any anthropological
dimension in the approach to the revision of so massive and long-
standing a ritual system' (Kavanagh, 1991: 71). Ritual patterns,

which have much to do with sustaining identity and social bonds, are essentially conservative and need to change gradually.

The most balanced and convincing recent appraisal of the reform, in my view, has come from Mannion (1998). He expresses succinctly what lies at the root of the inability of much contemporary Catholic worship to engage with a sense of the sacred when he speaks about the need to recatholicise the reform (1998: 11–48). By this he means that what is required is a return to the 'ethos' of Catholic liturgy: its spiritual depth, sacramental richness, religious exuberance and creative ecclesiology. This is best served by returning to the insights of the Eastern and Reformed traditions, to writers such as Gerardus van der Leeuw, Rudolf Otto and Mircea Eliade, to a revival of the liturgy's aesthetic dimension and to a reawakening of the true meaning of catholicity which rests upon a positive ecclesiology centred upon 'the glory of God flowing in its Trinitarian dynamism into the earth' (1998: 24).

The way forward for the reformed liturgy is not to encourage further changes or amendments, but to revitalise the spiritual richness of the liturgy, to rediscover the spiritual depths which lie at the heart of the reformed worship as it was conceived at the Council; to encourage 'a spiritual unfolding of the potentiality of the revised liturgical rites rather than their expansion' (1998: 28). What is required is a greater emphasis on the spiritual, the mystical and the devotional; the liturgy's doxological and praise-filled character must be reclaimed through attention being given to its eschatological and cosmic significance (1998: 29). In my next chapter I delineate in more detail some of the difficulties associated with the demise of these components in relation to the emergence of a largely cognitive and disembodied approach which has occurred since the reforms.

6

⸻►◉◄⸻

FORGETTING HOW TO REMEMBER

The previous chapter examined some of the central features in the document on worship issued at the Second Vatican Council, followed by a representative sample of the varied responses which occurred in relation to the proposals and ensuing liturgical practices which emerged. In this chapter, three strands are crucial to a more detailed critical analysis of the reforms themselves: first, I discuss how the Council Fathers' recommendation that greater active participation become the norm, failed to recognise the importance of symbolic participation; as a result, it was unable to address a vital and constitutive feature of such participation. Second, I demonstrate how a process of subjectification developed in relation to the Church's liturgy, which ended in confusion about its public and private nature. Third, I point to how the devaluation and virtual ignoring of the essentially embodied nature of rite within liturgy weakened its mnemonic power and potential. All three elements extend and clarify the issues surrounding the performative, symbolic and embodied nature of liturgy I have discussed earlier in my argument.

Participation

The weighty phrase 'full, conscious and active participation' occurs in paragraph 14 of *Sacrosanctum Concilium*. Such participation is paramount in the reformers' vision of liturgical renewal and is 'the aim to be considered before all else' (*SC*, paragraph 14). Indeed these five words were to become one of the fundamental principles underlying the liturgical renewal. It was also a phrase which was to appear again and again in the documents and letters of exhortation after the Council. Pope Paul VI in his address to a general audience on 6 April 1966 wrote,

'Participation' here is one of the ecumenical Council's most often repeated and most forceful affirmations bearing on divine worship, on the liturgy. . . . this affirmation can be termed one of the distinguishing principles of the conciliar teaching and reform (*DL* 1982: 126).

Nine years later on 26 March 1975 more justification for active participation is given by Pope Paul VI,

We cannot, then, simply be present at a liturgical rite as spectators. . . . we must become, to an extent, the actors in it. We must therefore see ourselves sitting at table at the Last Supper, standing along the *Via Crucis* lightning-struck at the mystery of the risen Jesus' appearances. . . In any believer who participates in the liturgy there is no sense of remoteness or of being on the outside. Consequently in celebrating the paschal mystery the believer is taken into and overcome by the dramatic power of the 'hour' of Christ, 'my hour' as he called it (see Jn 2:4, 12:23, 17:1 etc.) (*DL* 1982: 173).

'Conscious'

The reformers believed that participation would be enhanced by a congregation's awareness and understanding of worship. It is the duty of pastors to ensure that 'the faithful take part fully and are aware of what they are doing'. They must be able to grasp its meaning since 'through a good understanding of the rites and prayers they should take part in the sacred action, conscious of what they are doing, with devotion and full collaboration'. The Church's prayer should not be esoteric nor remote from people's comprehension. This absorption into the meaning of the liturgy is to be done even during the celebration itself, since it provides a marvellous arena for teaching and instruction: 'A more explicitly liturgical catechises should also be given in a variety of ways. Within the rites themselves provision is to be made for brief comments, when needed by the priest or a qualified minister' (*SC*, paragraph 35)

It was hardly surprising in the light of the Church's attention to *aggiornamento*, that much of the debate around the reform of the liturgy was focused on such moves to make worship more comprehensible, intelligible and consequently, more in tune with the contemporary mind. In the *Sacramentary* approved in 1973 by Pope Paul VI, it states with reference to *Sacrosanctum Concilium* that, 'Both texts and rites should be drawn up so that they express more clearly the holy things they signify' (1985: 9). This would apply in practice, for example, to the priest at the invitatory of the Mass,

who could use 'his own words' since by this means the celebration
can become 'more concrete and effective' (1985: 14). Rites were
to be 'restored to the vigour they had in the tradition of the
Fathers' and would lead 'to an inner participation in them' (1985:
20). It was affirmed that such comprehensibility would lead to
more meaningful inner participation by the heart and will.

Catechetical

As a result of such recommendations, participation and comprehension became inextricably connected. As previously recognised
at the Council of Trent, the Mass had the potential to be highly
catechetical and therefore it was fitting for priests to 'include some
explanation of the mystery of this sacrifice' (*Sacramentary* 1985: 21).
Indeed, the permission granted 'to interpose some commentary
during the sacred rites themselves' (1985: 21) was clearly in line
with much of the thinking towards a more pedagogic type of
worship. For example, one of the reasons given for receiving
Communion under both kinds was so that a deepening of the
understanding of the sacrament would occur. Such reforms would
accomplish 'a participation in body and spirit' (1985: 22). This
catechetical emphasis was also to become reflected in the architectural adaptations which were to lend themselves to 'noble simplicity,
not ostentation' and new arrangements were to be suited 'to foster
instruction of the faithful' (1985: 45). Indeed, all furnishing was to
'ensure the active participation of the faithful' (1985: 43).

   This strongly mentalist and cognitivist approach to worship
is only regarded as being secondary when children's liturgy is
discussed. The central significance of the liturgy as an activity of
both the body and the mind was to be reserved for children's liturgy
alone since, 'In view of the nature of the liturgy as an activity of the
entire person and in view of the psychology of children, participation by means of gestures and posture should be strongly
encouraged in Masses with children' (1985: 59). This is echoed in
the exhortation to use visual elements with young people since the
'liturgy should never appear as something dry and merely intellectual' (1985: 60). Although the *Sacramentary* does mention how
the 'beautiful expression' of the unity of the faithful is maintained
by the uniformity of actions in 'standing, sitting and kneeling'
(1985: 30), this is never given prominence over its central concern
about intelligibility, but stated as a warning against the danger of
individualism creeping into the unifying worship of the Church.

The Devaluation of Symbolism

This overriding desire to make the liturgy more meaningfully intelligible and participatory had the effect of marginalising the complex and ambiguous dynamic of liturgical symbolism, which always defies cognitive classification. Liturgy as essentially a symbolic rite was replaced by an emphasis on liturgy as catechetical opportunity and intelligible celebration. Leading liturgists have commented on this omission. Saliers' critique of the reforms is centred precisely around this issue:

> In our haste to render the liturgy intelligible and accessible to the worshippers, we easily neglect the complex matter of participation in symbol and symbolic efficacy (power and range). In our preoccupation with reformed texts and rubrics, we may have neglected the most difficult challenge: to uncover the intersection of human hopes and fears, longings and hungers, with the symbolic power and range of liturgical rites authentically celebrated (1992: 71).

Duffy seems to agree with him in his discussion of what he considers to be the erroneous identification of intelligibility with effective worship:

> We are now, I think, beginning to be in a position to draw up a balance sheet of loss and gain from changes which were based on the assumption that the mysteries celebrated in the sacraments could or should be understood with ease, that the liturgy was an activity concerned primarily with pedagogy, that liturgical rites should be short, clear and free from useless repetition (1996: 53–54)

For both Saliers and Duffy liturgy can never be easily grasped, since one of its defining constituents is its symbolic nature. Symbol defies classification and precisional analysis due to its ability to create layers of possible meanings. Liturgy always carries the potential to express a selected range of many levels of meaning inherent in its nature as a symbolic re-enactment of the saving events of Christ (*SC*, paragraph 21). Saliers argues that this 'primary' archaic power of symbol has been particularly eroded by increased attention being given to what he calls 'secondary' symbols which simply 'express the inclinations of the present cultural modes of communication' (1996: 73). He attempts to reclaim for Roman Catholic liturgy the emphasis Turner gives to the tripartite power of ritualised symbol: first, its multivocality or fusion of many levels of meaning; second, its unifying power of several different referents and experiences; and third, the meanings it accumulates around affective and morally normative values (quoted in Madden, 1992: 75). The 'ordinary things' in liturgy (wine, bread, oil), become infused with religious meaning, transformed from mere 'things'. The opportunity to become 'lightning-struck' by worship rests fundamentally for Saliers on this participatory engagement with Christian symbolism, not on an increase in cognitive understanding and explanation.

Such engagement can never be realised through cognitive participation, since symbols do not appeal primarily to the intellect. They cannot be deciphered once and for all by the grasp of the mind. In quoting Gelineau, Saliers advocates what he considers to be the central constitutive dimensions of liturgy: its parabolic, metaphorical, allegorical and symbolic nature:

> Ritual activity is not concerned with producing purely 'worldly' effects
> ... but the coming of the Kingdom. Thus in the liturgy we do not eat
> only to feed our bodies; we do not sing only to make music; we do not
> speak only to teach and to learn; we do not pray only to restore psychic
> equilibrium. The liturgy is a parabolic type of activity (which throws us
> aside), metaphorical (which takes us somewhere else), allegorical
> (which speaks of something else) and symbolic (which brings together
> and makes connections) (1992: 74).

Any renewal in liturgy must safeguard and restore a 'sense of history and *mysterion* to the symbols embedded in the ritual actions of the liturgy' (1992: 76), since it is the power of the public symbol which has the means to restore new life to worship and life. This is not a process of instantaneous or simple clarification, but a gradual peeling back of the variable and shifting nature of symbol. We never have access to the unmediated 'pure' meaning of symbols. The water, the bread and wine, the cross, the word, always reveal and conceal (Saliers, 1992). This mysterious ' hiddenness' within worship needs to be protected. Any attempt to articulate precisely the exact nature of symbol is doomed to failure, since its power and efficacy rests on its polyvalence and sense of remoteness.

Duffy similarly criticises attempts to simplify and dehistoricise the liturgy. Symbols are polyphonic and polysemous. They live within inherited patterns of meaning and are

> often palimpsests which grow by accretion, by the overlaying and juxta-
> position of layer upon layer of meaning and sign, which are often in
> tension with each other, and held together not by a single dominant
> explanation but by performance, by the complex of recitation,
> repetition, song, prayer and gesture through which we appropriate and
> enter into the web of realities symbolised by the rite, by which we live
> within the tradition (1996: 57).

The recommendations to simplify and make intelligible the symbolic core of liturgy are moves in the wrong direction. Liturgy works by performance, complexity and ambiguity rather than discursive reasoning and exactitude. This is not to suggest that each ritual re-enactment is always identically the same performance. Its structure might maintain a pattern and form which assures continuity with the past, but its concomitant defining feature is its 'looseness', its ability to be altered creatively and changed while still maintaining a formal structure, or as Duffy puts it,

> We *make* ritual, even inherited and prescribed ritual, because we bring to it a network of association and intention which shapes its meaning for us. Every rite is our own work of art and in every celebration of the liturgy there is always more going on than the words, rubrics or intentions of the celebrant or the liturgists explicitly envisage (1996: 58).

There is always a dynamic interplay between the form a ritual takes and the meanings individuals take to and draw from it.

Symbolic Lifestyles

This sense of a loss of the symbolic is a common theme running through many discussions about modern Roman Catholic devotion and liturgy since the reforms. Duffy echoes much of the earlier work of Douglas by arguing that institutional religion carries with it responsibilities and obligations to encourage the symbolic lifestyles of its adherents. He takes up the issue of fasting which he argues relies upon the notion of public and corporate identity. Individual choice, he claims, can never replace the importance of the corporate symbolic sign. The modern changes which took place regarding rules of fasting reflected ideas about inconvenience within a secular society. He writes, 'And many of the arguments against compulsory fasting are part of that minimising of symbolic distinctiveness, in the service of secular convenience' (1995: 116). Symbolic actions are powerful substantially because they are distinctive and are able to disrupt a secular way of doing things. In other words, they are significant due to their 'awkwardness'.

Romano Guardini's discussion of the 'spirit of liturgy' also resides around the use of symbolism. He argues that one of the major constituent elements in worship is the symbolic, since it is capable of presenting a truth far more strongly than verbal expression. People who really come to live by the liturgy will gradually realise that 'the bodily movements, the actions, and the material objects which it employs are all of the highest significance' (1935: 170). The body, movement and material objects used in liturgy complement and interact with each other symbolically as liturgies unfold and progress. In a liturgical sacrifice the victim is offered, not only by the hands, but in a vessel or dish. There is always a dynamic interplay between such elements used in liturgies which produce endlessly rich performances.

This decline in the importance attached to the power of the symbolic within religion is not confined to the Roman Catholic Church alone and reflects a more general religious trend of the 1960s, certainly within Britain (Davie, 1995). A recent Church of England report entitled 'Paying the Piper: Advertising and the Church' (1994), about the need to 'market' the Church more effectively, points to the necessity of identifying key questions to be asked in relation to the use of advertising in the Church. It suggests that appropriate use of advertising is a good and useful enterprise, arguing at one point that its vivid imagery, telling allusions and occasional humour makes it remarkably close in style to the biblical parable! It is not my intention to rehearse these arguments here, but to focus on a crucial element in the campaign – the extreme appeal to relevance and the consequent abandonment of traditional religious symbolism.

The advertising poster about the Christian celebration of Easter in 1995 will serve to illustrate my point. Instead of using the traditional symbol of the cross it was decided that such Christian images carried too much 'cultural baggage'. What exactly this meant was never fully explained by those responsible for the campaign, but I suppose it points to the idea that the symbol of the cross presents people today with an irrelevant image, no longer in tune with the kind of world in which we all live. One member of the group, the Rev. Robert Ellis, argued that people have rejected traditional symbols and there was a need for new ones. The word SURPRISE appears on the poster instead of the cross. Traditional symbols were regarded as being anachronistic and irrelevant – emotive words are much better at communicating the Christian message. Advertising manager, Kate Grieves, who helped launch the programme, commented, 'What is the obsession with the cross? We are trying to meet them where they are, rather than putting out cliché images which may be disregarded' (in *The Times*, 10 March 1995). Such statements reflect a well-intentioned but misguided understanding of the power of religious symbolism.

Symbolic Space

The use of symbolic space and positionings also fulfil a vital function in liturgy and are never only for the ease of congregational participation or a means simply of ensuring didactic attention (Roose-Evans, 1994). Primarily strategic, they add to the creative, mnemonic and symbolic dynamics which unfold during every celebration. As the French liturgist, Louis-Marie Chauvet comments, 'As liturgical space, it is a place which is "informed", in the Aristotelian and Scholastic sense of the term, by the tradition and collective memory of Christians' (Chauvet, 1995: 29). Each item or 'thing' within the space is held in symbolic harmony by the relationship between the different items, some of which are stationary and some which move according to the liturgical season. But it is the positioning of one to the other, in appropriate arrangement which constitutes the 'informed' symbolic space. With each celebration comes the potential for a new configuration of space (and, with it, new meaning or revelation). This is a matter of central importance, since,

> Oscillating between metaphor and metonym, depending on the instance, mute objects begin to speak; metonymically they link the assembly to past generations which have handed down to it the living tradition of the church and the totality of Christian communities which, by communion, form the church of Christ (1995: 30).

Such symbolic space is also initiatory, since it rests on and produces tradition. Chauvet argues that Christian initiation can only be brought about by an invitation to the heart, not by a command made to the intellect. The mystery of Christ can never be understood by propositions aimed at the intellect; it is essentially a bodily process: 'To be initiated is not to have learned "truths to believe" but to have received a tradition, in a way through all the pores of one's skin' (1995: 31). This bodily dimension of liturgy is crucial and continues the tradition of early Christianity when such initiation always occurred through a 'slow incubation in the body, the memory and the heart of each and every one... Even now we would be wrong to neglect this dimension in favour of taking only critical reason into account' (1995: 31).

Holy space also ensures that any actions and words within its parameters assume a highly symbolic dimension; the space itself 'speaks' before anyone opens his or her mouth, since the actions and bodily dispositions of the congregation tell of the 'otherness'

of the performance to which they have been invited, long before
they have begun to participate in the sacred rites themselves. As
Chauvet writes,

> Within the theological content communicated mutely by the archi-
> tecture of this or that church, the very form of the message which is
> transmitted is affected... the very bodies of the faithful have a grave
> bearing which manifests, to a degree superficially, the evocation of the
> mystery which bears in on them (1995: 33).[1]

Before the Enlightenment all space had been understood in this
way. It was not until the seventeenth century that space came to be
understood as void of matter, having been determined and
calibrated through scientific scrutiny; it came to rest on geometrical
and mathematical findings, and the cosmos began to lose all
symbolic and religious significance (Ward, 1997: xvii–xxii). In the

---

[1] Francesca Murphy's recent work on aesthetic theology draws attention
to the importance of both form and symbolism in her analysis of the christological imagination (1995). For Murphy analogical symbols are able to
express something of the infinite being of God; they represent qualities of
transcendent being. They are situated in the real and yet are able to
stretch up to God. She quotes Jacques Maritain: 'To bring together
various meanings at a single moment of action is to exercise... the
symbolic imagination... The symbolic imagination conducts an action
through analogy, of the human to the divine, of the low to the high, of
time to eternity' (quoted in Murphy, 1995: 53). Symbols are signs, the
means through which the transcendent beauty of God is transmitted and
conveyed. The pattern that the liturgy assumes is a 'transcendent, super-
eminent type of Christian art-form' (quoted in Murphy, 1995: 56).
Liturgy exposes a pattern which comes from beyond the human spirit's
perception of meanings within this world (Murphy, 1995: 56). The self-
transcending dynamism of human beings comes about through their
being lured by being and if religion is to have a transcendental ground, it
must be able to describe and explain reality, but having done so, must also
show how this public life is analogical and finds its ultimate meaning in
the transcendent. Unless it refers to such a transcending reality, the
culture has nowhere to point, except back at itself. Nowhere is this
analogical idea more perfectly witnessed than in the liturgy. Here Christ,
the form of beauty, is revealed in symbolic action and word. Only God is
beautiful in the strictest sense, but liturgy is able to offer the most intense
and radiant possibility of entering into that beauty, through the form it
takes and the world it creates by its absorption in the 'non-ordinariness' of
time and space. Christ, the form of beauty, is revealed in liturgical
symbolic action and word (Murphy, 1995).

premodern world, space had never been matterless, but was 'full', in the sense that it carried a symbolic reflection of the Divine creation, being a mirror into which one could glimpse the goodness and beauty of God (Jantzen, 1996). Such analogical use of space, as I have indicated earlier, was particularly witnessed in the traditions of many Religious Orders up to the Second Vatican Council, which modelled the use of earthly space on heavenly design (Curran, 1989). It is not too difficult to imagine how, as part of that analogical relationship between the earthly and the heavenly, the distinct arena of liturgical space was able to assume a special sacredness and sanctity in order to 'make holy' those who dwelt there.

David Brown and Anne Loades discuss this notion of symbolic space in terms of new co-ordinates. Liturgy develops its own 'distinctive medium, its own set of spatial and temporal co-ordinates' (1995: 3). Space and time are given a new measure and the co-ordinates which are adopted become significantly different from their secular counterparts. They are right to argue that this makes it possible for a congregation to enter more fully into a God-centred view of the world. The sanctified 'alternative geography' of liturgical space ensures its sacredness, a thing set apart. Ethical behaviour is a *constituent of and derives from* an absorption into the 'otherness' of symbolic space and is never dependent upon mere human bestowing. Susan White's attempt to equate sacred space with those places where ethical action towards the building of the kingdom occurs, emphasises an immanentist understanding of Christ's presence (White, 1995). Such a position sees little signifi-cance in *differentiated sacred spaces* except in relation to what is given by the individual mind or the community (Chiffley, 1998: 30). But as Chiffley reminds us, because 'modern man' finds himself alienated from the cosmos in a way his ancestors did not, 'It is important not to undervalue created reality as a means of commu-nicating the revelation and redemptive presence of Christ' (Chiffley; 1998: 27). However, where 'particular rites, space, texts, or persons are no longer seen as having any intrinsic connection to the Divine apart from what is attributed by the individual psyche or the community, it is difficult for rite to speak eloquently' (Chiffley: 1998: 30). This cosmic alienation is particularly demon-strated in the priest's liturgical orientation *versus populum* during the Mass since the reforms. Originally facing the east, earlier orien-tations of the priest and people ensured that worship was set within a sacramental frame of a divinely created order, in relation to the symbol of the rising sun (Chiffley, 1998: 28).

It is only in such symbolic spaces that individuals and communities can humble themselves before God. One of the essential properties of liturgy is that it invites the 'world being to the being-before-God (Lacoste, 1994). The 'fool' of liturgy, according to Lacoste, testifies that giving praise is a worthier occupation than exercising rationality. Significance and self-transformation emerge from an eschatological perspective, by being a 'fool' who symbolically inhabits Good Friday and whose destiny 'becomes intelligible only in the light of another destiny, that of the crucified one in whom and by whom God restores peace between human kind and himself' (quoted in Ward, 1997: 261).

Symbolic Communication

Cultural theorists have pointed to the importance of symbols in ensuring the maintenance of cultural and social meaning and their work sheds light on the implications of the use of symbolism for liturgy. The Swedish writer Johan Fornas argues that in late modernity where 'normative hegemony' is no longer easily upheld and where Yeats' line 'things fall apart at the centre' has become a slogan for many postmodern writers (1995: 57), the importance of symbolic communication has become a crucial, if problematic debate (Featherstone, 1995). He demonstrates that symbolic communication can be understood primarily from two sides: as a transportation of shared meaning from sender to receiver; and as a shaping of shared meaning in communal rituals. The first implies a fairly static operation – something is passed on, as a deposit, to someone else. The second is more dynamic and implies a creative process whereby transported meaning is shared and interpreted among people. The implications for liturgy are obvious and Fornas uses the example of Holy Communion to make his point. But while the symbol automatically carries with it this openness to interpretation, it is never wholly arbitrary. Quoting Ricoeur to support his contention, he writes that an 'essential characteristic of the symbol is the fact that it is never completely arbitrary. It is not empty; rather there always remains the trace of a natural relationship between the signifier and the signified' (1995: 186).

The liturgical context is the means of determining the non-arbitrariness of symbol. The discourse in which the symbol is used determines and locates the extent of the range of meanings possible. Inevitably new layers of meaning are always possible, but these emerge within the confines of the religious context. This is how the creative tension and power of symbol occurs – between the stock of meanings already given by tradition and the new significations which become possible through their use and adaptation as each new liturgy is celebrated. As Fornas writes,

> Symbols acquire life by the tension between their formal logic and their pointing at something else. No symbolic mode is totally closed or autonomous. It is woven into the totality of human *praxis,* and its relative, systemic independence is a tendency and the goal of a process rather than its starting point (1995: 187).

Liturgy allows such creative meaning to be refracted from the symbolic objects, words or gestures themselves. It is an arena of meaning that, if entered with our whole human make-up, makes experience of the sacred possible through deeper gratitude, awe, and a greater capacity for hope and compassion (Madden, 1992). Such experiences are always patterned and contextualised within a much greater framework of social meaning and history.

The 'primary semblance' (a phrase used by John Foley) between the divine and human worlds is able to occur once the symbolic and sacred is established by ritual. The processions to and from the altar symbolise the entrance and exit from a holy geographical realm. Foley discusses the overriding importance of this: 'All movements within the designated space, whether this be only the sanctuary or includes the whole interior of the church or room, work to establish the primary semblance: sanctified actions within God's sphere' (1994: 247). Appropriate liturgical language is therefore essential within such symbolic spaces. A priest's 'Good morning' might lead to a weakening of the sense of a sacred space. He quotes Northrop Frye to make his point: 'Full awareness of an audience makes speech rhetorical, and rhetorical means a conventionalised rhythm' (1994: 248). Because liturgy is 'other' and 'distanced' (ie. there is literally space between altar and congregation), a 'The Lord be with you' is often more appropriate. This conventionality, stylisation and distancing allows the ritual nature of liturgy to be itself. It promotes the establishment of an alternative world, 'other' to daily or 'normal' living.

Tying Meaning Down

Liturgy suffers when efforts are made to tie down its meaning. David Power writes that 'In the eucharist, the word and thing "bread" must have a demonstrable reference to what common sense recognises as a substance, but its meaning in the ceremony depends on its cultural and traditional polysemy' (1985: 65). This double meaning of symbol in liturgy occurs every time a liturgy is celebrated. According to Power, there is an unfortunate tendency in modern worship to do three things: to refuse the 'interplay of images' (by which he means focus simply on one thought or idea); to impose well-defined, unambiguous meaning on words and actions; and to revert to naive realism and remain in the world of the everyday and sense perceptions. Such attempts severely limit the power of liturgy. Discursive reasoning must always give way to the symbolism which ensures a part of its form. Using Langer's work, Power points to the capacity of symbols to 'take hold of experience and give it form and expression in such a way that it becomes accessible to thought' (1984: 65). But cognitive thought can never simply pin down the meaning of symbols to the present moment. Rather symbols are able to release thought from its contemporaneous concerns and are an 'abstraction and liberate thought from the immersion in the immediately present physical world' (1984: 69). This prevents liturgy from becoming superficially 'stuck' in the present moment.

Liturgy as Art Form

Foley's work on liturgy is particularly important since it attempts to discover the creative potential of liturgy by focusing on its relationship to the arts. He tries to answer the question whether a liturgical celebration is primarily an aesthetical event by comparing the liturgical act to a 'birthing' – tracing the conception, gestation and finally birth of the human child. Foley asks the question: 'Is art like birth? And is liturgy like art – both in its creativity and in its quality of craft?' (1994: 8). In the Introduction of Part II of his book, he attempts to answer the question is liturgy an art form, by considering its symbolic and organic nature. Liturgy is 'art – dialogue with God in symbolic form' and 'liturgical planners must see the liturgy as a drama, and therefore, they must conceptualise it as a whole.... It is only the totality of the liturgical event that will present a coherent image of an alternative world' (1994: 143).

Three elements dominate Foley's argument and echo my earlier emphases: first, liturgy is a symbolic construction; second, it has a coherent form; and third, it is involved in the creation of an alternative world. Foley develops the notion of a 'commanding form' to liturgy. Such a form rather than closing down opens up options and possibilities: 'Possibilities are found within the commanding form not realisations' just as in any creative process, 'As in any living organism, the rhythm and intricate relation of event to event happen when they happen, not when some rigorous, detailed plan dictates' (1994: 232). The 'commanding form' resists interpretation as a kind of precompacted work of routine and rather than repetition being redundant, it is crucial since it establishes what he calls, 'the primary semblance' meaning 'Repeated words and actions are like a stairway worn smooth; the daily act of ascending the stairs takes place without thought, even as the bestowal of the Spirit happens prior to thinking. With the comfort of repetition comes an ability to attend interiorly to what one already knows and barely listens to' (1994: 247).

The Subjectivisation of Liturgy

A process of subjectivisation has accompanied and been activated by the demise of symbolic participation. It was the 'self' which became sacred and the pivot around which much liturgical thinking revolved after the reforms. Cultural systems based upon shared symbolic systems became substituted by individual constructions of meaning. This deconstruction of the symbolic 'otherness' of liturgy has been well-traced by Francis Mannion. Referring to American Roman Catholic liturgy since the 1960s, he locates this shift from 'otherness' to familiarity in terms of a radical process of subjectification. Drawing on Bellah's, Lasch's and Sennett's work, he demonstrates how the reform of the liturgy over the last twenty-five years has acutely reflected this emphasis. Quoting Bellah he writes, 'This view, which *Habits of the Heart* describes as "ontological individualism" embodies the conviction that "the individual has a primary reality whereas society is a second-order, derived or artificial construct"' (1986: 102). The sacred became 'located inside' and 'closely attached to the self, not to rituals celebrated and shared in public'. The result is that modern Americans 'look for the holy to reveal itself, not in awe-inspiring rites of baptism and Eucharist, but in the awesome precincts of the self' (1986: 71). The primary and archaic symbols of liturgy have given way to secondary expressions connected to interior dispositions and feelings: 'In this climate, the liturgical performance of liturgical rites takes on an experimental and improvisory character. The search for liturgical expressions adequate to interior personal disposition, crisis or need appears as a constant and intense preoccupation' (1986: 106). Such an emphasis has significant repercussions for how liturgies are evaluated; they become cast in terms of appropriateness to individual needs: 'Indeed, ritual forms will be so evaluated that what appears as therapeutically valuable will move into higher relief while the more formal, complex, and ceremonial elements which mediate ecclesial significance will be reduced in importance' (1986: 106).

For Mannion this demise of the public sphere is reflected in what he calls the process of 'politicisation'. The symbolic structures of culture are substituted for individual systems of meaning. Signifying practices are replaced by personal signs, meaningful only to the individual: 'When cultural symbol systems collapse or become distorted, so too does the possibility of meaningful and civilised coexistence' (1986: 115). This process of deculturation reduces the sense of the sacred and transcendent in worship and is a direct result of the undermining and disinterestedness attached to the socially cohesive function of symbols which consequently brings about 'a critical loss of transcendence and a collapse of the proper relationships between individual, nature and society' (1986: 116).

Searle's critique of some of the unhelpful developments since the early reforms of the liturgy focuses further attention on this notion of subjectivisation. He argues that the earliest stirrings of a liturgical movement in the 1830s by Guéranger were based on a desire to reshape and reform the liturgy which had taken into its practice the presuppositions and norms of its own culture – for example, its leanings towards sacramental pragmatism and individualistic devotionalism. The liturgy needed to be rescued from such influences and become itself again. In other words, to regain its essential and definitive form and intention, so that from involvement in the liturgy a renewed self would be able to take the spirit of Christ into the world. For Searle, too, the reforms of Vatican II were promoted more as an accommodation to culture rather than as a call for conversion and baptism of culture. He argues that the Liturgical Movement that Guéranger launched in the 1830s was nothing less than an attempt to free the liturgy from the influences of the prevailing culture, but this vision of allowing the liturgy to speak for itself was lost sight of at the reforms (1990: 50). This has become manifest in the various modes of liturgy which have emerged, for example, in the way in which attempts have occurred to close social distance within liturgy (a previously vital means of maintaining a sense of the holy), as if somehow this was alien to good liturgy. He uses Richard Sennett's phrase, 'the ideology of intimacy' (1990: 42; Sennett, 1993) to suggest that in attempts to make the liturgy more participatory there occurred moves to introduce the private and personal into an arena or space which ought to be reserved for the public and communal. One instance of this would be the priest or eucharistic minister referring to the communicant by her Christian name before giving communion. He doubts whether such moves are intended to foster the same kind of participation that is demanded by the nature of the liturgy itself. Real and effective participation is the sharing in the priestly life of Christ, not simply about 'getting people to join in' or making the liturgy more personally meaningful: 'The most immediate and most urgent need is to let God be God in our liturgies. . . . Anything in the liturgy that does not direct us to that end – anything that focuses on togetherness, instruction, entertaining, even participation – is a distraction at best, idolatry at worst' (Searle, 1990: 48).

This charge of encouraging individualism rather than collegiality has also been taken up by the distinguished Oratorian liturgist Louis Bouyer. His work *The Decomposition of Catholicism* translated into English in 1989, draws attention to the 'take-over' of the liturgy by individuals and groups intent on distorting the liturgy for their own political or social ends. The prayer of the Church has now become a 'ballyhoo meeting' (quoted in Spurr, 1995: 31). Two paradoxes have resulted. First, although the reforms were intended for the laity, they have often been a largely clerical invention with the idiosyncrasies of the clergy dominating liturgical practice. Catholics now have the right only to experience the religion of their pastor, with all its limitations, mannerisms and futilities. Second, the allegation that preconciliar Catholicism was non-participatory is not the case. Barry Spurr documents the rise of dissatisfaction with the reforms of the liturgy by referring to the work of Campion in listing the 'participation' of Catholics before the reforms (1995: 32–34). These centred particularly on the popular devotions and the 'rich diversity' which made it a truly 'people's religion' (1995: 32). Although the priest might have been distanced at the altar, congregations participated personally and actively, since it was a religion that, 'spoke both to the emotions and the intellect' – to the needs of 'children or simple folk' while satisfying the more sophisticated 'in the rhetorical grandeur of the antique Latin ceremonies' (Spurr, 1995: 33). Unless liturgy symbolically reflects a world which comes from beyond the human being's own perception of meaning, it merely echoes a culture which has nowhere to go except back upon itself. Authentic liturgy is able to offer the most intense and radiant possibility of entering into the beauty of God since it offers the possibility of self-transcendence by its invitation to enter into what von Balthasar calls a 'Theo-drama' (Murphy, 1995).

Rite as a Public Action of the Church

The Church itself has not been unaware of the difficulties involved in substituting a public rite for a private one. The document on liturgy itself had pointed out that liturgical services are not private functions, but celebrations belonging to the Church itself. The Instruction *Doctrina et Exemplo* issued in December 1965 on the formation of future priests, laid stress on the public nature of worship: 'Celebration in liturgy is always through an act at once internal and external: external, because it is public; internal, because it is truthful and sincere' (*Sacramentary*, 1985: 45). Archbishop Bugnini (although one of the central champions of the reforms) similarly testifies to some of the latent dangers associated with the renewal in his discussion of one of the guiding principles of the reforms, 'the manifestation of the Church': 'Communal celebration is... always to be preferred to individual celebration. Communal celebrations show forth the nature of the Church as a hierarchically organized community' (1990: 42). All individualistic attempts are at odds with the ecclesial meaning of the liturgy and harmful to the Church's unity.

The Apostolic Letter of Pope John Paul II on the twenty-fifth anniversary of the promulgation of *Sacrosanctum Concilium* similarly stressed the view that the liturgy belonged to the universal Church, not to isolated individuals. Couched in terms of a warning to those who might be tempted to supplant their own idiosyncratic innova-tions in place of prescribed rites, the letter states: 'Since liturgical celebrations are not private acts but "celebrations of the Church", their regulation is dependent solely upon the hierarchical authority of the Church. The liturgy belongs to the whole body of the Church, the sacrament of unity' (*Briefing*, 19 (2) (1989). Liturgy is a cry from the Church's heart, not the psyche of the individual.

Although such statements seem to endorse the importance of

rite as a public action of the whole Church, they simultaneously reflect back to the dangers of individualism inherent in the reforms themselves. There has been considerable confusion between the strong encouragement given at the reforms to make the liturgy more pastorally sensitive and up-to-date and the claims about the need to insist on its public function. Liturgists have seized on this issue. Liturgical pastoral effectiveness does not consist in a process of intensifying or highlighting the individual preoccupations of its congregation, but rather from the trans-formation of those preoccupations. The experience of another world and another time during a liturgy exposes self-occupation as narcissistic and potentially deceiving. Liturgy always offers a divine mirror through which the self may be seen and then changed. Any solipsistic tendencies in liturgy denies its distinctiveness as a public arena and experience in which ontological transformations take place. Seasoltz is right to suggest that, 'The liturgy provides a context in which the celebrants can discover or rediscover who they are in the world and what the nature of the world is' (1993: 54). Liturgical experience always sets the self in relation to the Church's understanding of the world and the self. This self-discovery comes about through an engagement with the world enacted in the rite which is often described as being qualitatively different from individual perceptions and thoughts. As Seasoltz concludes, 'The world view set out in the celebration of Christian liturgies is at odds with the highly privatised view of religion and salvation that has often been espoused by Christians' (1993: 55).

This notion of liturgy as somehow establishing another world and cosmology is important. Keifer argues that the quality of a liturgical act rests substantially on its nature as a public act contextualised within a redeemed cosmology, an event, 'that enacts a worldview, that perceptibly functions as embracing the whole of life' (Hughes and Francis, 1991: 71). Kathleen Hughes also suggests that private manipulations of the liturgy undermine its public function: 'We do not gather in the presence of the Holy One in order to discuss what we intend to do but to surrender to God's designs for us, a surrender that cannot be predetermined or controlled because it is not up to the initiative of the community' (1991: 45). Ritual action provides this means of transformation by its performance of a pattern for changed understanding and behaviour and through its invitation to the participants to act and live their lives according to the values encouraged in the rite. The process of transformation can only take place within a public realm.

As I have already referred to, Guéranger had realised in the nineteenth century that the most effective means of achieving a pastoral liturgy was through the strict observance of ritual codes and prescribed patterns. Rites had the capacity to restore any lost sense of sociality and community since 'symbols, gestures and rituals can be shared by all classes' and they 'reinforce the community' (quoted in Franklin, 1976, 1979). Guéranger believed that liturgy would be strong and effective if it found its witness within its ritual apparatus (Guéranger, 1995; Flanagan, 1991). For Peter Taylor Scott, this essentially public dimension to liturgy comes about by being thrown 'into a drama larger than ourselves, and liberated from the increasing privatism and boredom of contemporary egoism' (1980: 104). Like theatre, liturgy 'pulls persons out of themselves and thrusts them into the public enactment of drama' (1980: 104). For Taylor Scott, the major problem is that too often the liturgy becomes an instrument for individual enrichment. The error lies in seeing the liturgy as a sort of scaffolding upon which individuals climb and from which they hang their own preoccupations without any regard to its inner form and structure. Liturgy is only effective when its own formal structures are safeguarded.

Liturgical Language and Dress

The maintenance of a distinct form of liturgical language is essential to this public function. Removed from the quotidian and subjective intentions of participants, language is neither propositional nor colloquial. The continuance of the sacred polis of liturgy is achieved through a deprioritisation, not a heightening, of the psyche (Pickstock, 1993). The patterning set up by the language and action during the rite enables the event to become an iconic analogue of the sacred cosmos. Collective pronouns replace personal ones as they 'awaken in the participants an affective disposition which discloses a specific field of reference, fortifying the participant's general preparedness in concrete form, enabling "a form of constitutive receptivity... which prepares the soul to hear what they propose and effect"' (Pickstock, 1993: 125). The performance of the words engages participants in a dialogic structure whose repetition is 'axiomatic to the cohesion of its community, to its assertion of cosmos over chaos, and to its establishment of a sacred temporal order' (131–32).

Liturgical clothing carries a similar responsibility. The wearing of habits for many Religious Orders is one primary social, cultural and visible means of expressing spiritual commitment. 'Religious clothing represents a witness to a tradition that denies the logic of modernity and all its works. Profoundly unfashionable, religious clothing denotes a disconnection from the values of cosmopolitan life and a wish to affiliate with heavenly realities' (Flanagan, 1991: 101). In liturgy, actors are expected to live up to the ideals the garments represent, particularly to notions of innocence and purity. The vestments worn by priests before the Second Vatican Council were symbolic reminders of their office and dedication to lives of holiness. The white alb was symbolic of the purity of the soul, the cincture (the cord worn around the priest's waist) symbolic of preparation for hard work and the need to hold the passions in check, the maniple, (a band worn on the left arm) symbolic of the reward of conscientious effort. Such garments were invariably put on during the reciting of prayers like, 'May I deserve, O Lord, to bear the maniple of weeping and sorrow in order that I may joyfully reap the reward of my labours.'

The liturgically clothed actor within the liturgy does not simply imitate the actions and intentions of the role being enacted, but *is* the actual and public embodiment of the performance, being represented again in the present. Religious habits 'effect something more than a mere covering of the actor. The wearer is believed to convey a quality of virtue and dedication to its pursuit. He is believed to express a link to the super-personal, and is given a right of access to handle the holy when so dressed' (Flanagan, 1991: 101). Religious clothing denies the arguments of consumerism that change and fashion are needed. Commodity production rejects the view that there might exist forms of life that are exemplary and unaffected by cultural moods (Connerton, 1995).

Mnemonic Potential of the Body

With the increase of more mentalist and personalist approaches to worship, the status given to embodied performances of liturgy has been eroded. This has had important repercussions for its mnemonic function. Bodily ritualised performances of sacred prototypical events are an effective means of securing a strong mnemonic sense and of not allowing the Christian metanarrative to be forgotten. Liturgy must ensure that a religious community never forgets the story out of which it was formed and in relation

to which its participants lead their lives. The timeless quality of
bodily movement and gesture make present again an event which
was transient and always in danger of being forgotten. Liturgy is
celebratory because it makes a remembrance of the works of God
by not only recalling events but actualising them in the present.
Anamnesis takes place when the liturgical assembly is called by the
anaphora prayer to remember, as participants see the actions of
Christ 'done again' or actually do them themselves. When writing
of the Roman Catholic Mass and the Islamic Muharram festival of
the Shiites, Connerton reminds us of the importance of somatic
repetition: 'both re-enact a holy narrative by gestural repetitions,
in the one case through an orchestration of frenzied grief, in the
other through a slow choreography of calm and ordered
sequence' (1995: 69). The life of the liturgy does not consist in
surprises and innovations, but in solemn repetition (Flanagan,
1991: 234–57).

This sense of solemn repetition is particularly encoded in the
gestures and movements performed in the liturgy. The present
variation in the collective bodily actions of congregations in different
Roman Catholic churches reflects the confusion and devaluation
such actions have experienced since the reforms. For example,
although three forms of bowing still apply – a minor inclination of
the head during various prayers, a moderate bow when the altar
server presents the bread for consecration and a deep bow when
moving in front of the altar – such actions have become secondary to
more cognitive and catechetical approaches to liturgy. Although
Sacrosanctum Concilium itself claims that the actions of the priest and
Christ's body, the Church, are the actions of Christ himself and that
the liturgy is the 'summit' of all actions, prayerful embodiment has
become less important since the reforms. This is problematic since
the sacred ritualised spaces, objects and gestural movements used
during liturgy strengthen the ability to remember. The altar,
sanctuary or baptismal font become the stable pivots around which
the continuation of the past into the present occurs. As Peter
Cramer argues in his study of twelfth-century baptistries in northern
Italy, the baptistery itself became active and performative. It was not
merely a temporary thing, but a physical means of re-enacting death
and resurrection: 'The baptistery performs... it is a coincidence of
form and matter which addresses the senses as much as the mind, or
addresses that part of the mind which is caught up in the senses, its
power of intuition' (Cramer, 1993: 70). Their stability is able to
separate them off from other 'formless' spaces since,

the irruption of the sacred does not only project a fixed point into the formless fluidity of profane space, a centre into chaos; it also affects a break in plane, that is, it opens communication between the cosmic planes (between heaven and earth), and makes possible ontological passage from one mode of being to another (Eliade, 1987: 63).

The body is particularly suited to securing such stable remembering. Paul Connerton argues that 'incorporating practices' centred around the body are often able to convey and sustain social memories much better than 'inscribing practices'. Rites function primarily by the actions, gestures and movements of the body. A 're-enactment normally includes a simulacrum of the scene or situation recaptures' (1995: 72), and this depends for much of its persuasiveness on prescribed bodily behaviour. 'Incorporating practices' are appropriate to mnemonic activity since they do not exist independently of being performed and the event has to be done again if collective memory is to be sustained. Acquired in such a way as not to encourage criticism about their performances, rituals are able to dissuade reflexive questioning offering an insurance against doubt and insecurity.

Connerton takes the example of the changes which occurred after the French Revolution to make his point. He argues that a distinctive and successful ritual forgetting was achieved through the public execution of Louis XIV. The dynastic principle was destroyed not by the assassination nor imprisonment nor banishment, but by putting Louis to death in such a way that official public abhorrence of the institution of kingship was actually expressed. The revolutionaries needed to find some ritual process through which the aura of inviolability surrounding kingship could be explicitly repudiated. In contrast, 'inscribing practices' offer many more opportunities for disagreement and rejection. Connerton argues in a strongly Durkheimian fashion, that insightful groups will entrust to bodily practices the values and categories which they are most anxious to conserve. They know how well the past can be kept alive by such strategies (1995: 72–104).

For centuries Roman Catholic liturgy kept this tradition of introducing its ritual participants to a permanent and universal metanarrative to be told until the end of time. Through its ritual retelling of the story of Christ, it developed the means of offering each member of the Church a part in the performance of its own sacred drama (Navone, 1990; Loughlin, 1996). Through its ritual retelling of the Christian metanarrative, the Church had become

its embodiment or 'bearer' and was able to offer a thoroughly
embodied and collective means of encountering that story. By
participation in the rites of the Church the congregation became
no longer witnesses of the drama but characters within it learning
to adopt the character of Christ. This was no mere pageant, but
an experience of *anamnesis*. As Mannion comments about the
liturgy of Good Friday, 'the solemn Good Friday liturgy is
infinitely richer and more significant than any passion play or
historical drama. Its purpose is not only to call to mind the
original event of Calvary, but to recognise and celebrate the cross
standing forth in the Church and the world to-day' (Mannion,
1998: 89).

   This initiation into the story of salvation begins at baptism, as
the boundaries between the earthly and heavenly are loosened and
ritual participants become 'grafted into the paschal mystery of
Christ' (*SC*, paragraph 6). Candidates are then offered an
alternative way of seeing and being in the world. All ritualised
liturgies carry this task of reorientation as their re-enactments of
important moments within the Christian metanarrative allow
participants to embody Christ's message and to be transformed by
its telling. As characters within the drama they learn to be Christ
themselves by reverencing and participating in His actions
(Ratzinger, 1986). It is by such actions, for example, in bending
the knees and offering the sign of peace (just as Christ did) that
Christians are able to signify that they are 'imitating and adopting
the attitude of him who "humbled Himself unto death"'
(Ratzinger, 1986: 75). From baptism they move on to other ritual
spaces which tell the story further and encourage the attitude
released by the first rite. Such spaces allow the Christian metanarrative to unfold and enfold the participants, as they become
moulded by the action of the rite experienced through their
sensory bodies. By knowing and starting to live by that story, the
futureless claims of postmodernity become resisted and contra-
dicted.

   The Christian metanarrative repeatedly enacted within a new
ritual timescale ensures that participants are able to remember
their salvific past which cuts into the present and becomes set in
relation to the future. Ritual action establishes the sacred and
eschatological world over the quotidian, allowing 'eternity's
flowing back to the present' (Pickstock, 1993: 134; 1998). The
normal linear sequence of everyday living is changed into eschatological time where events become re-enacted and cyclically

remembered. Time and space are imbuded with a new dimension as chronological time (*chronos*) becomes transmuted into sacred time (*kairos*), allowing the action to be secured within a redemptive framework. In the premodern world the liturgical calendar secured the social and working lives of individuals. However, the sixteenth century saw the secularisation and manipulation of time for economic purposes which unpicked the ritual year by wiping out local festivals and major events from the Sarum calendar (Duffy, 1992: 385; Ward, 1997: xiv). A sense of the eschatological framework of time became further eroded as the new geological and zoological discoveries of the seventeenth, eighteenth and nineteenth centuries marginalised scriptures' understanding of time in relation to its doctrine of redemptive creation.

In the acceptance of their own foundationlessness, rituals share at least one thing with postmodernism. Never able to defend themselves against other stories by reason, they have always enacted their own tales again and again in the conviction that others will be drawn in. As Loughlin comments, 'Christianity is postmodern because it is not founded on anything other than the performance of its own story. It cannot be established against nihilism by reason, but only presented as a radical alternative, as something else altogether' (1996: 21). The biblical narrative performed during liturgies has no 'modern' reasons to convince those on the outside; things happen collectively on the inside and only then does the story acquire power and significance. The distinctive and alternative world set up by the rite is not made sense of by the intellect nor ever encaptured by the mind. Its ability to transform rests on the performance itself, enacted again and again, as it becomes imbibed, embodied and felt by the sensory bodies of the participants. Forgetting of the Christian metanarrative occurs when re-enactments are undermined or underplayed and when discursive language starts to rationalise the story being performed.

The Sensual Body

Further problems arose for ritualised worship during modernity as the body assumed a myriad of fluctuating meanings within differing social contexts. Connerton argues that since the Enlightenment, the body has been understood simply as an object, along with others, which merely responds to and obeys mechanical processes; it became an arbitrary bearer of meanings,

acknowledged only in an etheralised manner. Such understanding
failed to realise the potential the body might assume as a bearer of
social meaning and value. Besides being an agency of mnemonic
power, anthropological research on the sensual body indicates the
importance of the body for creating collectivity and unity. For
example, Largey and Watson have argued that the burning of
incense during liturgies might fulfil various functions. For
example, it is able to create an 'intersubjective we-feeling' among
participants involved in a rite. It is not possible 'not to participate
in the effervescence (or fellow-feeling) of the odour' (Howes,
1991: 134). Referring to Boulgne's research on the importance of
olfaction in ritual events, he suggests how incense provides for the
senses a symbolic representation of the invisible action that is
taking place. Odours tend to destabilise discursive reasoning and
invariably either attract or repel us in a distinctive manner. Odour
is also a strong means of securing transition from one state to
another and (like the sound of percussion) this frequently
depends on a primal sensory/emotive experience to 'fill in the
gaps of logical/semantic structures' and thus 'instigate transition
between social categories' (Howes, 1991: 133).

Howes argues that there is a vital connection between olfaction
and personal and collective transitions and uses Turner's work on
the liminal stage to support his position. This transition involves
the neophyte being dirty, smelly and indefinable, since odour
contains an elusive quality which is able to promote transition
from one definable realm to another. The synchronising effect of
odour is equally important; odours create both a sense of social
solidarity and produce social and emotional change. The decline
in the modern period of the importance of olfaction is located in
the new awareness of 'the self' which developed in the eighteenth
century (Classen, 1993). Kant omitted the sense of smell in his
aesthetics. The elevation of 'the self' in modernity reflected this
dissociation of odour with the emerging individual and placed its
focus primarily around the sense of sight. If there is an awakening
of the importance of odour within contemporary culture it is
primarily through consumerist participation in deodorising rituals.

Concluding, therefore, we can say that by emphasising the need
for active participation through 'conscious' understanding, the
reformers wasted an opportunity to focus on the sensual body as a
crucial means for such participation. We 'learn' to share in the
divine life of Christ primarily by the engagement of our bodily
senses, not by increasing attention being given to the stimulation

of our minds. The power of ritual is achieved through the symbolic use of the body. The nature of liturgical symbol means that in order for us to be participants, the whole human being must be engaged through the senses. This omission of the reformers was to have severe repercussions on later liturgical practices.

CONCLUDING REMARKS

What has been learnt from the previous chapters? At the start of this book, I suggested that a vital and constitutive dimension of liturgy was its ritual expression and that it needed to maintain its organic form if it was to achieve the necessary transformative effect upon those participating in the rite. Ritual expression contains specific, delineating characteristics which ensure its distinction and distancing from ordinary, quotidian occurrences. Primarily bodily, it operates within a highly prescribed code, tightly centred around spatial positionings, movement and gesture. This codified action implies a 'traditional' character which often resists change and alteration. A Christian rite, therefore, is a collective means of enabling the self to develop in relation to the sacred world the rite upholds and through which it is invited into the story of redemptive Christianity. It has the capacity to re-enact that story which it passes on from one generation to the next.

I argued that this emphasis on the importance of the symbolic body within the context of highly ritualised liturgy was severely eroded at the Second Vatican Council. What the Council Fathers emphasised above all else was the need for liturgy to engage the people of God through a much more cognitive approach and by means of more active participation. They seemed to misunderstand the creative potential of ritual and suggested that 'ritualism' had become the norm. An oppressive and retrograde tendency to perform liturgy mechanically had characterised significant historical developments within Roman Catholic worship. Radical change, the reformers believed, was obviously necessary.

In discussing this changed understanding of the nature of liturgy, however, my plea throughout this book has not been to advocate a return to a pre-Vatican II model of Roman Catholic worship. Although I have pointed to some lessons that might be

196

learnt from the worship of the Middle Ages, I have also been concerned to defend the view that a better future for Roman Catholic liturgy might well reside, not in attempts to explain its meaning (and in the process devalue its symbolic richness), but in a recognition of the potential of the symbolic body within ritual forms. In my view, future discussions about worship need to revolve much more around its intrinsic nature as *somatic actions to be performed* rather than texts to be deciphered.

Restoring the Significance of the Liturgical Body

Recent social and anthropological research, as I have shown, indicates that the body has assumed considerable semiotic power in contemporary culture and reflects a myriad of conflicting assumptions dependent upon its context and position. It would be a mistake, therefore, to underestimate the symbolic and beneficial power the ritualised body might signify in future liturgical expression and contexts. Bodily gesture and movement can assume considerable importance within the sacred spaces of worship. These corporeal modes of expression need to be explored more fully. It would be ironic if the Roman Catholic Church, so insistent on the need for unity and the 'common good' (*Common Good*, 1997), in what it sees as a highly fragmented age, continued to underplay the unifying power of ritualised liturgy, which Durkheim and Guéranger had so skilfully identified in the nineteenth and twentieth centuries.

I have suggested throughout this book that the appropriation of modern assumptions, especially those concerned with subjectivity (in particular the 'knowing autonomous self' and the use of private experience), have tended to dominate both twentieth-century theology and Christian worship. The objective 'form' that a rite needs to preserve in order to transform individuals and communities, has become increasingly invaded by a series of 'personal' and erratic interruptions, encouraged and endorsed by 'official' recommendations of the Church itself. It is not surprising that the sense of identity which Roman Catholicism secured so successfully in the past, strongly underpinned and supported by its uniformity of worship, became significantly eroded as more individualised liturgies increased (Archer, 1986). No longer are the 'bodies' of Roman Catholics doing and acting the same things with any degree of commonality in their liturgy, as they did before the reforms. This diversity of bodily response testifies alone to the growing privatisation of liturgy in the present age. The priest and the people continue to invent what *they* consider to be the most appropriate means of worshipping. Such tendencies similarly apply to liturgical language when members of the congregation are heard to override the 'sexist' vocabulary of the Church with their own inclusive corrections.

I discussed how some of the dominant cultural and social assumptions of modernity began to influence Christian worship. It is not (as Kathryn Tanner remarks about the issue of modern christologies) that responding to such assumptions is always inappropriate or disastrous, but rather that such assumptions have often never been given 'the requisite critical scrutiny' (Gunton, 1997: 248) they deserve. For example, as I have indicated, the emphasis accorded to instrumental reason after the Enlightenment, as the primary agency for 'mastering' social and natural worlds, was clearly reflected in the concerted moves by members of the Liturgical Movement and the Second Vatican Council to 'rationalise' and explain, often through a process of catechesis, God's story as performed and 'told' during the liturgy. The worship of God became a much more explanatory lesson, whereby individuals were encouraged to take hold of and grasp the meaning of the liturgy. The performance, on its own, seemed wanting and insufficient. There were lasting repercussions involved in such shifts.

Control or Chaos?

I suggested that this approach frequently resulted in strategies to encourage a form of 'control by explanation' over the liturgy by priests and lay participants. It was as if the symbolic ambiguity of the liturgical performance itself would somehow only be made effective and meaningful if attempts to stake out its significance, primarily through discursive reasoning, occurred. I argued how Bauman has already warned us how the use of instrumental reason in the modern period invariably became a means of securing power over other people and other 'things'. This type of dominating power allowed men during modernity to imagine that they were somehow being 'successful' when often, in fact, they were involved in some of the worst acts of self-deception and oppression. Roman Catholic worship since the Second Vatican Council is less guilty, but it does show signs of a far more 'rational' and controlling approach. Such attempts to 'tame the lion of Judah' became rooted in attempts by priests and people to aggregate the worship of God to themselves. Once they started to imagine that they needed to understand what the liturgy really meant, they inevitably began to take control of it and to imagine they were 'safe' in its midst.

Any such tendencies betray the very grounds on which liturgy is built. The 'knowing subject' within liturgy is always invited into an arena in which she or he is confronted by a radically alternative world – sacred, out of time, within an unfamiliar space. A sense of being 'lost' and an experience of 'unknowing' often characterises such times. The experience of 'chaos' and of being located on the 'edge of darkness' that Kavanagh speaks about (1984, 1992) is not a cause for panic, but allows the participant to enter a liminal state of 'nakedness' so that transformation may occur. Turner has demonstrated well how such experiences lead to a new ontological self and to a new identity (Turner, 1967; 1974). The modern subjectivist tendency to claw back from any experience of threshold liminality in which the self is laid bare and stripped of those things which are familiar, rests easily within a culture which advocates progress through a cognitivist and precise classificatory form of 'knowing'. But, as we know, darkness and transcendence are never so easily explained.

I also argued that the Roman Catholic tradition of worship which had been historically so highly attentive to the authoritative and transformative potential of ritual, was abruptly taken in another direction during the period leading up to and beyond the Second Vatican Council. This liturgical turn centred around giving supreme importance to the mind, away from the body, which openly reflected many of the dominant assumptions about the shifting axis of power between the mind and body in the modern period. As a result, a far more classificatory, instrumental and cerebral approach began to characterise modern Roman Catholic worship.

As a consequence, pastoral practices in relation to liturgy became largely based on false premises. Attempts to see to the needs of 'modern man' invariably focused on participation and catechesis. A much greater emphasis on a congregation's understanding of liturgy was to take place in the pursuit of a more pastorally framed liturgy. With this shift in direction, I argued that such cognitive approaches to worship resulted in far more arid forms of worship. They ignored the creative potentialities of ritual expression and deconstructed the essentially symbolic nature of worship. A degeneratively personalised and politicised liturgy often emerged from such adaptations, exacerbated by a loss of the collective mnemonic nature of worship which had been previously maintained primarily by the bodily actions, gestures and movements of the celebrant and congregation. The Christian metanarrative was beginning to be forgotten and a sense of the sacred, which Durkheim had argued was so necessary for the flourishing of religion, was slowly ebbing away.

Learning from the Past

If there is any returning to the past, then like Guéranger, we might like to situate ourselves in the Middle Ages to discover an experience of the sacred and transcendent. Liturgy was at the centre of the medieval religious and social world. Issues of life and death revolved around the Church's rites, the supreme means by which life was made sense of and individual destinies given hope. The ritualised body was at the hub of devotional and spiritual practices, just as it had been during the first centuries of Christian sacramental worship. The body itself became a symbol and measurement of spiritual advancement. As Mellor and Shilling write in their critique of the shifting historical patterns of re-forming the body, 'Church rituals stimulated a structured opening of the medieval body to its sacred surroundings, exhausted the meaning of discourse, and made the flesh into a route for religious experience' (1997: 38). The practice of Christianity entailed an embodied experience.

In contrast, the modern period became dominated by a far more rationalist and instrumental approach to discovering knowledge and truth. The Protestant emphasis on the word coupled with the emergence of a highly suspicious attitude to the body, ensured that a far more cerebral approach to the sacred occurred, with the types of bodily ritual practices which had been prevalent during the Middle Ages starting to be equated with superstition or even sorcery. Descartes' later influence and the increase of more 'inscribing practices' after the invention of printing, exacerbated the view that the mind rather than the body was the most appropriate site for self-identity and religious formation.

The ensuing attempts at cognitive control during the advancement of the modern period resulted (not surprisingly) in largely neurotic operations of social classification. Nothing was to be left unexamined or unturned; the taming of nature and the body had begun. Doubt and ambiguity had to be eradicated through a process of systematic *mathesis*. This was to have harmful and damaging effects as a process of bodily disengagement from the 'natural' world unfolded relentlessly. As Kevin Vanhoozer writes of the trajectory of reason within the modern period, this resulted in a process of disengagement from the world: 'To be rational or "objective" is to position oneself over and against the world "out there"' (1997: 168). Continuing this theme, I sought to show how the Enlightenment narrative of rationality, although having immense social and cultural influence, eventually itself came under increasing attack. The 'death of reason' thesis became a dominant feature of many 'postmodern' critiques. Instrumental reason began to be openly exposed for not delivering the plan of 'progress' it claimed it would and for reducing human culture to the information one might find on a computer disc. The fleshy self could not be so easily ignored as the Enlightenment thinkers had suggested.

In one sense, therefore, this book itself might be regarded as a kind of 'postmodern' liturgical critique of those modern forms of worship which attempt to give precedence to more cerebral approaches which prioritise the mind over the body and reflect an inadequate and limited understanding of the body and its implications for ritualised forms of liturgy. The mistakes which have been made in worship had been seen before in the cultural and political programmes which dominated the post-Enlightenment era. Many postmodern critiques have helped liturgists to re-think the direction worship might take in the future.

The Future Direction of Roman Catholic Worship

What can be done in the future? It has become apparent that this shift from a more objective tradition of corporeal worship to a more internalised, personal and individualised cognitive model prevalent during the 'modern' period, reflects the more general process of 'detraditionalisation' identified by sociologists. Any sense of an Augustinian acceptance of a pregiven order of the world was rapidly replaced by more 'reliable', modern, secular assumptions about inventing and constructing order. Clearly, there is no easy going back to such an Augustinian view of the world.

Religious groups themselves continue to encourage a more personal understanding of faith, transposing authority from 'without' to 'within' (Heelas, 1996, Heelas, Lash and Morris, 1996). This 'inner movement', defended in terms of personal authenticity, clearly reflects the process of increased reflexivity which became a characteristic of the modern period. Many of the criticisms of more traditional approaches to religion rest upon their perceived authoritarian and exclusivist stances, which they contend offer tradition for tradition's sake and squash any signs of creative individuality. As Heelas argues in his analysis of the process of detraditionalisation, such responses are highly suspicious of the order of the self, which had always been in the premodern world 'by definition collectivistic or communal' (Heelas, Lash and Morris, 1996: 4). Consequently, they ignore Durkheim's claim that 'the individual personality is lost in the depths of the social mass' (quoted in Heelas, Lash and Morris, 1996: 4).

However, in contrast to such tendencies, I have discussed how ritual has an inherent capacity to achieve the kinds of personal and social goals many are aspiring to in the postmodern age. Once ritual began to suffer a severe loss of status during the modern period problems arose, particularly in relation to the construction of the 'self' and the formation of a culture which was able to enjoy shared values collectively. Inherently 'traditional', it had served Christianity well in maintaining a sacred and timeless order. Never corrosive upon the transformation of the self but rather precisely organised around it, ritual expression, maintained by a unique 'form', was able to secure corporate unity *and* existential stability. Rites existed over and above individuals and at the same time were performed by, and penetrated into, the heart of their fleshy selves. The self and society were not abandoned but renewed in collective rites. Difficulties only arose when new and experimental liturgical devices and strategies became staged and the Church itself forgot the significance of its own ritual past; freedom to experiment with or adapt traditional rites largely resulted in more confusion. Ineffective liturgies increased because rites, by their very nature, are inviolate and dissuade individualised alteration and challenge.

In the modern period, the traditional ritual forms of Catholic worship began to be altered since it was assumed that ritual itself was obstructive to the pastoral aims the liturgical reformers had set themselves. Ritual was regarded as being no longer an effective vehicle for addressing modern concerns. However, developments outside the Christian Church were to tell another story. To suggest that postmodern people do not indulge in and respond to 'traditional' forms of ritual expression is untenable. For example, the new age movement, the *bête noir* of established Christianity, often reworks traditional forms to its own ends. This network of associated groups is at times highly dependent on past narratives and the reinvention of ritual practices. It invariably draws on traditions, while bypassing their more dogmatic beliefs and moral teachings (Heelas, 1996b). Within more secular contexts, too, ritual often finds expression, particularly at times of intense doubt or fragility after tragic events. Davie's account (1995) of the highly ritualised behaviour at the Anfield football ground after the Hillsborough disaster and the numerous ritual layings of flowers at the spots where people have been killed or murdered suggests that rituals have far from disappeared in modern consciousness and still hold existentialist meaning and importance. The national response to the death of Diana, Princess of Wales, tells a similar story. Such rituals might be far removed from those ecclesiastically managed during the medieval period, but they do point to the need for many people to mark important stages in life with ritualised actions which help secure order and meaning.

If a more cognitive approach to worship has characterised the modern period, then as the next millennium begins it is tempting to surmise what new forms worship might take and what encouragement there might be from the various churches. Outside Catholicism much more emotionally virulent forms of worship seem to have erupted. The charismatic movement has demonstrably shown how the god Dionysis has become far more influential than the god Apollo. Its body language and attempts at more emotional contact with the divine suggest a return to new forms of embodied liturgical experience, even if far removed from the controlled but nevertheless bodily 'feel' of medieval Christian worship. Within the broad range of liturgical expressions in the Anglican Church perhaps the most significant is the lesson to be learnt from The Nine O'Clock Service in Sheffield. Originally endorsed by the Anglican Church in its early days, it reflected an institutional move to make worship much more technologically vibrant, 'theatrical' and relevant to the contemporary age. Influenced by the worship of the Spirituality Centre run by Matthew Fox, the Planetary Mass attempted to be (according to its leader the Rev. Chris Brain) a weekly celebration of life, ritual celebrations and a time of repentance (Howard, 1996). The demise of the service, associated with the sexual abuse of some of

the congregation by Chris Brain, testifies to the potentially
dangerous attempts to present worship in the form of a stylistically
brilliant hi-tech spectacle.

Experimentation with new forms of liturgy continues within
Roman Catholicism. Relevance and appeal to individual
worshippers is still common. For example, the practice of
repeating the Christian name of the communicant (if known),
before saying 'the body of Christ', is still widespread, one attempt
among many of trying to make the liturgy more personal and
individually meaningful. But there is a growing field of opinion
which suggests that there are numerous lessons to be learnt from
the liturgical changes which have taken place over the last thirty
years. As I have documented, more recent criticisms of Roman
Catholic worship make a plea for a return to a more formalised
rite, while recognising the good work the Second Vatican Council
did as a whole.

For critics such as Nichols and Duffy, as well as newly formed
groups like the Society for Catholic Liturgy, the way forward is
to stem the tide of liturgical 'philistinism' and secularism which
they claim has occurred since the Council. Nichols' measures
include encouraging the use of manuals like Elliott's *Ceremonies
of the Modern Roman Rite: The Eucharist and the Liturgy of the Hours*
which give helpful rubrical direction and more emphasis to the
visual and aural setting of the Mass (Nichols, 1996: 118). He also
argues for the redesignation of the Missal of 1969 as the *ritus
communis* to act as a solid foundation for further liturgical development (1966: 122). Other criticisms revolve around a move
away from 'inscribing practices' in liturgy towards more 'incorporating practices.' Numerous 'inscribing practices' need to be
replaced by an emphasis on symbolic action and gesture, accompanied by a more thorough engagement of the senses. For many
in the churches it might require no more than raising the eyes
from the text of a service book in order for the senses to
become engaged in a rite, through sight and sound, movement
and gesture, colour and odour. A more deliberate attention to
the significance of communal posture, gesture and mutuality in
liturgical assemblies is also recognised, particularly by the
Women's Movement, as one of the methods by which a new
symbolic liturgy might occur. In other words, a renewed
emphasis on Christian anthropology as a foundation for liturgical thinking is now being advanced as one of the most fruitful
ways forward in worship.

Educational Implications

Such criticism is not solely confined to liturgical thinking. Cliff Harris has already reminded us of the important place ritual can assume in Religious Education. He argues, 'Far too little attention has been paid to ritual in the past' (1992: 11). Within recent educational debates focus has been redirected to those forms of meaning-making which children experience before they learn to read and write. Kress' research (1997) into the kinds of activities young children engage in emphasises its two, three and four dimensional means, as well as the different methods used by children to open up different bodily engagements with the world: 'If we concede that speech and writing give rise to particular forms of thinking, then we should at least ask whether touch, smell, taste, feel, also give rise to their specific forms of thinking' (1997: xvii–xviii). He rejects the sparse understanding of 'cognition' that exists at present which tends to separate thought from emotion, feeling and affect. As I suggested in my earlier analysis of Foucault, so Kress argues that 'Just at the point when electronic technologies are promising or threatening (or both) to take us further from our bodies, it may be essential to insist on all the potentials which we have as bodily humans and which, for most of us, we are not encouraged to develop and use' (1997: xviii).

David Hay's research into children's spirituality similarly endorses the view that Religious Education must find new ways of engaging the body as well as the mind. The modern culture of rationalism, based largely upon Cartesian dualism, has repressed the innate spirituality of many young people with the result that many male pupils at the age of ten are terrified of expressing views about their own spiritual experiences. The social construction of scepticism is the obstacle RE specialists must deal with if they are to be effective teachers. Hay argues that 'embodied knowing' is one of the most natural means of learning to understand and appreciate the world. It is 'the natural knowing of young children before they become inducted into the Cartesian intellectualism that is our cultural heritage' (1997: 9). Like Whelan (1993), he endorses the positive value of somatic experience and its implications for educational and spiritual development.

Returning to a Sense of the Sacred

At a time when sociologists and cultural theorists are suggesting that consumption is the axis upon which identity is framed in the postmodern world, the opportunities for people to experience a sense of the sacred are becoming more rare. If the Christian Church is to offer its members anything of lasting value in such a culture, then it is surely through its attempts to perform the story of salvation in as effective and engaging manner as possible. Its liturgical function, in other words, becomes vital to its mission, its vitality and its flourishing.

There are hopeful signs that this function is being revived as the third millennium begins (Caldecott, 1998). The Cartesian cognitivism which dominated earlier modern reforms of the liturgy is beginning to be increasingly rejected in favour of a new model which gives due weight to notions of embodiment, symbolism and ritual. As I discussed in the previous chapters, a new 'liturgy of embodiment' is now being recognised as the most appropriate and inventive way forward for the Church. It is now accepted far more readily than before that ritual patterns which employ bodily gestures and movement are not merely instrumental or educative, but life-giving and potentially self-transformative means and vehicles for an experience of the divine. Social anthropology is beginning at last to be acknowledged as a close ally of liturgy. As we move towards the next stage of liturgical revision, there are strong indications that the dry mentalism and cerebral focus which have characterised much Roman Catholic liturgy since the 1960s is being pushed aside for a renewed liturgical vision, one that endorses Tertullian's conviction that we will most readily respond to the Spirit of God when we 'Look to the body' (quoted in Brown, 1991: 77).

BIBLIOGRAPHY

Ackroyd, P. (1998) *The Life of St Thomas More*. London: Chatto and Windus.

Adam, A. (1981) *The Liturgical Year: Its History and its Meaning After the Reform of the Liturgy*. New York: Pueblo Publishing Co.

Anderson, B. (1991) *Imagined Communities: Reflections on the Origin and Spread of Nationalism*. Revised edn. London: Verso.

Arbuckle, G. (1985) 'Dress and Worship: Liturgies for the Culturally Dispossessed' *Worship* 59 (5): 426–35.

Arbuckle, G. (1990) *Earthing the Gospel*. London: Geoffrey Chapman.

Archer, A. (1986) *The Two Catholic Churches: A Study in Oppression*. London: SCM Press.

Ariès, P. (1974) *Western Attitudes Towards Death from the Middle Ages to the Present*. Baltimore: The Johns Hopkins University Press.

Ariès, P. (1981) *The Hour of Our Death*. New York: Alfred A. Knopf.

Asad, T. (1993) *Genealogies of Religion: Discipline and Power in Christianity and Islam*. Baltimore: The Johns Hopkins University Press.

Austin, J. (1975) *How To Do Things With Words*. Oxford: Oxford University Press.

Barauna, W. (ed.) (1966) *The Liturgy of Vatican II. Vol. 1*. Chicago: Franciscan Herald Press.

Barba, E. and Savarese, N. (1991) *A Dictionary of Theatre Anthropology: The Secret Art of the Performer*. London: Routledge.

Baudrillard, J. (1983) *Simulations*. New York: Semiotext(e).

Baudrillard, J. (1993) *Symbolic Exchange and Death*. London: Sage.

Bauman, Z. (1987) *Legislators and Interpreters*. Cambridge: Polity Press.

Bauman, Z. (1989) *Modernity and the Holocaust.* Cambridge: Polity Press.

Bauman, Z. (1991) *Modernity and Ambivalence.* Cambridge: Polity Press.

Bauman, Z. (1992a) *Intimations of Postmodernity.* London: Routledge.

Bauman, Z. (1992b) *Mortality, Immortality and Other Life Strategies.* Cambridge: Polity Press.

Bauman, Z. (1993) *Postmodern Ethics.* Oxford: Blackwell.

Beck, U. (1992) *Risk Society: Towards a New Modernity.* London: Sage.

Belenky, M., Clincy, B., Goldberger, N. and Tarule, J. (1986) *Women's Ways of Knowing: The Development of Self, Voice and Mind.* New York: Basic Books.

Bell, C. (1992) *Ritual Theory, Ritual Practice.* Oxford: Oxford University Press.

Bellah, R., Maddsen, R., Sullivan, W. M., Swindler, A. and Tipton, S. M. (1985) *Habits of the Heart: Individualism and Commitment in American Life.* New York: Harper and Row.

Bentley, E. (ed.) (1992) *The Theory of the Modern Stage.* Harmondsworth: Penguin.

Berger, P. (1972) *The Sacred Canopy: Elements of a Sociological Theory of Religion.* New York: Anchor Books.

Berger, P. (1974) *The Homeless Mind: Modernisation and Consciousness.* Harmondsworth: Penguin.

Berger, T. (1990) 'The Women's Movement as a Liturgical Movement: A Form of Inculturation?' *Studia Liturgica* 20 (1): 55–64.

Berman, M. (1982) *All that is Solid Melts Into Air: The Experience of Modernity.* London: Verso.

Berry, J. (ed.) (1993). 'Liberating Worship – Pastoral Liturgy and the Empowering of Women' in Graham, E. (ed.) *Life Cycles: Women and Pastoral Care.* London: SPCK.

Berry, P. and Wernick, A. (eds) (1992) *Shadow of Spirit: Postmodernism and Religion.* London: Routledge.

Binski, P. (1996) *Medieval Death: Ritual and Representation.* London: British Museum Press.

Blondel, M. (1984) *Action: Essay on a Critique of Life and a Science of Practice.* trans. Blanchette, O. Notre Dame, IN: University of Notre Dame Press.

Bossy, J. (1983) 'The Mass as a Social Institution', *Past and Present* 100: 29–61.

Bossy, J. (1985) *Christianity in the West 1400–1700.* Oxford: Oxford University Press.

Bourdieu, P. (1997) *Language and Symbolic Power.* Cambridge: Polity Press.

Bouyer, L. (1965) *Life and Liturgy.* London: Sheed and Ward.

Bouyer, L. (1969) *The Decomposition of Catholicism.* New York: Franciscan Herald Press.

Boyle, N. (1995) 'The End of History', Part 1, *New Blackfriars* March, 76 (891): 109–19.

Bradley, I. (1995) *The Power of Sacrifice.* London: Darton, Longman and Todd.

Bradshaw, P. (1992) *The Search for the Origins of Christian Worship.* London: SPCK.

Bradshaw, P. (1996) *Early Christian Worship: A Basic Introduction to Ideas and Practice.* London: SPCK.

Bradshaw, P. and Spinks, B. (eds) (1993) *Liturgy in Dialogue.* London: SPCK.

Brittan, A. (1989) *Masculinity and Power.* Oxford: Blackwell.

Brown, D. and Loades, A. (eds) (1995) *The Sense of the Sacramental: Movement and Measure in Art and Music, Place and Time.* London: SPCK.

Brown, D. and Loades, A. (eds) (1996) *Christ: The Sacramental Word: Incarnation Sacrament and Poetry.* London: SPCK.

Brown, P. (1991) *The Body and Society.* London: Faber and Faber.

Bugnini, A. (1990) *The Reform of the Liturgy 1948–1975.* Collegeville: The Liturgical Press.

Burgard, C. (1960) *Scripture in the Liturgy.* London: Challoner Publications.

Burnham, A. (1994) 'Maundy Thursday Chrism', *Theology* March/April 114–20.

Burrett, A. (1966) 'The Revision of the Rites of the Mass' in Crichton, J. (ed.) *The Liturgy and the Future.* Tenbury Wells: Fowler Wright.

Bynum Walker, C. W. (1987) *Holy Feast and Holy Fast: The Religious Significance of Food to Medieval Women.* Berkeley: University of California.

Bynum Walker, C. W. (1991) *Fragmentation and Redemption: Essays on Gender and the Human Body in Medieval Religion.* New York: Zone Books.

Caldecott, S. (1998) 'Conclusion: The Spirit of the Liturgical Movement' in Caldecott, S. (ed) *Beyond the Prosaic: Renewing the Liturgical Movement.* Edinburgh: T&T Clark.

Cameron, E. (1991) *The European Reformation*. Oxford: Oxford University Press.

Campbell, C. (1987) *The Romantic Ethic and the Spirit of Modern Consumerism*. Oxford: Blackwell.

Caron, C. (1993) *To Make and Make Again: Feminist Ritual Thealogy*. New York: Crossroads.

Chadwick, O. (1990) *The Reformation*. Harmondsworth: Penguin.

Chadwick, O. (1993) *The Secularization of the European Mind in the Nineteenth Century*. Cambridge: Cambridge University Press.

Chandlee, H. (1972) 'The Liturgical Movement' in Davies, J. G. (ed.) *A Dictionary of Liturgy and Worship*. London: SCM Press.

Chapman, R. and Rutherford, J. (eds) (1989) *Male Order: Unwrapping Masculinity*. London: Lawrence and Wishart.

Chauvet, L-M. (1995) 'The Liturgy in Symbolic Space' in Chauvet, L-M. and Lumbala, F. (eds) *Concilium: Liturgy and the Body* June (3). London: SCM Press.

Chiffley, E. (1998) 'The Altar: Place of Sacrifice and Sacred Space in the Religious Building' in *Altar and Sacrifice*. The Proceedings of the Third International Colloquium of Historical, Canonical and Theological Studies on the Roman Catholic Liturgy. London: The St Austin Press.

Chupungco, A. (1989) *Liturgies of the Future: The Process and Methods of Inculturation*. New York: Paulist Press.

Classen, C. (1993) *Worlds of Sense: Exploring the Senses in History and Across Cultures*. London: Routledge.

Collins, P. (1992) *Bodying Forth: Aesthetic Liturgy*. New York: Paulist Press.

Connerton, P. (1995) *How Societies Remember*. Cambridge: Cambridge University Press.

Congar, Y. (1985) *Lay People in the Church*. London: MD.

Cramer, P. (1993) *Baptism and Change in the Early Middle Ages*. Cambridge: Cambridge University Press.

Crichton, J. (1966) *The Liturgy and the Future*. London: Fowler Wright.

Crichton, J. (1995) 'Worshipping with Awe and Reverence', *Priests and People* December, 9 (12): 451–55.

Crichton, J., Winstone, H. and Ainslie, J. (eds) (1979) *English Catholic Worship: Liturgical Renewal in England since 1900*. London: Geoffrey Chapman.

Critchley, S. (1994) *The Ethics of Deconstruction: Derrida and Levinas*. Oxford: Blackwell.

Curran, P. (1989) *Grace Before Meals: Food Ritual and Body Discipline in Convent Culture.* Urbana and Chicago: University of Illinois Press.

Daly, G. (1980) *Transcendence and Immanence: A Study in Catholic Modernism and Integralism.* Oxford: Clarendon Press.

Davie, G. (1995) *Religion in Britain since 1945: Believing Without Belonging.* Oxford: Blackwell.

Davies, J. G. (ed.) (1978) *A Dictionary of Liturgy and Worship.* London: SCM Press.

Davis, C. (1994) *Religion and the Making of Society: Essays in Social Theology.* Cambridge: Cambridge University Press.

de Coppet, D. (1992) *Understanding Rituals.* London: Routledge.

Descartes, R. (1983) *Discourse on Method and the Meditations.* Trans. Sutcliffe, F. Harmondsworth: Penguin.

Dix, G. (1983, 1945) *The Shape of the Liturgy.* New York: Seabury Press.

Dollimore, J. (1992) *Sexual Dissidence: Augustine to Wilde, Freud to Foucault.* Oxford: Clarendon Press.

Douglas, M. (1966) *Purity and Danger: An Analysis of Concepts of Pollution and Taboo.* London: Routledge and Kegan Paul.

Douglas, M. (1970) *Natural Symbols: Explorations in Cosmology.* London: Barrie and Jenkins.

Drew, M. (1998) 'The Spirit or the Letter? Vatican II and Liturgical Reform' in Caldecott, S. (eds) *Beyond the Prosaic.* Edinburgh: T&T Clark.

Dreyer, E. (1983) 'Bonaventure' in *A Dictionary of Christian Spirituality.* London: SCM Press.

Driver, T. (1991) *The Magic of Ritual: Our Need for Liberating Rites that Transform Our Lives and Communities.* New York: HarperSanFrancisco.

Duffy, E. (1992) *The Stripping of the Altars: Traditional Religion in England c. 1400–c. 1580.* New Haven: Yale University Press.

Duffy, E. (1995a) 'An Open Letter to the Bishops', *Priests and People* March, 9 (30): 112–16.

Duffy, E. (1995b) 'Holy Pictures', *Priests and People* December, 9 (12): 462–67.

Duffy, E. (1996a) 'The Lay Appropriation of the Sacraments', *New Blackfriars* January, 77 (899): 53–68.

Duffy, E. (1996b) 'Praying in Bad Language: The Stripping of the Liturgy', *The Tablet* July: 882–83.

Dupré, L. (1993) *Passage to Modernity: An Essay in the Hermeneutics of Nature and Culture.* New Haven: Yale University Press.

Durkheim, E. (1951 [1897]) *Suicide*. London: Routledge and Kegan Paul.

Durkheim, E. (1995 [1912]) *The Elementary Forms of Religious Life*. London: The Free Press.

Eagleton, T. (1991) *Ideology: An Introduction*. London: Verso.

Eagleton, T. (1997) *Illusions of Postmodernism*. Oxford: Blackwell.

Easthope, A. and McGowan, K. (eds), (1992) *A Critical and Cultural Theory Reader*. Buckingham: Open University Press.

Eliade, M. (1957 [1987]) *The Sacred and the Profane: The Significance of Religious Myth, Symbolism, and Ritual Within Life and Culture*. San Diego: Harcourt Brace Company.

Emsley, N. (1998) 'Light in the Easter Vigil', *Priests and People* March 12 (3): 105–09.

Falk, P. (1994) *The Consuming Body*. London: Sage.

Featherstone, M. (1991) *Consumer Culture and Postmodernism*. London: Sage.

Featherstone, M. (1995) *Undoing Culture: Globalization, Postmodernism and Identity*. London: Sage.

Featherstone, M., Hepworth, M. and Turner, B. (eds) (1995) *The Body: Social Process and Cultural Theory*. London: Sage.

Fenn, R. (1987) *The Dream of the Perfect Act*. London: Tavistock.

Fenn, R. (1992) *Liturgies and Trials: The Secularisation of Religious Language*. Oxford: Blackwell.

Fenn, R. (1997) *The End of Time: Religion, Ritual and the Forging of the Soul*. London: SPCK.

Ferguson, H. (1992) *The Religious Transformation of Western Society*. London: Routledge.

Flanagan, K. (1981) 'Competitive Assemblies for God: Lies and Mistakes in Liturgy', *Research Bulletin*. University of Birmingham Institute for the Study of Worship and Religious Architecture: 20–69.

Flanagan, K. (1987) 'Resacralizing the Liturgy' in 'Class and Church. After Ghetto Catholicism. Facing the Issues Raised by Anthony Archer's *The Two Catholic Churches*', *New Blackfriars* 68 (802): 64–75.

Flanagan, K. (1990) *Sociology and Liturgy: Re-Presentations of the Holy*. London: Macmillan Press.

Flanagan, K. (1996a) *The Enchantment of Sociology: A Study of Theology and Culture*. London: Macmillan Press.

Flanagan, K. (1996b) 'Postmodernity and Culture: Sociological

Wagers of the Self in Theology' in Flanagan, K. and Jupp, P. (eds) *Postmodernity, Sociology and Religion*. London: Macmillan Press.

Flanagan, K. and Jupp, P. (eds) (1996) *Postmodernity, Sociology and Religion*. London: Macmillan Press.

Flannery, A. (ed.), (1992) *Vatican Council II: The Conciliar and Post Conciliar Documents. Revised Edn. Study Edition*. Dublin: Dominican Publications.

Flood, G. (1997) *An Introduction to Hinduism*. Cambridge: Cambridge University Press.

Foley, J. (1994) *Creativity and the Roots of Liturgy*. Washington: The Pastoral Press.

Fornas, J. (1995) *Cultural Theory and Late Modernity*. London: Sage.

Foucault, M. (1965) *Madness and Civilisation: A History of Insanity in the Age of Reason*. London: Tavistock.

Foucault, M. (1981) *The History of Sexuality. Vol. 1: An Introduction*. Harmondsworth: Penguin.

Foucault, M. (1991) *Discipline and Punish: The Birth of the Prison*. Harmondsworth: Penguin.

Franklin, W. (1976) 'Guéranger and Pastoral Liturgy: A Nineteenth Century Context', *Worship* 50 (2): 146–62.

Franklin, W. (1979) 'The 19th Century Liturgical Movement', *Worship* 53 (1): 12–39.

Fromm, E. (1995) *The Fear of Freedom*. London: Routledge.

Gamber, K. (1993) *The Reform of the Roman Liturgy: Its Problems and Background*. California: Una Voce Press.

Geertz, C. (1973) *The Interpretation of Cultures*. New York: Basic Books.

Gellner, E. (1992a) *Reason and Culture*. Oxford: Blackwell.

Gellner, E. (1992b) *Postmodernism, Reason and Religion*. London: Routledge.

Giddens, A. (1990) *The Consequences of Modernity*. Cambridge: Polity Press.

Giddens, A. (1991) *Modernity and Self-Identity*. Cambridge: Polity Press.

Gill, R. (1989) *Competing Convictions*. London: SCM Press.

Girard, R. (1977) *Violence and the Sacred*. Baltimore: The Johns Hopkins University Press.

Gledhill, R. (1995) 'Church's Easter Message Dispenses with the Cross', *The Times*, 10 March.

214   *Losing the Sacred*

Gluckman, M. (1963) *Order and Rebellion in Tribal Africa.* Glencoe, Ill. Free Press.

Goffmann, E. (1990) *The Presentation of the Self in Everyday Life.* Harmondsworth: Penguin.

Gombrich, E. (1949) 'Ritualised Liturgy and Expression in Art', *The Philosophical Transactions of the Royal Society of London.* Series B: 393–401.

Graham, E. (1995) *Making the Difference: Gender, Personhood and Theology.* London: Mowbray.

Grey, M. (1989) *Redeeming the Dream: Feminism, Redemption and the Christian Tradition.* London: SPCK.

Grey, M. (1997) 'Christian Theology, Spirituality and the Curriculum'. Unpublished paper for 'Engaging the Curriculum: A Theological Programme', Project of the Council of Church and Associated Colleges. Director, Professor Ian Markham.

Grimes, R. (1982) *Beginnings in Ritual Studies.* Washington DC: University of America Press.

Grimes, R. (1990) *Ritual Criticism.* Columbia: University of South Carolina Press.

Guardini, R. (1935) *The Church and the Catholic.* London: Sheed and Ward.

Guéranger, P. (1995) *Introduction à l'année liturgique.* Bouere: Dominique Martin Morin.

Guiver, G. (1996) *Pursuing the Mystery.* London: SPCK.

Gunton, C. (ed.) (1997) *The Cambridge Companion to Christian Doctrine.* Cambridge: Cambridge University Press.

Gutting, G. (ed.) (1994) *The Cambridge Companion to Foucault.* Cambridge: Cambridge University Press.

Hall, S. and Jefferson, T. (eds) (1976) *Resistance through Rituals: Youth Subcultures in Post-War Britain.* London: Hutchinson.

Hand, S. (ed.) (1992) *The Levinas Reader.* Oxford: Blackwell.

Harris, C. (1992) *Creating Relevant Rituals.* Celebrations for Religious Education. Newtown: E. Dwyer.

Harris, M. (1990) *Theatre and Incarnation.* London: Macmillan Press.

Harvey, D. (1990) *The Condition of Postmodernity.* Oxford: Blackwell.

Hastings, A. (ed.) (1991) *Modern Catholicism. Vatican II and After.* London: SPCK.

Hauweras, S. (1994) *Dispatches from the Front: Theological Engagements with the Secular.* London: Duke University Press.

Hay, D. (1997) 'Contemporary Research on Spirituality'. Unpublished paper given at Liverpool Hope University College, 7 October.

Heelas, P. (1996) *The New Age Movement: The Celebration of the Self and the Sacralization of Modernity.* Oxford: Blackwell.

Heelas, P., Lash, S. and Morris, P. (1996) *Detraditionalization.* Oxford: Blackwell.

Held, D. (1980) *Introduction to Critical Theory: Horkheimer to Habermas.* Berkeley and Los Angeles: University of California Press.

Held, D. and Thompson, J. (eds) (1991) *Anthony Giddens and His Critics.* Cambridge: Cambridge University Press.

Herbert, A. (1935) *Liturgy and Society.* London: Faber and Faber.

Hodgson, P. and King, R. (eds) (1985) *Readings in Christian Theology.* London: SPCK.

Holloway, R. (ed.) (1991) *Who Needs Feminism? Men Respond to Sexism in the Church.* London: SPCK.

Howard, R. (1996) *The Rise and Fall of the Nine O'Clock Service: A Cult Within the Church?* London: Mowbray.

Howes, D. (ed.) (1991) *The Varieties of Sensory Experience: A Sourcebook in the Anthropology of the Senses.* Toronto: University of Toronto Press.

Hughes, K. and Francis, M. (eds) (1991) *Living No Longer for Ourselves: Liturgy and Justice in the Nineties.* Collegeville: The Liturgical Press.

Huizinga, J. (1949) *Homo Ludens.* London: Routledge and Kegan Paul.

Huizinga, J. (1965) *The Waning of the Middle Ages.* Garden City, NY: Doubleday.

Irvine, C. (1994) *Making Present: The Practice of Catholic Life and Liturgy.* London: Darton, Longman and Todd.

Jameson, F. (1991) *Postmodernism or the Cultural Logic of Late Capitalism.* Durham: Duke University Press.

Jantzen, G. (1995) *Power, Gender and Christian Mysticism.* Cambridge: Cambridge University Press.

Jantzen, G. (1996) 'Reflections on the Looking Glass', Inaugural John Rylands Professorial Lecture. University of Manchester, 30 October.

Jay, N. (1992) *Your Generations Forever: Sacrifice, Religion and Paternity.* Chicago: University of Chicago Press.

Jeffery, P. (1992) *A New Commandment: Toward a Renewed Rite for the Washing of Feet.* Collegeville: The Liturgical Press.

Jenkins, C. (1995) *A Passion for Priests.* London: Headline.

Jenks, C. (ed.) (1995) *Visual Culture.* London: Routledge.

John Paul II (1994) *Crossing the Threshold of Hope.* London: Jonathan Cape.

John Paul II (1995) *Orientale Lumen.* Apostolic Letter. London: Catholic Truth Society.

Jones, D. (1998) 'Liturgy's Mystery Man', *The Catholic Herald* 10 April: 7.

Jones G., Wainwright, G., Yarnold, E. and Bradshaw, P. (1992) *The Study of Liturgy.* Revised edition. London: SPCK.

Jungmann, J. (1962) *Pastoral Liturgy.* London: Burns and Oates.

Jungmann, J. (1964) *Liturgical Renewal.* London: Burns and Oates.

Jungmann, J. (1966) 'A Great Gift of God to the Church' in Barauna, W. (ed.) *The Liturgy of Vatican II. Vol. 1.* Chicago: Franciscan Herald Press.

Kavanagh, A. (1990a) *Elements of Rite: A Handbook of Liturgical Style.* Collegeville: Pueblo Publishing Company.

Kavanagh, A. (1990b) 'Liturgical Inculturation: Looking to the Future', *Studia Liturgica* 20 (1): 95–106.

Kavanagh, A. (1991) 'Liturgy' in Hastings, A. (ed.) *Modern Catholicism: Vatican II and After.* London: SPCK.

Kavanagh, A. (1992) *On Liturgical Theology.* Collegeville, Minnesota: The Liturgical Press.

Keating, T. (1987) *The Mystery of Christ: The Liturgy as Spiritual Experience.* New York: Amity House.

Keifer, R. (1991) 'Liturgy and Ethics' in Hughes, K. and Francis, M. (eds) *Living No Longer for Ourselves: Liturgy and Justice in the Nineties.* Collegeville: The Liturgical Press.

Kenny, M. (1997) *Goodbye to Catholic Ireland.* London: Sinclair-Stevenson.

Kerr, F. (1989) *Theology After Wittgenstein.* Oxford: Blackwell.

King, U. (1996) *Spirit of Fire: The Life and Vision of Teilhard de Chardin.* New York: Orbis Books.

Kirby, M-D. (1998) 'Sung Theology: The Liturgical Chant of the Church' in Caldecott, S. (ed.), *Beyond the Prosaic: Renewing the Liturgical Movement.* Edinburgh: T&T Clark.

Klauser, T. (1969) *A Short History of Western Liturgy.* London: Oxford University Press.

Kolve, V. (1960) *The Play Called Corpus Christi.* London: Edward Arnold.

Kress, G. (1997) *Before Writing: Rethinking the Paths to Literacy.* London: Routledge.

Krondorfer, B. (1993) 'Play Theology as a Discourse of Disguise', *Journal of Literature and Theology* December, 7 (4): 365–80.

Kung, H. (1995) *Christianity: The Religious Situation of Our Time.* London: SCM Press.

Lacoste, J-Y. (1994) *Expérience et absolut.* Paris: Presses Universitaires de France. Extract translated as 'Liturgy and Kenosis' in Ward, G. (ed.) (1997) *The Postmodern God: A Theological Reader.* Oxford: Blackwell.

Langer, S. (1979) *Philosophy in a New Key: A Study in the Symbolism of Reason, Rite, and Art.* London: Harvard University Press.

Lasch, C. (1991) *The Culture of Narcissism: American Life in an Age of Diminishing Expectations.* New York: W. W. Norton.

Lathrop, G. (1993) *Holy Things: A Liturgical Theology.* Minneapolis: Fortress Press.

Leonard, J. and Mitchell, D. (1994) *The Postures of the Assembly During the Eucharistic Prayer.* Chicago: Liturgy Training Publications.

Le Pivain, D. (1998) 'Meal and sacrifice in the magisterium of the Church' in *Altar and Sacrifice.* The Proceedings of the Third International Colloquium of Historical, Canonical and Theological Studies on the Roman Catholic Liturgy. London: The St Austin Press.

Lévi-Strauss, C. (1981) *The Naked Man: Introduction to a Science of Mythology. Vol. 4.* New York: Harper and Row.

Lewis, G. (1980) *Day of Shining Red: An Essay on Understanding Ritual.* Cambridge: Cambridge University Press.

Lindbeck, G. (1970) *The Future of Roman Catholic Theology.* London: SPCK.

Loisy, A. (1902) *L'Évangile et L'Église.* Paris: Presses Universitaires de France.

Loughlin, G. (1996) *Telling God's Story: Bible, Church and Narrative Theology.* Cambridge: Cambridge University Press.

Loughlin, G. (1997) 'René Girard (b. 1923): Introduction'. in Ward, G. (ed.) *The Postmodern God.* Oxford: Blackwell.

Lukes, S. (1975) 'Political Ritual and Social Integration', *Sociology* 9 (2): 289–308.

218 *Losing the Sacred*

Lyon, D. (1994a) *The Electronic Eye: The Rise of Surveillance Society.* Oxford: Polity Press.

Lyon, D. (1994b) *Postmodernity.* Buckingham: Open University Press.

Lyotard, J-F. (1984) *The Postmodern Condition.* Manchester: Manchester University Press.

MacCulloch, D. (1996) *Thomas Cranmer: A Life.* New Haven: Yale University Press.

MacIntyre, A. (1996) *After Virtue: A Study in Moral Theory.* London: Duckworth.

Macquarrie, J. (1981) *Twentieth Century Religious Thought.* London: SCM Press.

Madden, L. (1992) *The Awakening Church: 25 Years of Liturgical Renewal.* Collegeville: The Liturgical Press.

Maffesoli, M. (1996) *The Time of the Tribes: The Decline of Individualism in Mass Society.* London: Sage.

Mannion, F. (1986) 'Liturgy and the Present Crisis of Culture', *Worship* 62 (2): 98–123.

Mannion, F. (1998) 'Holy Week As Living Mystery', *Priests and People* March 12 (3): 87–91.

Martimort, A. (1987) *The Church at Prayer. Vol. 1. Principles of the Liturgy.* London: Geoffrey Chapman.

Martin, D. (1980) *The Breaking of the Image: A Sociology of Christian Theory and Practice.* Oxford: Blackwell.

Martin, D. (1995) 'Christian Foundations, Sociological Fundamentals'. Unpublished paper for 'Engaging the Curriculum: A Theological Programme.' Director, Professor Ian Markham.

Maxwell, W. (1936) *An Outline of Christian Worship.* London: Oxford University Press.

McClintock Fulkerson, M. and Dunlap, S. (1997) 'Michel Foucault (1926–1984): Introduction' in Ward, G. (ed.) *The Postmodern God: A Theological Reader.* Oxford: Blackwell.

McDade, J. (1991) 'Catholic Theology in the Postconciliar Period' in Hastings, A. (ed.), *Modern Catholicism: Vatican II and After.* London: SPCK.

McDade, J. (1998) 'Kissing the Cross', *Priests and People* 12 (3): 96–100.

McNay, L. (1994) *Foucault: A Critical Introduction.* Oxford: Polity Press.

McSweeney, B. (1981) *Roman Catholicism: The Search for Relevance.* Oxford: Blackwell.

Mellor, P. (1992) 'Regionalisation and the Theology of Space', *New Blackfriars* 73 (860): 276–84.

Mellor, P. (1993) 'Reflexive Traditions: Anthony Giddens, High Modernity, and the Contours of Contemporary Religiosity', *Religious Studies* 29: 111–27.

Mellor, P. A. and Shilling, C. (1997) *Reforming the Body: Religion, Community and Modernity*. London: Sage.

Merquior, J. (1991) *Foucault*. London: Fontana Press.

Meštrović, S. G. (1991) *The Coming Fin de Siècle: An Application of Durkheim's Sociology to Modernity and Postmodernity*. London: Routledge.

Milbank, J. (1993) *Theology and Social Theory: Beyond Secular Reason*. Oxford: Blackwell.

Milbank, J. (1997) *The Word Made Strange: Theology, Language and Culture*. Oxford: Blackwell.

Miles, M. (1992) *Carnal Knowing*. Tunbridge Wells: Burns and Oates.

Miller, J. (1994) *The Passion of Michel Foucault*. London: Flamingo.

Mitchell, K. (1989) 'Ritual and Pastoral Care', *Journal of Pastoral Care* 43: 68–77.

Mitchell, N. (1990) *Cult and Controversy: The Worship of the Eucharist Outside Mass*. Collegeville: The Liturgical Press.

Mitchell, N. (1995) 'Emerging Rituals in Contemporary Culture' in Chauvet, L-M. and Lumbala, F. (eds) *Concilium: 'Liturgy and the Body'* June, (3). London: SCM Press.

Moleck, F., Mauch, M., Searle, M., Nowell, I. and Weakland, R. (1990) *Liturgy: Active Participation in the Divine Life*. Collegeville: The Liturgical Press.

Moltmann-Wendel, E. (1994) *I Am My Body*. London: SCM Press.

Morrison, K. (1995) *Marx, Durkheim, Weber: Formations of Modern Social Thought*. London: Sage.

Murphy, F. (1995) *Christ the Form of Beauty: A Study in Theology and Literature*. Edinburgh: T&T Clark.

Navone, J. (1990) *Seeking God in Story*. Collegeville: The Liturgical Press.

Nelson, J. (1992) *The Intimate Connection: Male Sexuality, Masculine Spirituality*. London: SPCK.

Newton, D. (1986) 'Sociology of Worship' in Davies, J. G. (ed.) *A New Dictionary of Liturgy and Worship*. London: SCM Press.

Nichols, A. (1989) *Yves Congar*. London: Geoffrey Chapman.

Nichols, A. (1996) *Looking at the Liturgy: A Critical View of its Contemporary Form*. San Francisco: Ignatius Press.

Nocent, A. (1994) *A Rereading of the Renewed Liturgy*.

Collegeville: The Liturgical Press/San Francisco: Ignatius Press.

Ortner, S. (1977) *Sherpas through their Rituals*. Cambridge: Cambridge University Press.
Otto, R. (1982) *The Idea of the Holy*. London: Oxford University Press.

Parkin, D. (1992) 'Ritual as Spatial Direction and Bodily Division' in de Coppet (ed.) *Understanding Rituals*. London: Routledge.
Parkin, F. (1992) *Durkheim*. Oxford: Oxford University Press.
Pateman, C. (1994) *The Sexual Contract*. Cambridge: Polity Press.
Pickering, W. S. F. (1984) *Durkheim's Sociology of Religion*. London: Routledge and Kegan Paul.
Pickstock, C. (1993) 'Liturgy and Language: The Sacred Polis' in Bradshaw, P. and Spinks, B. (eds) *Liturgy in Dialogue*. London: SPCK.
Pickstock, C. (1998) *After Writing: On the Liturgical Consummation of Philosophy*. Oxford: Blackwell.
Poster, M. (1990) *Foucault, Marxism and History: Mode of Production Versus Mode of Information*. Oxford: Polity Press.
Poster, M. (ed.) (1992) *Jean Baudrillard: Selected Writings*. Oxford: Polity Press.
Pottebaum, G. (1992) *The Rites of People: Exploring the Ritual Character of Human Experience*. Revised Edition. Washington: The Pastoral Press.
Power, D. (1984) *Unsearchable Riches: The Symbolic Nature of Liturgy*. Pueblo Publishing Co.
Prokes, M. (1996) *Toward a Theology of the Body*. Edinburgh: T&T Clark.
Pryce, M. (1996) *Finding a Voice: Men, Women and the Community of the Church*. London: SCM Press.

Rabinow, P. (ed.) (1991) *The Foucault Reader*. Harmondsworth: Penguin.
Rahner, K. (1978) *Foundations of Christian Faith: An Introduction to the Idea of Christianity*. New York: Crossroad.
Ramshaw, E. (1987) *Ritual and Pastoral Care*. Philadelphia: Fortress Press.
Ranchetti, R. (1969) *The Catholic Modernists: A Study of the Religious Reform Movement 1864–1907*. Oxford: Oxford University Press.

Rappaport, R. (1979) *Ecology, Meaning and Religion.* California: North Atlantic Books.

Ratzinger, J. (1986) *Feast of Faith: Approaches to a Theology of the Liturgy.* San Francisco: Ignatius Press.

Readt, P. (1997) 'Pierre Guéranger'. Unpublished paper given at the Ecclesiastical History Society Conference, 'Continuity and Change in Christian Worship', University of St Andrews. July.

Reardon, B. (1970) *Roman Catholic Modernism.* London: A&C Black.

Reid, S. (ed.) (1996) *A Bitter Trial: Evelyn Waugh and John Carmel Cardinal Heenan on the Liturgical Changes.* Curdridge: The Saint Austin Press.

Richards, H. (1966) 'God's Word in the Liturgy' in Crichton, J. (ed.) *The Liturgy and the Future.* London: Fowler Wright.

Richardson, M. (1995) 'The Spatial Sense of the Sacred in Spanish America and the American South and its Tie with Performance' in Schechner, R. and Appel, W. (eds) *By Means of Performance: Intercultural Studies of Theatre and Ritual.* Cambridge: Cambridge University Press.

Riches, J. (ed.) (1986) *The Analogy of Beauty: The Theology of Hans Urs von Balthasar.* Edinburgh: T&T Clark.

Ritzer, G. (1993) *The McDonaldization of Society.* New York: Pine Forge Press.

Roll, S. (1994) 'Women's Liturgy: Dancing at the Margins'. *Doctrine and Life* Sept: 387–96.

Roose-Evans, J. (1994) *Passages of the Soul: Ritual Today.* Shaftesbury: Element Books.

Rorty, R. (1996) *Philosophy and the Mirror of Nature.* Oxford: Blackwell.

Rubin, M. (1991) *Corpus Christi.* Cambridge: Cambridge University Press.

Ruether, R. (1985) *Women Church.* San Francisco: Harper and Row.

Rutherford, J. (1988) 'Who's that Man?' in Chapman, R. and Rutherford, J. (eds) *Male Order: Unwrapping Masculinity.* Lawrence and Wishart.

Saliers, D. (1992) 'Symbol in Liturgy, Liturgy as Symbol: The Domestication of Liturgical Experience' in Madden, L. (ed.) *The Awakening Church: 25 years of Liturgical Renewal.* Collegeville: The Liturgical Press.

Sanders, D. (1995) 'The Work of Our Redemption', *Priests and People* December, 9 (12): 450.

Schechner, R. (1977) *Essays on Performance Theory 1970–1976.* New York: Drama Book Specialists.

Schechner, R. (1993) *The Future of Ritual*. London: Routledge.

Schechner, R. (1995) 'Magnitudes of performance' in Schechner, R. and Appel, W. *By Means of Performance: Intercultural Studies of Theatre and Ritual*. Cambridge: Cambridge University Press.

Schechner, R. and Appel, W. (eds) (1995) *By Means of Performance: Intercultural Studies of Theatre and Ritual*. Cambridge: Cambridge University Press.

Schreiter, R. (ed.) (1984) *The Schillebeeckx Reader*. Edinburgh: T&T Clark.

Scruton, R. (1997) *The Aesthetics of Music*. Oxford: Oxford University Press.

Searle, M. (1990) 'Culture' in Moroney, J. (ed.) *Liturgy: Active Participation in the Divine Life*. Collegeville: The Liturgical Press.

Searle, M. (1992) 'Ritual' in Jones, C., Wainwright, G., Yarnold, E. and Bradshaw, P. (eds) *The Study of Liturgy*. London: SPCK.

Seasoltz, K. (1980) *New Liturgy, New Law*. Collegeville: The Liturgical Press.

Seasoltz, K. (1993) 'Liturgy and Social Consciousness' in Stamps, M. (ed.) *To Do Justice Upon the Earth*. Collegeville: The Liturgical Press.

Segal, L. (1994) *Slow Motion: Changing Masculinities, Changing Men*. London: Virago Press.

Segal, R. (ed.) (1998) *The Myth and Ritual Theory: An Anthology*. Oxford: Blackwell.

Seidler, V. (1991) *Recreating Sexual Politics*. London: Routledge.

Seidler, V. (1994a) *Recovering the Self: Morality and Social Theory*. London: Routledge.

Seidler, V. (1994b) *Unreasonable Men: Masculinity and Social Theory*. London: Routledge.

Sennett, R. (1993) *The Fall of Public Man*. London: Faber and Faber.

Sennett, R. (1994) *Flesh and Stone: The Body and the City in Western Civilization*. London: Faber and Faber.

Shilling, C. (1993) *The Body and Social Theory*. London: Sage.

Shorter, A. (1988) *Toward a Theology of Inculturation*. London: Geoffrey Chapman.

Silverman, H. (ed.) (1993) *Questioning Foundations: Truth, Subjectivity, Culture*. London: Routledge.

Skelley, M. (1991) *The Liturgy of the World: Karl Rahner's Theology of Worship*. Collegeville: The Liturgical Press.

Slee, N. (1996) 'The Power to Re-member' in Hampson, D. (ed.)

Swallowing a Fishbone? Feminist Theologians Debate Christianity.
London: SPCK.

Smart, B. (1989) *Foucault, Marxism and Critique.* London:
Routledge.

Smith, R. (1889) *Lectures on the Religion of the Semites.* First Series, 1st
edn. Edinburgh: A&C Black.

Spurr, B. (1995) *The Word in the Desert: Anglican and Roman Catholic
Reactions to Liturgical Reform.* Cambridge: The Lutterworth Press.

St Augustine (1985) *St Augustine's Confessions.* Trans. Pine-Coffin,
R. Harmondsworth: Penguin.

St Bonaventure (1978) *Bonaventure: The Soul's Journey Into God. The
Tree of Life: The Life of St Francis. The Classics of Western Spirituality.*
Trans. and Intro. Cousins, E. London: SPCK.

Stamps, M. (ed.) (1993) *To Do Justice Upon the Earth.* Collegeville:
The Liturgical Press.

Stanislavski, C. (1937, 1993) Trans. Hapgood, E. *An Actor Prepares.*
London: Methuen.

Stevenson, K. (1989) *Accept this Offering: The Eucharist as Sacrifice
Today.* London: SPCK.

Stuart, E. (1996) *Spitting at Dragons: Towards a Feminist Theology of
Sainthood.* London: Mowbray.

Swanson, R. (1997) *Religion and Devotion in Europe, c.1215–c.1515.*
Cambridge: Cambridge University Press.

Synnott, A. (1993) *The Body Social: Symbolism, Self and Society.*
London: Routledge.

Tambiah, S. (1979) 'A Performative Approach to Ritual',
Proceedings of the British Academy 65: 113–69.

Tanner, K. (1997) 'Jesus Christ' in Gunton, C. (ed.) *The Cambridge
Companion to Christian Doctrine.* Cambridge: Cambridge University Press.

Taylor, C. (1992) *Sources of the Self: The Making of Modern Identity.*
Cambridge: Cambridge University Press.

Taylor Scott, P. (1980) 'The Likelihood of the Liturgy: Reflections
Upon Prayer Book Revision and its Liturgical Implications',
Anglican Theological Review 62: 103–20.

Tester, K. (1993) *The Life and Times of Post-modernity.* London:
Routledge.

Thomas, K. (1991) *Religion and the Decline of Magic.*
Harmondsworth: Penguin.

Torevell, D. (1995) 'The Terrorism of Reason in the Thought of
Zygmunt Bauman', *New Blackfriars* March, 76 (891): 141–53.

Torevell, D. (1997) 'Taming the Lion of Judah: Masculinity, the Body and Contemporary Christian Liturgy', *Journal of Contemporary Religion* 12 (3): 383–400.

Touraine, A. (1995) *Critique of Modernity*. Oxford: Blackwell.

Turner, D. (1995) *The Darkness of God: Negativity in Christian Mysticism*. Cambridge: Cambridge University Press.

Turner, V. (1967) *Forest of Symbols: Aspects of Ndembu Ritual*. Ithaca, New York: Cornell University Press.

Turner, V. (1969) *The Ritual Process: Structure and Anti-Structure*. London: Routledge and Kegan Paul.

Turner, V. (1972) 'Passages, Margins and Poverty: Religious Symbols of *Communitas*', Part 1 *Worship* 46 (7): 390–412.

Turner, V. (1976) 'Ritual, Tribal and Catholic', *Worship* 50 (6): 504–26.

Underhill, E. (1936) *Worship*. London: Nisbet & Co. Ltd.

Vagagini, C. (1966) 'Fundamental Ideas of the Constitution' in Barauna, W. (ed.) *The Liturgy of Vatican II. Vol. 1*. Chicago: Franciscan Herald Press.

Vanhoozer, K. (1997) 'Human Being, Individual and Social' in Gunton, C. (ed.) *The Cambridge Companion to Christian Doctrine*. Cambridge: Cambridge University Press.

Verheul, A. (1987) *Introduction to the Liturgy: Towards a Theology of Worship*. Wheathampstead: Anthony Clarke.

Von Balthasar, H. (1982) *The Glory of the Lord: A Theological Aesthetics. Vol. I. Seeing the Form*. Edinburgh: T&T Clark.

Wagner, P. (1994) *A Sociology of Modernity: Liberty and Discipline*. London: Routledge.

Wakefield, G. (1983) 'Sacred Heart' in Wakefield, G. (ed.) *A Dictionary of Christian Spirituality*. London: SCM Press.

Ward, B. (1990) 'Saints and Sybils: Hildegard of Bingen to Teresa of Avila', in Soskice, J. (ed.) *After Eve: Women, Theology and the Christian Tradition*. London: Marshall Pickering.

Ward, G. (ed.) (1997) *The Postmodern God: A Theological Reader*. Oxford: Blackwell.

Ward, G. (1999) 'Bodies' in Milbank, J., Pickstock, C. and Ward, G. *Radical Orthodoxy*. London: Routledge.

Weber, M. (1992 [1904–5]) *The Protestant Ethic and the Spirit of Capitalism*. London: Routledge.

Webster Goodwin, S. and Bronfen, E. (eds) (1993) *Death*

and Representation. London: The Johns Hopkins University Press.

Wessels, A. (1994) *Europe: Was it Ever Really Christian?* London: SCM Press.

Whelan, W. (1993) 'Bodily Knowing: Implications for Liturgy and RE', *Religious Education* Spring 88 (2): 273–81.

White, J. (1989) *Protestant Worship: Traditions in Transition*. Louisville: John Knox Press.

White, J. (1992a) *Introduction to Christian Worship*. Revised Edition. Nashville: Abingdon Press.

White, J. (1992b) *Documents of Christian Worship: Descriptive and Interpretive Sources*. Edinburgh: T&T Clark.

White, S. (1990) *Art, Architecture and Liturgical Reform*. New York: Pueblo Publishing Co.

White, S. (1994) *Christian Worship and Technological Change*. Nashville: Abingdon Press.

White, S. (1995) 'The Theology of Sacred Space' in Browne, D. and Loades, A. (eds) *The Sense of the Sacramental: Movement and Measure in Art and Music, Place and Time*. London: SPCK.

Williams, R. (1986) 'Balthasar and Rahner' in Riches, J. (ed.) *The Analogy of Beauty: The Theology of Hans Urs von Balthasar*. Edinburgh: T&T Clark.

Wollaston, I. (1996) *A War Against Memory? The Future Of Holocaust Remembrance*. London: SPCK.

Yi-Fu Tuan (1995) 'Space and Context' in Schechner, R. and Appel, W. (eds) *By Means of Performance: Intercultural Studies in Theatre and Ritual*. Cambridge: Cambridge University Press.

Documents and Reports

Documents on the Liturgy 1963–1979 (1982), Collegeville: The Liturgical Press.

The Catechism of the Catholic Church (1994), London: Geoffrey Chapman.

The Oxford Declaration on Liturgy (1996).

The Society for Catholic Liturgy. *Brochure* (1995).

Paying the Piper: Advertising and the Church (1994), London: Church House Publishing.

The Common Good (1997), The Catholic Bishops' Conference of England and Wales.

Sacramentary (1985), New York: Catholic Book Publishing.

General Instruction of the Roman Missal (1975) in *Documents on the Liturgy 1963–1979* (1982), Collegeville: The Liturgical Press: 465–533.

The Roman Missal (1981), 3 Volumes, London: Collins/Geoffrey Chapman.

'On the Sacred Liturgy'. Apostolic letter of the Supreme Pontiff John Paul II on 25th Anniversary of the Promulgation of *Sacrosanctum Concilium. Briefing* 19, [2] (1989).

Index of Names

Ackroyd, Peter 50
Ainslie, J. 123, 123n, 125
Ambrose 51
Anderson, B. 121
Aquinas, Thomas 12
Archer, Antony 162–64, 197
Ariès, Philippe 88
Asad, Talal 33, 118
Augustine of Hippo 51–52, 52n
Austin, J. 24

Balthasar, Hans Urs von 143–45
Barauna, W. 148
Barba, Eugenio 30
Bauman, Zygmunt 15, 80–96
Bell, Catherine 24, 26
Bellah, Robert 16
Bentham, Jeremy 110–11
Berger, Peter 15, 17, 68–70
Binski, Paul 56, 60, 61, 63–64
Blondel, Maurice 131–32, 135, 136
Bonaventure 52–55
Bossy, John 57, 58–59, 88
Bourdieu, Pierre 160–61
Bouyer, Louis 127, 185
Bradley, Ian 91
Bradshaw, Paul 11, 49, 145
Brown, David 179
Brown, Peter 49, 206
Bugnini, A. 128–29, 157–58
Burnham, A. 60

Burrett, A. 157
Bynum-Walker, C. 64

Caldecott, Stratford 206
Cameron, Euan 13, 67, 119
Campbell, Colin 117–18
Casel, Odo 164
Chadwick, Owen 67
Chandlee, H. 119–20, 127
Chateaubriand, François 120
Chauvet, L.-M. 177–78
Chenu, Marie-Dominique 138
Chiffley, E. 179
Chupungco, A. 158
Classen, Constance 194
Collins, Patrick 23
Congar, Yves 138, 139
Connerton, Paul 191
Crichton, John 122–23n, 161
Curran, Patricia 45–47

Daly, Gabriel 123, 134, 135
Davie, Grace 176
de Lubac, Henri 138, 139
Descartes, René 72–79
Dix, Geoffrey 59
Dollimore, Jonathan 106
Douglas, Mary 9, 175
Dreyer, E. 55
Driver, Tom 30, 34, 59, 111
Duffy, Eamon, 19, 20, 54, 61, 91, 173, 174–75, 204
Duns Scotus, John 72
Dupré, Louis 72, 73

Index of Subjects